LADDERS TO LITERACY

LADDERS TO LITERACY

A Preschool Activity Book

by

Angela Notari-Syverson, Ph.D.
Washington Research Institute
Seattle, Washington

Rollanda E. O'Connor, Ph.D.
University of Pittsburgh
Pittsburgh, Pennsylvania

Patricia F. Vadasy, M.P.H.
Washington Research Institute
Seattle, Washington

·P·A·U·L·H·
BROOKES
PUBLISHING C<u>O</u>

Baltimore · London · Toronto · Sydney

Paul H. Brookes Publishing Co.
Post Office Box 10624
Baltimore, Maryland 21285-0624

Typeset by A.W. Bennett, Inc., Hartland, Vermont.
Manufactured in the United States of America by
Versa Press, East Peoria, Illinois.

The project on which this book is based was funded by Grant #H024B20031 from the U.S. Department of Education, Office of Special Education and Rehabilitative Services, Early Education Program for Children with Disabilities. The content, however, does not necessarily reflect the position of the U.S. Department of Education, and no official endorsement should be inferred.

The illustrations throughout this book are provided, with permission, from the following individuals: Tiana Bolden, Lauralee Brainard, Mary Delaney Gallien, Sonia Fierst, Heidi Gainer, Linda Gil, Dakota Madera, Clarissa Scott, and Amy Sundquist.

The clipart on pages 154, 178, 180, and 269 is courtesy of Corel Corporation.

Library of Congress Cataloging-in-Publication Data
Notari-Syverson, Angela.
    Ladders to literacy : a preschool activity book / by Angela Notari-Syverson, Rollanda E. O'Connor, Patricia F. Vadasy.
        p.   cm.
    Includes bibliographical references and index.
    ISBN 1-55766-317-3
    1. Handicapped children—Education (Preschool)—United States.   2. Reading (Preschool)—United States.   2. Reading (Preschool)—United States.   3. Education, Preschool—Activity programs—United States.   4. Literacy—United States.   I. O'Connor, Rollanda E.   II. Vadasy, Patricia F.   III. Title.
    LC4028.5.N68   1998
    371.9′0444—dc21   97-37862
                                                                                                              CIP

British Library Cataloguing in Publication data are available from the British Library.

Contents

About the Authors ix

Forewords   *Kevin N. Cole* xi

   Juliann J. Woods Cripe xiii

Acknowledgments xv

Introduction 1

**I Theoretical Framework for Early
   Literacy and Language Assessment and Curriculum** 11

Chapter 1 The Development of Early Literacy 13

Chapter 2 The Role of Scaffolding 27

Chapter 3 Implementing *Ladders to Literacy* 35

II Print/Book Awareness 45

   Shared Storybook Reading 51

   Snack/Lunch Menu 56

   Following Recipes 60

   Making Signs 64

   Many Ways to Write 68

   Morning/Afternoon Message and News 72

   I Found 76

   Name Cups 79

   Classroom Post Office 81

   Fill in the Blanks 84

   Making Books 87

   Photography 91

   Sorting Objects 94

   Blocks 98

   Recording Constructions 101

   Treasure Hunt 104

   Science Projects 107

   Obstacle Course 111

   Long Jump 114

   My First Journal 118

   Landscapes and Maps 122

   Museum Exhibit 126

III Metalinguistic Awareness 133

    Sound Representations 138

    Musical Instruments 141

    Rhythmic Activities 144

    Listening to Songs 147

    Clap the Syllables 150

    Syllable Puzzles 153

    Nursery Rhymes 156

    The Rhyming Book 159

    Rhyming Games 162

    Playing with the Sounds of Words 165

    Sound Isolation 168

    Letter Sound of the Week 171

    First Sound Song 175

    Guess the Word (Blending) .179

    I'm Thinking of a . . . (Blending by Category) 181

    Word to Word Matching Game: First Sound 184

    Play with Miniature Toys 187

    Pretend Play—The Store 190

    Pretend Play—Magic Password 193

IV Oral Language 201

    Show and Tell 206

    Food Talk 210

    Talking About Books 213

    Enacting Storybooks 218

    Book Buddy 222

    Portraits 225

    What Did You Hear? 228

    Feeling Objects 231

    I See, You See 234

    Treasure Boxes 237

    Water Play: Floating Objects 240

    My Dream 243

    Special Words 246

    What Does This Mean? 250

    Let's Say it Another Way! 253

    Interviews 256

    Movie Reviews 259

    Brainstorming 263

    From This to That 267

    Let's Find Out! 271

    Showtime 276

References 283

Appendix A: *Ladders to Literacy* Preschool Checklist 291

Appendix B: Early Literacy Activities for Children and Parents:
         A Parent's Guide to Easy Times to Do These Activities 327

Appendix C: Glossary 361

Appendix D: Additional Resources 365

Index 369

About the Authors

Angela Notari-Syverson, Ph.D., Research Associate, Washington Research Institute, 150 Nickerson Street, Suite 305, Seattle, Washington 98109
Dr. Notari-Syverson is a research associate at the Washington Research Institute in Seattle, Washington. Dr. Notari-Syverson holds degrees in child psychology and in language disorders from the University of Geneva, Switzerland, and a doctoral degree in early childhood special education from the University of Oregon in Eugene. In Geneva, Dr. Notari-Syverson worked in a clinical setting with children with a variety of oral and written communication disorders. In the United States since 1985, she has directed or co-directed federal research, model demonstration, and outreach projects at the Washington Research Institute and at the University of Washington in Seattle focused on early language and literacy intervention. She has published chapters and journal articles on early intervention assessment and curriculum as well as on the language, literacy, and cognitive development of young children with disabilities.

Rollanda E. O'Connor, Ph.D., Assistant Professor, Department of Instruction and Learning, University of Pittsburgh, 4H01 Forbes Quadrangle, 230 South Bouquet Street, Pittsburgh, Pennsylvania 15260   Dr. O'Connor is a reading specialist and an assistant professor at the University of Pittsburgh and has a doctoral degree in special education from the University of Washington in Seattle. Dr. O'Connor taught reading in special and general education classrooms for 16 years, directed an in-service consortium for general and special educators on strategies for educating children with disabilities in general education classes, and conducted research on developing literacy skills in young children with disabilities. Dr. O'Connor's research has focused on two themes: the feasibility and effectiveness of incorporating phonological awareness instruction into programs for children at risk for reading difficulties in general education classes and factors that influence accessibility of reading instruction. She has taught teachers to use activities designed to improve the reading development of their children during large- and small-group instruction. The factors identified in these studies have been incorporated in the activities in *Ladders to Literacy*.

Patricia F. Vadasy, M.P.H., Research Associate, Washington Research Institute, 150 Nickerson Street, Suite 305, Seattle, Washington 98109   Patricia Vadasy is a research associate at the Washington Research Institute in Seattle, Washington. She has published extensively in the areas of early childhood special education and family support programs during her work at the University of Washington's Experimental Education Unit. Since 1989, she has directed federal research and demonstration projects at the Washington Research Institute in programs involving students from differing ethnic backgrounds and early reading instruction.

Foreword

In the not too recent past, it was highly unlikely that educators of young children would consider themselves involved in "reading instruction." In fact, to many early childhood educators, reading instruction conjured up images of drill and practice, worksheets, and developmentally *inappropriate* practices. We had a strong understanding of the importance of language development for young children and an awareness that, at some point in the early elementary grades, reading instruction was essential. It was unclear, however, what the precise connection was between early childhood education practices and later reading development. In the 1980s, the bridge between early experience and later reading ability began to come into focus. Children's oral language development, exposure to storybook reading by adults, knowledge of rhyming, and other preschool activities were found to be strong predictors of later reading ability. Research on what was later labeled *emergent literacy experience* indicated a strong causal relationship to later reading success. In a brilliant review of research on early reading development, Adams (1990) concluded that children who entered school with exposure to these important early experiences (estimated to be *at least* 1,000 hours of interaction in a typical middle-class family) would be much more prepared to benefit from formal reading instruction in the early elementary grades. However, children who did not experience the hours and hours of storybook reading, nursery rhymes, storytelling, conversing, playing with words and sounds, manipulating magnetic refrigerator letters, and so forth, were at a tremendous disadvantage before they ever began kindergarten. Until now there has been no application of this new information that uses carefully designed lessons based on proven instructional techniques that will help all children, including those with disabilities, enter school ready to learn to read. This curriculum is, I believe, the first set of materials designed to help early intervention professionals close the gap in reading readiness in an effective and developmentally appropriate way.

This volume has a great deal to offer to early childhood service providers. It is designed to be ecologically valid, embedding activities into daily classroom routines and home activities. It is also developmentally appropriate, alleviating any fears that activities related to reading success will be too difficult or too tedious for young children. The organization of the materials into print/book awareness, metalinguistic awareness, and oral language activities encourages interdisciplinary involvement between speech-language pathologists and teachers. In addition, the activities are designed for a continuum of developmental levels, allowing them to be used more easily in inclusive and mainstreamed settings.

This volume represents cutting-edge knowledge of research in emergent literacy combined with an organized, practical set of materials. It will enable early childhood educators and special education professionals to target the language and preliteracy skills that can make the difference between children's success and failure in school.

Kevin N. Cole, Ph.D.
Research Faculty
University of Washington
Seattle

REFERENCES

Adams, M.J. (1990). Beginning to read: Thinking and learning about print. Cambridge, MA: MIT Press.

Foreword

Through exposure to typical everyday events, preschool children begin to develop early literacy skills such as turning pages in a book, rhyming words, or making scribbles. These seemingly simple tasks set the stage for a future of reading and writing, the very methods through which further knowledge is gained in school and throughout life. Unfortunately, young children with disabilities, especially those with communication and language delays, often do not gain these same early literacy skills without direct intervention. The lack of early literacy opportunities serves to increase the significance of a child's disability by denying him or her access to a crucial learning methodology.

Early intervention programs have not consistently included literacy skills in their early childhood special education curriculums. Because of the perception that literacy is a "later developing skill" and because of the paucity of information regarding the relevance of early literacy to later learning for young children with disabilities, it has not received the attention it deserves. More pragmatically, early childhood special educators were unfamiliar with the specific skills to be taught and appropriate instructional methodology. The importance of early literacy was not included in early childhood special education personnel preparation programs or readily promoted in staff development or in-service training.

Ladders to Literacy: A Preschool Activity Book and *Ladders to Literacy: A Kindergarten Activity Book* are timely and significant contributions to the field linking research on emergent literacy development in young children with and without disabilities to practice for early childhood education and early childhood special education. *Ladders to Literacy* offers direct services providers a synthesis of the most relevant and recent theoretical and empirical knowledge about early literacy in a highly readable and understandable format. Other components provide a scope and sequence of skills to be taught and field-tested, developmentally appropriate strategies for intervention. The checklist in Appendix A of this volume identifies children's existing knowledge and then provides a curriculum linked to the assessment to ensure that the skills are taught.

Ladders to Literacy supports inclusive practices by delineating activities appropriate to a variety of child-directed preschool curriculums and, therefore, can be incorporated into the many different settings in which young children with disabilities are served. The interventions are useful with heterogeneous groups of children at varying stages of development because of the modifications illustrated. By presenting the interventions in an activity-based format, the children are offered choices, direct their own learning, and have multiple opportunities to practice skills throughout the day in their preferred activities. The materials further enhance literacy skills and family-guided practices by including a family participation component that, too, is easily adaptable, culturally responsive, practical, and fun.

The authors are to be commended for their careful attention to detail in their development of the materials. Not only do the materials provide the key components for the implementation of early literacy training, they do so in an easy to read and apply format. More important, *Ladders to Literacy* provides a framework for learning that encourages the educator to take an active role in problem-solving the most appropriate strategies for each child within the area (i.e., print/book awareness, metalinguistic skills, or oral language) to be taught. It is not a "cookbook" with a recipe for literacy or a "scrapbook" of fun and interesting, yet generally unrelated, literacy activity suggestions. The books delineate the critical concepts for early literacy development; provide supportive examples for their application, a sequence for development, and strategies for implementation; and suggest modifications for individualization and methods for monitoring progress.

The *Ladders to Literacy* activity books are an excellent example of educational "interactivity," showing the interrelatedness of learning in early development domains; the partnerships between home, school, and community; the linkages between assessment and intervention; and the multiplicity of learning that occurs within daily routines and activities with thoughtful planning. *Ladders to Literacy* is an important addition to the educator's endeavor to promote lifelong learning within a literate society. Little could be more important for all young children.

Juliann J. Woods Cripe, Ph.D.
Associate Professor
Valdosta State University
Valdosta, Georgia

Acknowledgments

Our thanks to the many preschool and Head Start teachers, children, and families in the Seattle public schools; the Northwest Center Child Development Program; the United Indians Daybreak Star Child Development Program; and the Islamic School of Seattle, Washington; for their participation in the field-testing of these activities. A particular thanks goes to preschool teachers Heidi Gainer, Sonia Fierst, and Lauralee Brainard for their many helpful suggestions and to Ann Hazelwood for her assistance in the data collection. We would also like to thank Drs. Juliann J. Woods Cripe and Christine Marvin for reviewing the curriculum and providing invaluable feedback. We are especially grateful to Mary Delaney Gallien for her invaluable contributions in the typing, design, and preparation of the many experimental versions of the manuscript. We are grateful for the support provided by the U.S. Department of Education, Office of Special Education and Rehabilitative Services, Early Education Program for Children with Disabilities, for the development and field-testing of the curriculum.

LADDERS TO LITERACY

Introduction

The most important academic task that children accomplish in the elementary school years is the development of formal literacy. However, many children enter kindergarten and first grade without critical early literacy experiences and skills. This volume is designed to help children develop early literacy skills through engaging activities that can be incorporated into programs for children at risk for reading failure, including children with disabilities and their typically developing peers. These activities address the areas that research suggests are most strongly related to later reading development—print/book awareness, metalinguistic awareness, and oral language—and promote the competence that can help children become receptive to beginning reading instruction in the early grades. The activities in *Ladders to Literacy* were field-tested in inclusive preschool settings with small and large groups of children reflecting a range of interests and abilities.

A NEW PERSPECTIVE ON LITERACY

Since the 1980s, educators and researchers have revised their views regarding how and when children begin to learn about literacy. Known as the *emergent literacy perspective,* this view considers literacy a complex sociological, psychological, and linguistic activity. Learning about literacy begins at a very early age and is a continuous process that is directly linked to early oral language and social interactions. It is an integral and functional component of everyday living (Teale, 1984). Several lines of research suggest that a child's experience with literate activities prior to first grade makes a significant difference in his or her language and literacy skills (e.g., Dickinson & Smith, 1996; Maclean, Bryant, & Bradley, 1987; Scarborough, Dobrich, & Hager, 1991; Snow & Weisman, 1996; Wells, 1985; Whitehurst et al., 1994; Whitehurst et al., 1988). In this book, which uses Snow's (1983) definition of literacy activities and skills associated directly with the use of print, literacy is not restricted to *reading and writing*. Children learn about literacy when they listen

1

to stories, help adults follow cooking recipes, memorize logos, draw pictures, scribble unintelligibly, or invent spellings. These experiences help children construct their understanding about what it means to be literate in our[1] culture. This knowledge forms a foundation for later, more specific learning about literacy in the early school years.

THEORETICAL AND RESEARCH BASES

This volume is based on three major theoretical perspectives: 1) the ecological model of human behavior (Bronfenbrenner, 1979), which views the development of the child within the broader familial and societal context; 2) the constructivist approach derived from Piaget's (1971) theory, which views the child as an active learner; and 3) Vygotsky's (1978) social-interactionist perspective, which emphasizes the role of social interactions with adults in the child's learning process. Because of the complex cultural, psychological, and linguistic nature of literacy, children's acquisition of reading and writing involves early experiences with multiple aspects of literacy. The learning of these aspects will vary at different points in development as a function of children's changing interests and abilities. Research has highlighted that early exposure to literacy events and metaphonological aspects of language is important for successful performance in school-based literacy activities. The acquisition of literacy results from the interaction among these experiences (Sulzby & Teale, 1991) that can be broadly categorized into three major areas: print/book awareness, metalinguistic awareness, and oral language. Instructional programs based on a comprehensive approach to early literacy have been successful in promoting early literacy and language skills of young children who are at risk for or who have disabilities (Notari-Syverson, O'Connor, & Vadasy, 1996; Whitehurst et al., 1994).

Print/Book Awareness

Children's awareness of the forms and functions of literacy has been shown to predict later school success (e.g., Adams, 1990; Wells, 1985). This knowledge begins to develop during the preschool-age years through informal exposure to literate activity. Story reading with parents is the most common type of informal literate event for preschool-age children and has been linked concurrently and predictively to literacy and language measures (Bus, van Ijzendoorn, & Pellegrini, 1995). Frequency of story reading in the home and the amount of parent–child engagement in story reading are correlated with later literacy achievement (Chomsky, 1972; Crain-Thoreson & Dale, 1992; Wells, 1985). Teaching parents to read more interactively

---

[1]"Our" culture in this book refers to the United States. These experiences, however, are common to children in many other literate societies.

with their children enhances language development in both typically developing preschool-age children (Whitehurst et al., 1988) and in young children with disabilities (Dale, Crain-Thoreson, Notari-Syverson, & Cole, 1996; Swinson & Ellis, 1988).

Story reading is only one kind of preschool activity that promotes literacy. Parents and teachers also draw children's attention to print conventions and letter names and sounds, often in the context of writing activities or manipulation of magnetic letters (Clay, 1993; Snow, 1983). These kinds of activities help the child to become aware of the formal print conventions (e.g., letter shapes, directionality). Children's knowledge of such print conventions is an important predictor of later literacy achievement (Clay, 1979; McCormick & Mason, 1986; Wells, 1985). Katims (1991) found that a group of preschool children with mild to moderate delays made significant gains on formal and ecological measures of literacy after a year-long exposure to structured literacy activities involving daily storybook reading by adults, a classroom writing center, and visits to the classroom library.

Metalinguistic Awareness

Metalinguistic awareness enables one to reflect on and manipulate the structural features of *spoken* language, such as phonemes, words, sentences, and propositions (Tunmer, Herriman, & Nesdale, 1988). Studies have powerfully demonstrated the connection between the ability to manipulate sounds in spoken words (metalinguistic awareness) and learning to read (Blachman, 1994; Catts, 1993; Maclean et al., 1987; Share, Jorm, Maclean, & Matthews, 1984). Moreover, one of the best predictors of success in first-grade literacy activities is metalinguistic awareness (Felton, 1992; Juel, 1988; Share et al., 1984). This knowledge about sounds and the ability to manipulate them develops naturally for many children but are often missing elements in the repertoires of children with disabilities. Instructional studies of preschool and kindergarten children at risk and with language delays (Ben-Dror, Bentin, & Frost, 1995; O'Connor, Jenkins, Slocum, & Leicester, 1993; Slocum, O'Connor, & Jenkins, 1993; Torgesen, Morgan, & Davis, 1992) have demonstrated that we can teach these fundamental skills to children who are not expected to acquire them independently. The link between improved metalinguistic awareness in kindergarten and improved reading in first grade has also been established (Blachman, 1994; Byrne & Fielding-Barnsley, 1993; Byrne, Freebody, & Gates, 1992; O'Connor, Notari-Syverson, & Vadasy, 1996, 1998). Metalinguistic experiences can be integrated with meaningful home and school literacy experiences. These include engaging children in nursery rhymes, rhymed stories, and rhyme production; musical activities involving clapping and dancing to syllabic rhythms; and reading and writing activities during which opportunities can occur naturally to segment sentences into individual words, investigate word length, and practice isolation and identification of phonemes (Adams, 1990; Lundberg, Frost, & Peterson, 1988; Maclean et al., 1987; Morrow, 1989; Notari-Syverson, O'Connor, Jenkins, & Drinkwater, 1997; Schickedanz, 1989; Sulzby & Teale, 1991).

Oral Language

Storybook reading with parents and teachers is another way that children acquire language and real-world knowledge and learn how to construct meaning from their environments (Crain-Thoreson & Dale, 1992; Whitehurst et al., 1988). Most important, children assimilate cultural ways of learning from books and develop discourse patterns, the absence of which may contribute significantly to the failure in school of children from different cultural backgrounds (Dickinson, Du Temple, Hirschler, & Smith, 1992; Dickinson & Snow, 1987; Heath, 1982; Hoff-Ginsberg, 1991). From an emergent literacy perspective, learning to read and write is viewed as a social phenomenon, especially during the earliest stages of acquisition. Studies on storybook reading have highlighted specific linguistic and nonlinguistic interactions between child and adult and have shown that adults use a variety of strategies known to facilitate the development of oral language. Examples of such strategies include adult expansions on previous child utterances; open-ended questions; questions that demand clarification of the child's utterances; and scaffolding, which refers to the adult's assistance in arranging tasks in a manner to facilitate the child's response (Bruner, 1983; Cross, 1978; Snow, 1983). These skills can be successfully taught to parents, with resultant gains in their child's vocabulary acquisition and overall language complexity (Whitehurst et al., 1988). These same characteristics of adult–child interaction that support language acquisition also appear to facilitate early reading and writing development (Snow, 1983). During storybook reading, children learn different aspects of literacy at different ages, beginning with vocabulary knowledge (Ninio & Bruner, 1978), then moving on to syntactic structures (Snow & Goldfield, 1983), and progressing toward knowledge of print conventions and story structures (Sulzby, 1985; Teale, 1984). As the child gains experience, the language used during discourse around storybook reading acquires characteristics that are similar to those of written language.

Learning to read and write requires the child to reconceptualize his or her language, which has its beginnings in oral contexts and functions (Sulzby, 1985). Early oral language takes place in one-to-one social interactions and is highly dependent on the immediate context (Snow, 1983). Written language is decontextualized, with the writer and the reader being removed from one another in time and in space. The acquisition of literacy involves a transition from oral to written language (Cook-Gumperz & Gumperz, 1981); and storybook reading, which includes aspects of oral *and* written language, may facilitate this transition.

SUPPORTING LITERACY DEVELOPMENT IN YOUNG CHILDREN

This volume of preschool activities attempts to form a comprehensive and cohesive framework that brings together theory, research, and practice across diverse disciplines: early literacy and language development, early childhood, and early childhood special education. Theory and research as well as actual classroom practices guided the development of the activities. Similarly, theoretical foundations as well as ideas for practical applications are presented in this volume for users to make their own and adapt to their particular circumstances. Following is a description of the major features of the curriculum (see Table 1 for an overview of these features).

General Knowledge Features

This volume provides teachers and parents with knowledge and skills in four areas: 1) understanding the development of literacy in young children, 2) providing a literacy-rich physical environment in the home and school, 3) promoting early literacy through child-responsive teaching strategies, and 4) assessing children's literacy development in developmentally appropriate ways.

Table 1.   Major features of the *Ladders to Literacy* preschool curriculum

General knowledge features

Information on child development and emergent literacy

Recommendations for materials, activities, and routines to support literacy development at home and in the classroom

Strategies that facilitate responsive adult–child interactions

Procedures that provide for teachers and parents to assess early literacy learning

Activity features

Ecologically and environmentally sensitive activities that promote literacy development at home and in school

Developmentally appropriate activities that encourage children to experience and experiment with their own words, ideas, and stories

Responsive to the particular needs of young children at diverse developmental levels

Meaningful across a variety of cultures and ethnic groups

Based on a solid foundation of literacy theory and research

Instructional features

Useful in group instruction; adaptable to heterogeneous groups

Supports that can be integrated with other curricula

Developmentally appropriate activities

Provision of guidelines for child-responsive teaching strategies

Provision of suggestions for including families

Provision of recommendations for individualized family service plan/individualized education program goals and objectives

Formal and informal assessment procedures

- **Knowledge about literacy development**—Information is provided on child development and applications of emergent literacy research to the curriculum to ensure thorough understanding of the processes involved in the development of literacy in young children.
- **Literacy-rich physical environment**—The curriculum provides recommendations for materials, activities, room arrangements, and organizations of daily routines that support children's literacy experiences in the home and at school. These include listening to storybook readings, participating in structured writing center activities, and visiting the classroom library.
- **Adult–child interaction**—The curriculum provides teachers and parents with information on the use of child-responsive teaching strategies, drawn from the social-interactionist research (Diaz, Neal, & Vachio, 1991; Pellegrini, Perlmutter, Galda, & Brody, 1990; Snow, 1983; Wertsch, 1985). Some of these strategies have been used successfully in early intervention programs (Mahoney & Powell, 1988) to facilitate mother–child interaction and early language development of children with disabilities. Examples of child-responsive teaching strategies include varying levels of task demands and support in response to the child's level of competence in a task, facilitating language through information-talk, expanding on the child's utterance, asking open-ended questions, following the child's lead, and taking turns.
- **Assessment of early literacy**—The curriculum provides developmentally appropriate and ecological procedures for teachers and parents to assess young children's early literacy learning, such as informal observations, structured performance samples (e.g., Teale, 1988), and a checklist.

Activity Features

- **Ecologically sensitive**—This volume emphasizes the importance of providing children with a broad literacy-rich environment (i.e., physical and social) both at home and at school. Teaching is activity based (Bricker & Cripe, 1992), with literacy skills encouraged within meaningful everyday life activities.
- **Developmentally appropriate**—Activities encourage children to experience and experiment with literacy activities by reconstructing meanings of books and events through their own words and expressing their own ideas and stories.
- **Responsive to individual differences**—Activities are designed specifically to respond to the particular needs of young children with a variety of disabilities. The social-interactionist perspective of our curriculum and, in particular, the use of scaffolding (Wood, Bruner, & Ross, 1976) provide a framework for addressing the variety of individual needs experienced by children with disabilities who are learning together with their

typically developing peers. The activities immerse children in an authentic literate environment. The emergent literacy experiences that have been associated with school success are introduced not as isolated segments but through a series of activities in which each child can participate and learn at his or her individual level of functioning. To facilitate learning, activities include developmentally appropriate teaching strategies. Adults can provide different levels of assistance, arrange tasks and situations, and match the goals of the interaction with the individual child's understanding of the tasks (Wertsch, 1985).

The teaching strategies and adaptations for specific needs of children with disabilities are guided by the notion of scaffolding (Wood et al., 1976), a dynamic type of adult–child interaction in which the adult provides high levels of support and low demands to assist the performance of a child who is less competent (see Figure 1 in Chapter 2). Researchers have identified a number of adult interactive behaviors that positively affect children's literacy and language outcomes (Morrow, 1989). These include strategies such as questioning, giving information, clarifying and restating information, expanding on the child's utterances, and offering praise and feedback. These strategies have also been used to facilitate language in young children with disabilities (Fey, 1986). Use of these approaches allows for individualization in a child-responsive manner, making the curriculum ideal for use in an inclusive program in which children of many ability levels may be grouped in the same classroom.

- **Multiculturally sensitive**—Literacy is deeply embedded in the culture of the family and the community (Heath, 1982; Sulzby & Teale, 1991). This volume offers literacy activities that are meaningful across and within a variety of cultures and ethnic groups and that address the issue of culture-specific adult–child interaction styles.

- **Grounded in research theory**—Effective implementation of any curriculum depends on a solid understanding by the users of the philosophy and principles on which it is founded (Adams, 1990). Each teaching activity is accompanied by relevant theoretical and empirical information to enable users to understand the purpose of each activity.

Instructional Features

The following features enable teachers and parents to use the activities in a variety of settings and with children at different stages of literacy development:

- **Useful in group instruction; adaptable to heterogeneous groups**—The curriculum is designed to ensure that children of different ability levels can be served in inclusive groupings. Each experience includes activities for a range of developmental levels so that teachers can respond to individual differences.

- **Supports that can be integrated with other curricula**—*Ladders to Literacy* will enhance rather than replace existing curricula. This makes the curriculum flexible and easy to include with classroom curricula and routines.
- **Activities that are developmentally appropriate**—Activities are functional and meaningful for the child and facilitate behaviors in multiple areas. Each educational activity identifies a developmental sequence of activities to accommodate children of different developmental levels.
- **Provision of guidelines for child-responsive teaching strategies**—For each activity, guidelines for teaching strategies are described to facilitate children's participation and to allow for adjustments of demands and support according to the child's level of task competence.
- **Provision of suggestions for including families**—A series of activities are available specifically for use by parents and other family members.
- **Provision of recommendations for individualized family service plan/individualized education program goals and objectives**—The educational activities contain examples of child behaviors that can be expected to be facilitated during the activity. This is to assist teachers and parents in identifying goals and objectives.
- **Inclusion of formal and informal assessment procedures**—Guidelines are recommended for using portfolios to document children's progress. Informal assessment procedures, observation forms, and checklists are proposed to assist teachers in determining children's progress toward specific objectives.

RESEARCH ON *LADDERS TO LITERACY* DEVELOPMENT

The activities in this volume have been extensively field-tested over a 4-year period in a variety of preschool settings, including child development programs, Head Start programs, and early childhood special education classrooms. Sites included an inclusive child development center serving primarily Caucasian middle-class children; a multicultural program in an Islamic School; two Head Start programs, one attended primarily by African American children and the other primarily by Native American children; and self-contained special education preschools in public schools attended by children from a variety of cultural backgrounds and presenting a broad range of disabilities. A total of 26 teachers and teaching assistants participated in the field-testing. The professional training of the teachers ranged from a child development associate to a master's degree in early childhood special education. Most teachers implemented each activity at least once. Generally, activities such as Storybook Reading, Snack/Lunch Menus, Journals, and Morning/Afternoon Message took place daily. Activities such as Show and Tell and Musical Activities took place weekly, whereas activities that required more intensive planning and materials preparation (e.g., Long Jump, Following Recipes, Making Maps) were implemented only once during the school year. Teachers reported that they liked the activities and found them developmentally appropriate, culturally sensitive, and easy to include within their daily classroom routines. To meet the needs of heterogeneous groups of children, the activities in this volume were designed for participation by children functioning across a range of levels typical of inclusive settings. In one particular study, we explored the effects of conducting activities on the early language and literacy development of young children with disabilities, children at risk, and typically developing children (Notari-Syverson et al., 1996). Overall, all children benefited from participation in the activities. Children at risk and children with disabilities in particular made significant gains on standardized and nonstandardized measures of early literacy and expressive and receptive language.

SECTION I

Theoretical Framework
for Early Literacy
and Language Assessment
and Curriculum

Chapter 1

The Development
of Early Literacy

The development of literacy begins in the very early years. Early experiences such as adult–child interactions around picture books, exposure to environmental print, and familiarity with multiple forms and uses of symbols to represent objects and ideas (e.g., words, drawings, pretend play) all prepare children for more formal learning of reading and writing later in school.

As with other developmental domains, early literacy skills also progress according to a consistent and orderly sequence leading to the acquisition of reading and writing. Although skills may take different forms at different ages, behaviors within a domain are linked together developmentally, with each new behavior resulting from and integrating previous behaviors. For example, early gestures (e.g., pointing to objects, waving bye-bye) and words are two different but developmentally related forms of communication. Being able to place a child at a particular stage in a developmental sequence of skills helps in interpreting current behaviors and understanding where a child is coming from and where a child is heading. Children's early scribbling and drawing, for example, take on special meaning if they are recognized as early forms of graphic symbols that are related to more complex skills such as writing.

The following sections describe the major steps in the development of skills in the areas of print/book awareness, metalinguistic awareness, and oral language. These behaviors have also been compiled in the form of a checklist (presented in Appendix A) and organized according to a logical developmental sequence so that teachers can use the checklist as a guide for observing and assessing children's current early literacy behaviors as well as for gleaning information on which behaviors the child is most likely to develop next. The checklist covers the three areas of print/book awareness, metalinguistic awareness, and oral language. (The corresponding portions of the preschool checklist appear at the end of Sections II, III, and IV.)

Because of the complex cultural, psychological, and linguistic nature of literacy, children's acquisition of reading and writing skills involves early experience with multiple aspects of literacy. Children's learning of these aspects will vary at different points in development as a function of their changing interests and abilities. Research has highlighted that early exposure to literacy events and metaphonological aspects of language is important for successful performance in school-based literacy activities. The acquisition of literacy results from the interaction among these experiences (Sulzby & Teale, 1991), which can be broadly categorized into the three major areas covered in Sections II–IV and in the *Ladders to Literacy* Preschool Checklist: print/book awareness, metalinguistic awareness, and oral language. Table 1 presents an overview of early literacy and language concepts and behaviors across these three major areas.

PRINT/BOOK AWARENESS

Children's awareness of the forms and functions of literacy has been shown to be a predictor of later school success (Adams, 1990; Wells, 1985). During the preschool years, children become aware of print and books by developing their concepts of literacy. There is a developmental progression in children's acquisition of print conventions. The print/book awareness section of the curriculum cov-

Table 1.   Early literacy and language behaviors and concepts across curriculum areas

Print/book awareness	Metalinguistic awareness	Oral language
Symbolic representation • Play • Pictures • Graphics Print • Book conventions • Awareness of graphic symbols • Letter identification • Writing Letter–sound correspondence • Single sounds/letters • Words	Perception and memory for sounds • Environmental sounds • Words • Phrases • Phonemes Word awareness • Words Phonological skills • Rhyming • Alliteration • Blending • Segmentation	Vocabulary • Words and sentences Narrative skills • Narrations of real events • Book • Narrations of fictional story Literate discourse • Conversations • Categorical organization • Decontextualization • Interpretive/ analytical discourse

ers three major areas: symbolic representation, conventions of representing language in print, and letter–sound correspondence.

Symbolic Representation

A major developmental task for young children is to understand the nature of symbols. Very early in life, children begin to use symbols in play, when, for example, they use a block to represent a car. Two-dimensional representations of objects such as pictures and drawings are early forms of graphic symbols that relate to the later understanding that printed words are symbols that represent objects, events, people, ideas, and feelings. Early skills consist of using symbols in play; recognizing that people, objects, and actions are represented in pictures; scribbling; assigning a meaning to drawings; and drawing figures that are recognizable.

Conventions of Representing Language in Print

Children need to understand the specific conventions of our reading and writing system. The curriculum addresses four areas of print convention: book conventions, awareness of graphic symbols, letter identification, and writing. Book conventions include book-handling behaviors (e.g., turning pages, orienting the book correctly, knowing where the book begins and ends) as well as knowing that the print, not the pictures, tells the story and that text begins at the top left corner of the page and is read from left to right. Children begin very early to recognize environmental print (e.g., logos, road signs, brand marks on cereal boxes) and to read a few familiar words in print, including their name. Children then learn about the alphabet and identify single letters, both in upper- and lowercase. At an early age, children pretend to write messages by scribbling lines or making shapes that resemble letters on sheets of paper. They begin to reproduce and distinguish correctly simple shapes (e.g., lines, crosses, circles, squares) and then proceed to copy letters and a few words from a model. Usually preschool children are able to write a few familiar words correctly (e.g., name) and use familiar letter sequences to create other words and begin to create words using invented spellings (Sulzby, 1985).

Letter–Sound Correspondence

Children learn about the sound-based nature of our reading and writing system and about the connection between print and language by discovering that a written word represents a spoken word.[1] They learn that letters stand for individual sounds in the

---

[1]The basic sound unit for the orthographic system varies among languages. In English, the phoneme (as represented by the letter) is the basic unit for the writing system, but there are other languages (e.g., Japanese) that use a writing system based on the syllable or word as the basic unit.

language and then become able to combine individual sounds to spell words.

METALINGUISTIC AWARENESS

Metalinguistic awareness refers to the ability to reflect on and to manipulate the structural features of spoken language, such as phonemes, words, sentences, and propositions (Tunmer et al., 1988). Several studies have demonstrated the connection between young children's abilities to manipulate sounds in spoken words (phonological awareness) and learning to read (Ball & Blachman, 1991; Bentin & Leshem, 1993; Cunningham, 1990; Lundberg et al., 1988; Maclean et al., 1987). The metalinguistic awareness section of the curriculum covers three major areas: perception and memory for sounds, word awareness, and phonological skills.

Perception and Memory for Sounds

Learning that sounds represent objects in their environment helps children understand the symbolic nature of language. Playing with sounds helps children learn about the phonological structure of language. Children begin to demonstrate awareness of the sounds of language by repeating words, phrases, and phonemes and discriminating between different phonemes. In order to manipulate sounds and words, children must be able to hold them in memory. Poor readers are less able to retain sequences of words and phonemes than better readers (Fowler, 1991).

Word Awareness

An important development occurs when children become able to decenter or separate the sound of the word from its referent or meaning. They learn that sentences are composed of words and that words are collections of smaller speech units such as syllables and phonemes.

Phonological Skills

Phonological skills include rhyming, alliteration, blending, and segmenting sounds.

- **Rhyming**—Nursery rhymes offer children an early opportunity to analyze sounds in words. Children who can recite rhymes at the age of 3 tend to become better readers (Maclean et al., 1987). Gradually, children learn that some words share a common feature, the sound of the ending part, that leads to recognizing and producing words that rhyme. Rhyming may be the first step toward the awareness of phonemes (Maclean et al., 1987).

- **Alliteration**—Alliteration refers to children's recognition or production of words with common initial sounds. This ability requires a sensitivity to parts of words that are smaller than the syllable (Ball, 1993). Children as young as 3 years of age are able to recognize alliteration (Maclean et al., 1987).
- **Blending**—Children's ability to represent sounds moves from holistic to analytical. Blending meaningful units such as those in compound words (e.g., butter-cup, cow-boy) is easier than blending syllables, and blending syllables is easier than blending onset-rime and phonemes. To decode a word independently, children must be able to say the sound of each letter in a word and blend those sounds together (c + a + t = cat). By the age of 4, children begin to blend two sounds (e.g., m-at) (O'Connor et al., 1993; Slocum et al., 1993). As children become older, they are able to blend three to four phonemes into words (b-u-s).
- **Segmentation**—Segmenting, or saying each individual sound in a spoken word, helps children acquire the alphabetical principle, which is a necessary step toward understanding how the sounds in words map onto, or correspond to, the letters of the alphabet. Young children are able first to represent and manipulate the more holistic units of speech such as syllables before they become able to segment phonemes (Fowler, 1991). Children learn to identify the initial sound of a word, then to isolate the initial sound from the rest of the word (onset-rime), and later to segment one-syllable words into three to four phonemes.

ORAL LANGUAGE

The development of oral language skills is an integral part of literacy development that results from the continuous interactions among meaning, language, and representation. Oral language can be viewed as a continuum from conversational, context-dependent language to decontextualized literate forms that contain features of written language (Tannen, 1982). Several aspects of language development have been linked to early exposure to literate events, such as story reading with parents (e.g., Whitehurst et al., 1988). The oral language section of the curriculum covers three major areas: vocabulary, narrative skills, and literate discourse.

Vocabulary

At the earliest developmental levels, children learn labels for objects through story reading (Ninio & Bruner, 1978). As children become older, they begin to listen to and remember syntactic constructions from stories and reuse these patterns in their speech (Snow & Goldfield, 1983). Skills in processing semantics (meaning) and syntax (language structure) facilitate reading (Morrow, 1989).

Familiarity with both semantics and syntax helps the reader antic-ipate the format and content of sentences in print.

Narrative Skills

Children's abilities to organize and structure discourse begins with understanding that events have a beginning, a middle, and an end. Later, children elaborate their recount into a cohesive relationship with explicit causal and temporal connections between events. When reading books, children and adults tend to use a hybridized form of oral language that contains features of written language such as telling stories in which the author is impersonal, the setting is distanced, and prior knowledge is assumed on the part of the lis-tener (Sulzby, 1985). Initially, young children attend to and label the pictures in the book. They then provide longer descriptions and comments on individual pictures and gradually become able to link events and form stories based on the pictures. Later, children use language with more appropriate wording for written rather than oral discourse and intonational patterns that sound like reading rather than conversing or storytelling. The understanding of stories is positively correlated to early reading (Dickinson & Snow, 1987). At a very early age, young children listen to adults telling stories. Gradually, storytelling becomes more interactive as children begin to add simple comments and ask questions. Eventually, children are able to retell a story and acquire the concept of story structure. They learn to introduce the story with its beginning and setting and describe the theme, plot episodes, and resolution. They demon-strate their understanding of story details and sequence by orga-nizing all of these elements in a coherent manner.

Literate Discourse

Literate discourse refers to particular kinds of oral language associ-ated with texts, such as analysis and interpretation (Watson, 1989), that have been linked to children's successful transition to school-ing and their acquisition of literacy skills (Heath, 1983; Snow, 1983). Characteristics of literate discourse include the use of super-ordinate levels of category labels, decontextualized language, and interpretive and analytic discourse. These skills are used in the comprehension of text.

- **Conversation skills**—Conversation skills lay the foundation for later extended discourse skills characteristic of literate lan-guage. Shared book reading is a common and important in-stance of early joint-action routines.

    The collaborative, predictable, and repetitive nature of shared book-reading routines makes them an ideal context for young children to learn to become effective communicators and to de-velop essential conversation skills (Kirchner, 1991). The same characteristics of repetition and predictability representative of early language acquisition have been found to contribute to the development of reading skills (Bridge, Winograd, & Haley, 1983).

- **Categorical Organization**—The use of superordinate category labels (e.g., animals, food), as opposed to basic level labels (e.g., dog, cookie), categorizes objects and events at an abstract, general level and implies children's ability to interpret and analyze (Markman, 1987).
- **Decontextualization**—Decontextualized language is a literate form of language characterized by the removal from the here and now and the separation of the writer from the reader or the speaker from the listener (Snow, 1983). The decontextualization of oral discourse involves the ability to think abstractly and to use language to display and transmit knowledge (Heath, 1982). Early skills that reflect decontextualization include transcending the immediate context and drawing from personal experience; providing explanations; making predictions, interpretations, and judgments; and explicitly distinguishing fiction from real events.
- **Interpretive/analytic discourse**—An important aspect of literacy is the ability to interpret and analyze text. The use of certain metalinguistic and metacognitive types of oral language is evidence of early interpretive and analytical abilities (Watson, 1989) and is predictive of later literacy (Galda, Pellegrini, & Cox, 1989). These abilities include making metalinguistic requests as to the meanings and definitions of words and using words that refer to affective inner states (e.g., want, like, happy, sad); cognitive verbs that reflect mental states, beliefs, or attitudes rather than facts (e.g., idea, memory, know, understand, remember, think); and words that refer to the uses of language (e.g., say, tell, call, read).

ASSESSMENT

In addition to normative information on how children develop early literacy skills, teachers and clinicians are concerned with individual variations and the unique characteristics of a particular child. Systematic observation is essential in making sure that children are progressing in their acquisition of new skills and most helpful in identifying teaching strategies for a child who needs additional assistance and support (see the scaffolding strategies discussed in Chapter 2). Assessment of a child's skills in the areas of print/book awareness, metalinguistic awareness, and oral language ensures that activities are tailored to meet individual needs and that tasks and teaching strategies are developmentally appropriate. Also, the developmental sequence of skills in the *Ladders to Literacy* Preschool Checklist (see Appendix A) helps teachers identify appropriate teaching goals and objectives for children requiring individualized education programs (IEPs). A variety of methods in addition to the *Ladders to Literacy* Preschool Checklist can be used to document children's early literacy behaviors. Children's drawings and dictations, teachers' anecdotal observations, and parent reports all can be assembled to form a portfolio for each child that can then serve as a common document for sharing information between families and professionals.

Assessment Portfolio

An assessment portfolio is a purposeful collection of a child's work that can be used to document the child's efforts, progress, and achievements over time (Arter & Spandel, 1991). Portfolio assessment is a means to provide a comprehensive view of the child's performance across a variety of situations and settings. Portfolio assessment systems have been described for use with young children without disabilities (Meisels, 1993; Puckett & Black, 1994) and young children with disabilities (Hanline & Fox, 1994). Although children's work samples are the major component of the portfolio, teacher and parent observations also can be included (Hanline & Fox, 1994; Meisels, 1993). Children's products may include work samples such as artwork, picture journals, dictations, audiotapes of conversations and songs, photographs of block construction, clay and dough manipulations, and science projects. Portfolios may also contain records of systematic observations made by teachers, including anecdotal observations and checklists as well as parent reports. Test results from curriculum-based and standardized assessments can also be included in the portfolio. There are no specific rules for what a portfolio should look like. One can use ring notebooks, file boxes, or other means to organize and store materials. A portfolio, however, should be organized so that relevant materials can be located with minimal effort.

Conducting portfolio assessments goes beyond merely collecting children's work in a folder. Teachers who use portfolios should formulate a specific purpose for the portfolio (e.g., monitoring the child's progress, communicating with parents) and determine clear criteria for selecting and evaluating the content. Specific criteria for evaluating the child's daily performance should be determined by the professionals, parents, and, in some cases, the child. Children can play a role in the selection and evaluation of the content (Cohen & Spenciner, 1994), although with young children, adults are more likely to play the major role. Young children, however, can be offered the opportunity to participate in this process. They can choose favorite works to include in the portfolio, and the teacher can record the children's reasons for why they like or dislike a piece and what they may have learned from it. The overall portfolio can be evaluated in diverse ways (Cohen & Spenciner, 1994). An optimal approach is to review the contents with other professionals, parents, and the child; summarize the child's strengths and weaknesses; and formulate recommendations in a written evaluative narrative.

Collecting Early Literacy and Language Documentary Data

At the beginning of the school year, prepare a file folder for each child. As the year goes by, collect samples of the child's work on an ongoing basis and place them in the child's portfolio. Make the child aware of the portfolio so that he or she can also decide to save samples of work. At the end of the year, an overview of the portfolio should provide a fun and interesting record of the child's progress to review with the child and the family.

At least three samples of each type of the following documentation should be collected during the school year: drawings and writing, anecdotal notes, dictations, interviews, and literacy and communication materials. Be sure that you have at least one from the beginning, one from the middle, and one from the end of the year. It is important to remember to date all samples and mark the child's name. The content and the type of information to be collected should reflect and be guided by the overall program curriculum and by the child's individual goals and objectives. The following are some good examples of documentation:

Drawings and Writing

Drawings can include having the child draw a picture of him- or herself (e.g., draw-a-person) or of another person and print his or her name on the sheet. Also ask the child to write something about the picture. Mark the date and the child's comments about the drawing.

Anecdotal Notes

Anecdotal notes can be taken to document children's behaviors regarding interest in books and print, language (e.g., relating stories and events), and phonemic awareness skills (e.g., saying nursery rhymes, finding words that rhyme, playing with the sounds of words, separating words into sounds and putting them back together). Anecdotal notes are brief narrative descriptions of verbal (including direct quotations) and nonverbal behaviors that the observer judges to be important (Cohen & Spenciner, 1994). Events should be recorded as close in time as possible to the actual observation. Notes can be written informally on sheets of paper, yellow sticky tabs, or small notebooks or more formally recorded on observation forms or journals. Figures 1 and 2 show examples of observation forms for recording early literacy behaviors. (At the end of Sections II, III, and IV, there are blank observation forms for you to photocopy and use with the children. You can note your observations about literacy and language behaviors children display during the curriculum activities as well at other times during

Early Literacy Observation Form

Child's name: _____

Print/Book Awareness: Things about my play, drawing, and writing, and what I know about print and books.

Date	What I did or said	Where/with whom

Metalinguistic Awareness: What I know about sounds, words, and sentences; nursery rhymes; and word play (breaking down words into syllables and phonemes, putting sounds together, finding the first sound and words that sound the same).

Date	What I did or said	Where/with whom

Oral Language: Words I know; things I say about what I do, what I feel, and what I think; and stories I can tell.

Date	What I did or said	Where/with whom

Figure 1. An example of an early literacy observation form.

Ladders to Literacy: A Preschool Activity Book
by Angela Notari-Syverson, Rollanda E. O'Connor, and Patricia F. Vadasy
©1998 Paul H. Brookes Publishing Co., Baltimore

Early Literacy Weekly Notes

Week of: _____

What we did and said this week.

Child's name	Date	What I did or said

Figure 2.   An example of a form for recording anecdotal notes.

Ladders to Literacy: A Preschool Activity Book
by Angela Notari-Syverson, Rollanda E. O'Connor, and Patricia F. Vadasy
©1998 Paul H. Brookes Publishing Co., Baltimore

the day. These forms allow you to monitor children's progress over time and to share your observations with parents and other colleagues in a descriptive and informal manner.)

Dictations

Dictations include stories, thoughts, and ideas written by the adult but dictated by the child. The adult is the scribe for the child's verbal expression of real or imaginary happenings, related by the child spontaneously or following adult elicitation. Some examples of comments the adult may use to elicit dictations include the following: "Let's write a story together. You tell me the story, and I'll write it down," or "Is there something you would like to tell me about? I'll write down the story for you." Write exactly what the child says, as it is said. Read back the dictation to the child. If the child wishes to add, delete, or correct something, then do so. Ask whether the child wishes to keep the story or to draw a picture about it. If so, give the original to the child, and place a photocopy of the story and the drawing in the child's portfolio.

Interviews

Have a brief conversation with the child about events related to early literacy. The purpose of the interview is to discover the child's interest and way of understanding and interpreting events. Record what both the adult and the child say. Some examples of questions to ask include the following: "What is your favorite book/story (at home, at school, from the library)?" "Do you go to the library? What books do you take out? Do you like going to the library?" "Do you go to the bookstore? What books did you see?" "What's your favorite song/nursery rhyme? Can you sing it for me? What is it about?" "Do you like drawing pictures? What do you like best to draw?" "Do you like to write messages/letters to your friends?" "Does anyone write notes/letters to you?" "If you were to write a book, what would it be about?" and "Do you go to see/hear plays, puppet shows, storytelling? Tell me about what you saw/heard."

Literacy and Communication Materials

Additional information on children's behaviors and use of materials related to literacy and communication can be recorded through various visual and narrative means (e.g., photographs, videotapes, objects, written notes, parent reports). Photographs of children's work and participation in events at home and at school are useful and powerful forms of documentation. For children with specific disabilities, information on and examples of alternative reading, writing, and communication systems (e.g., sign boards, relief drawings, text in braille) that the child uses should be included.

Documenting and Monitoring of Progress on Individualized Education Program and Individualized Family Service Plan Goals and Objectives

Practitioners can also use the portfolio assessment to document children's progress on the IEP and individualized family service plan (IFSP) goals and objectives. The following procedures are critical to the assessment:

Identification of Goals and Objectives

- Identify goals and objectives for children in the areas of early literacy and language using the *Ladders to Literacy* Preschool Checklist or other curriculum-based assessments.

Data Collection

- Develop a plan for data collection on IEP/IFSP objectives (i.e., determine schedule for data collection, types of data, and portfolio format).
- Collect data, and place in portfolio.

After the previous steps are completed, the practitioner will be ready for the following stages.

Instructional Program Decision Making

Review information in the portfolio on a regular basis during team meetings, and evaluate progress on IEP goals and objectives. Continue the intervention plan if progress meets expectations. If not, then revise the plan. Following are some suggestions:

- Change teaching strategies by increasing levels of support. For example, if Sammy's drawings are not becoming more recognizable, then provide concrete models (e.g., objects, photographs) for him to copy.
- Change setting, activities, or materials. For example, if Sammy is not making progress in telling oral stories during classroom activities, then try the activity in a quiet, individual setting or use short, simple books with pictures that clearly illustrate the story line.
- Modify the objective. For example, if Sammy is having trouble reciting the entire rhyme, then change the objective to reciting the first two lines independently.

Evaluation of Yearly Progress

Toward the middle (if possible) and at the end of the school year, complete the *Ladders to Literacy* Preschool Checklist using information collected in the portfolio as well as direct observations of children's behaviors and compare it with beginning of year performance.

CONCLUSION

Portfolio assessment is an excellent tool for assessing children's progress within the context of meaningful events that reflect real-life situations (Notari-Syverson & Losardo, 1996). It provides a framework for organizing and integrating information from multiple methods and sources across multiple contexts. It can help facilitate collaboration among team members and families as well as provide continuity of documentation during transitions from one program to another.

Chapter 2

The Role of Scaffolding

Scaffolding is a metaphor introduced by Wood et al. (1976) to describe a process first observed in parent–child interactions. In scaffolding, the adult guides and supports the child's learning by building on what the child is able to do. The notion of scaffolding was later applied to classroom practice (Tharp & Gallimore, 1988) and language intervention (Norris & Hoffman, 1990). Because it is highly responsive to the individual characteristics of children and emphasizes the importance of the social environment, scaffolding has valuable applications for teachers and other professionals working in inclusive settings in which adults interact with children who are functioning at diverse developmental levels. Scaffolding approaches have been used successfully to assess and teach language and literacy skills to young children with language delays (Olswang, Bain, & Johnson, 1992), children at risk (Juel, 1996), and children from diverse cultural backgrounds (Gutierrez-Clellen & Quinn, 1993).

The notion of scaffolding derives from Vygotsky's (1978) concept of the zone of proximal development (ZPD). Vygotsky observed that children could improve their performance on tasks when provided with adult assistance. He used the term *ZPD* to refer to the difference between what a child can achieve independently and what the child can achieve with assistance. Teachers provide the necessary amount of support to help the child master emerging skills as defined by the child's ZPD. Only if tasks are at an appropriately challenging level within the child's ZPD will scaffolding be successful in moving the child to a more advanced level (Olswang et al., 1992; Pressley, Hogan, Wharton-McDonald, & Mistretta, 1996). The ZPD is different for each child, varies as a function of context and task, and changes constantly as the child learns new skills (Bodrova & Leong, 1996; Pressley et al., 1996). Some children may require high support and make small gains, whereas other children will learn quickly with minimal assistance. The same child may respond differently to various types of assistance and in various areas of development. Teachers need to be sensitive to both the level of task difficulty and the competence of the child. The amount of scaffolding or support the adult provides should be inversely related to the child's level of task competence. The more difficulty the child has in achieving a goal, the more directive the intervention of the adult should be (Fry, 1992). Effective scaffolding is flexible, is responsive to the child, draws on a variety of strategies, and may vary considerably across cultures (Berk & Winsler, 1995). The scaffolding process involves active coparticipation of the adult and the child. The amount and type of support is constantly being adjusted to the child's behavior and gradually reduced as the child assumes more responsibility for learning (Bruner, 1983; Rogoff, 1986; Tharp & Gallimore, 1988).

Applications of scaffolding range from low-structured approaches with minimal adult assistance (e.g., asking questions to help children discover their own solutions) to high-structured approaches with more direct and explicit modeling and instruction (e.g., eliciting questions, giving directions) (Norris & Hoffman, 1990; Peña, 1996). Means of assistance can be verbal, visual, or physical, including words, symbols, drawings, maps, arrangement of materials, and shaping (Bodrova & Leong, 1996; Tharp & Gallimore, 1988). Adults should constantly vary the degree of support, providing minimal guidance at first and increasing assistance as needed by the child. (At the end of Sections II, III, and IV, there are blank scaffolding checklists for you to photocopy and use with the children. These forms will help you identify which scaffolding strategies may work best for a particular child. Also, you may notice changes over time in the types and itensity of supports a child may need.)

SCAFFOLDING CATEGORIES

Following are *descriptions* of different scaffolding strategies organized from lower to higher levels of support and grouped into six main categories. (Each scaffolding strategy has a corresponding icon that will be used throughout the book for easy reference to the strategy.)

?

Open-ended questioning

The adult asks questions that encourage children to elaborate on their own ideas and communicate them to others. Open-ended questions are questions with unknown answers that have no one correct response. These include questions that relate to the immediate context ["What do you see?"]; questions that relate to past events ["What happened?"]; questions that require explanations ["Why?"]; questions that help the child go beyond the here and now by relating events to his or her own experiences ["Did this ever happen to you at home?"]; and questions that require hypotheses about novel situations and cause-and-effect inferences ["What should we do next?" "What if?"].

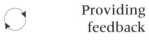

Providing feedback	The adult provides information on the child's performance to increase the child's sense of competence (e.g., encouragements, praise) and ability to monitor and regulate behaviors (e.g., evaluations, thinking aloud, clarification requests, interpretations, information talk).
Cognitive structuring	The adult provides structure for thinking and acting (Tharp & Gallimore, 1988) and facilitates children's logical reasoning and problem-solving abilities (e.g., making explicit rules and logical relationships, sequencing, pointing out contradictions).
Holding in memory	The adult shares the task by assuming part of the memory demands to enable the child to focus on the response or solution to the problem (e.g., restating goals, providing summaries and reminders).
Task regulation	The adult modifies certain aspects of the situation to facilitate child mastery by increasing the value of the task for the child (e.g., matching interests and experience) or by simplifying and clarifying the task (e.g., making it more concrete, rearranging elements, reducing alternatives).
Instructing	The adult provides highly structured direct assistance that has an explicit influence on the child's behavior. These strategies include modeling, orienting the child's attention to relevant aspects of the situation, asking direct questions, prompting elicitations, and co-participation.

For each of the six main strategies described previously, we have identified specific scaffolding strategies that teachers may use to assist children's learning of literacy and language skills. Figure 1 presents an overview of these strategies. Each activity in this book contains *suggestions* for types of scaffolding or teaching strategies. Each strategy is illustrated by specific examples, *meant to serve as ideas or models* for practitioners to adapt and modify. The following are *examples* of each scaffolding strategy.

Open-Ended Questioning

- **Descriptions**—The adult asks questions that help the child describe and talk about events and objects ["What do you see?" "What happened?" "What's this story about?"].
- **Predictions and Planning**—The adult helps the child go beyond the immediate context, generalize to novel situations, predict and plan future events, propose alternatives, hypothesize about possibilities, and anticipate eventual difficulties ["What are the things we need to do?" "What else could we use to reach up to the cupboard door?" "What else could you use to count the number of blocks you need?" "What do you think

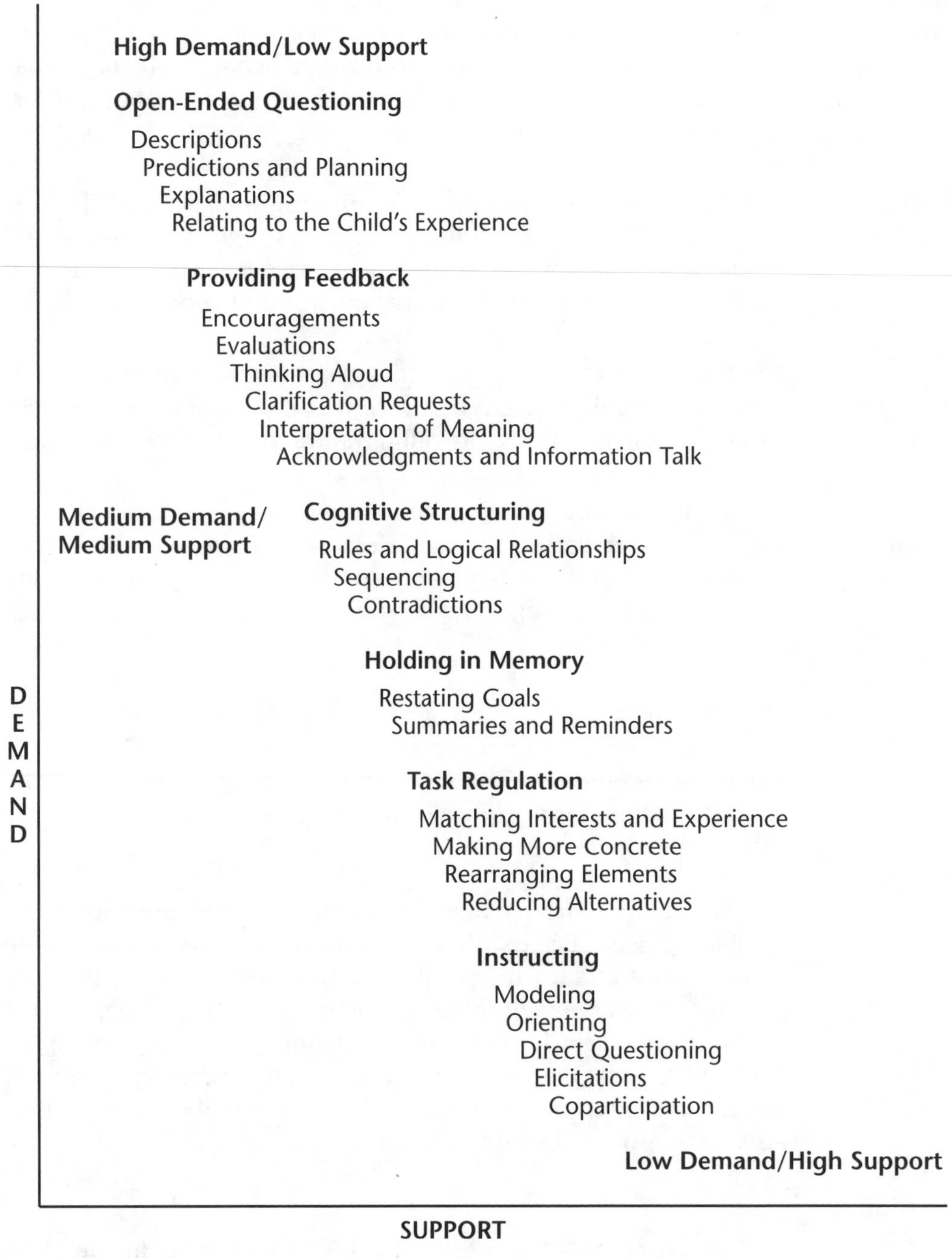

High Demand/Low Support

Open-Ended Questioning

Descriptions
Predictions and Planning
Explanations
Relating to the Child's Experience

Providing Feedback

Encouragements
Evaluations
Thinking Aloud
Clarification Requests
Interpretation of Meaning
Acknowledgments and Information Talk

Medium Demand/   **Cognitive Structuring**
Medium Support

Rules and Logical Relationships
Sequencing
Contradictions

Holding in Memory

Restating Goals
Summaries and Reminders

Task Regulation

Matching Interests and Experience
Making More Concrete
Rearranging Elements
Reducing Alternatives

Instructing

Modeling
Orienting
Direct Questioning
Elicitations
Coparticipation

Low Demand/High Support

D E M A N D

SUPPORT

Figure 1.   A continuum of scaffolding strategies.

might happen if . . . ?" "What could go wrong?" "How could you do this at home?"].

- **Explanations**—The adult helps the child provide explanations and explain causes ["Why do you think that happened?" "How is this different from what we saw yesterday?" "What did the wheel do when you poured the water?" "What did you do to make a sound with the drum?"].
- **Relating to the Child's Experience**—The adult helps the child relate a new situation to something the child may have experienced directly ["Has this ever happened to you before?" "Have you ever seen something like this?"].

Providing Feedback

- **Encouragements**—The adult offers simple verbal and nonverbal encouragements and praise to increase the child's confidence and sense of self-competence ["That's a good idea!" "That's interesting!"].
- **Evaluations**—The adult encourages the child to check the results of his or her own actions and to judge the appropriateness of his or her own actions ["Did it work?" "Did it move when you blew on it?" "Does that look right?"].
- **Thinking Aloud**—The adult helps the child describe aloud what he or she is doing or thinking in order to encourage awareness of the processes involved in solving problems ["Tell me what you are doing"].
- **Clarification Requests**—The adult encourages the child to provide reasons for his or her ideas and actions in order to help solve a problem, or the adult asks for more specific information to make an action or message clearer ["Why did you put the piece that way?" "Why are you writing to Safa?"].
- **Interpretation of Meaning**—The adult offers interpretations and explains underlying meanings to help the child complete a task, reach a solution, or understand reasons for success or failure of an action ["I don't think Katie understood what you said"; "The lady was upset because you talked too loudly in the library"; "Oh, you mean he couldn't come because he was sick?"].
- **Acknowledgments and Information Talk**—The adult acknowledges the child's actions and statements by making appropriate comments or describing the child's actions ["Now you're pouring water into the big jar"].

Cognitive Structuring

- **Rules and Logical Relationships**—The adult makes explicit underlying rules and helps the child notice relationships (e.g., cause and effect, similarities and differences) between events and characteristics of objects ["Did you notice how when the blue one gets smaller, the red one gets bigger?" "These two are the same size," "A husky and a poodle both are dogs," "A dinosaur is bigger than a bird"].

- **Sequencing**—The adult helps the child find a starting point or continue an action or narrative in a correct sequence ["Which puzzle piece should you choose first?" "What comes after the green one?"].
- **Contradictions**—The adult helps the child recognize inconsistencies and contradictions between actions, events, and facts ["You said that you needed a big block, but this one is very small"].

Holding in Memory

- **Restating Goals**—The adult reminds the child of the activity's purpose and of the behaviors expected ["Remember, we are writing this card to tell Tim about our visit to the zoo"].
- **Summaries and Reminders**—The adult summarizes events and actions and offers important information to help the child complete a task ["Remember, the one we saw was soft and fuzzy"; "We've decided that we are going to the Museum of Natural History tomorrow, and we are going to take the bus. What do you need to bring?"].

Task Regulation

- **Matching Interests and Experience**—The adult modifies aspects of the task to match closer the interests of the child (e.g., substitutes blocks with toy dinosaurs), to relate the task to the child's experience ["That's cold like ice cream"], or to make the task more familiar by using familiar materials or teaching tasks in a familiar setting or routine (e.g., rhyming words within familiar storybook-reading routines).
- **Making More Concrete**—The adult modifies a situation by decreasing the level of symbolic representation and memory demands, for example, by providing visual and other nonlinguistic cues (e.g., making gestures, substituting written words with pictures and real objects).
- **Rearranging Elements**—The adult changes the arrangement of materials to help the child complete the task or solve the problem (e.g., places together puzzle pieces that go together, turns objects in the right directions).
- **Reducing Alternatives**—The adult simplifies the task by reducing the number of choices ["You can make an animal with playdough or draw an animal with crayons," "Should we pick the yellow or the blue?" "Is this for real or pretend?" "Is this an animal or a bird?"].

Instructing

- **Modeling**—The adult exposes the child to models of problem-solving strategies and oral and written communication by demonstrating or pairing the child with a more experienced peer so that the child learns through observation and collaboration. The adult may, for example, write words for the child to copy, name letters, label objects, reword an incorrect sentence, or recast or expand on the child's utterances by adding new information.

- **Orienting**—The adult proposes appropriate tools or strategies to facilitate the child's performance, verbally describes how to perform a task, or draws the child's attention to relevant aspects of the situation ["How about using a typewriter?" "Do you think we could paste them together?" "I would push the green one," "You could ask Dave to help you," "Look at the top of the page"].

- **Direct Questioning**—The adult directs the child to a specific action or response by asking questions ["What's the name of this animal?" "What shape is this?"].

- **Elicitations**—The adult directly requests a specific action or verbalization ["Juice. Say juice," "Take the small block"].

- **Coparticipation**—The adult encourages the child to accompany the adult in performing an action (e.g., reciting a nursery rhyme together), to participate in completing a task (e.g., the adult begins building a tower with blocks and has the child place the top one), and to fill in the blanks in an utterance ["The eagle flew on top of the . . . ?"].

EXAMPLES OF ACTUAL SCAFFOLDING INTERACTIONS

Adults will use a variety of strategies to teach a skill. Two major guidelines are useful in choosing strategies: 1) observe the child's responses and determine which type of support will best suit the child's needs in that specific situation, and 2) begin with the least intensive assistance and add more support as needed. The following example illustrates an adult (A) helping a child (C) read a word in the presence of a peer (P):

A: What will we eat today? (**Open-ended questioning**/*prediction*)

C: (points to a word)

A: That's a complicated word. Let's look at the letters I wrote down here. First here's an /s/, then there's a /p/-Spa (**Cognitive structuring**/*sequencing*)

C: Spa

A: Here's a g, which makes which sound? (**Task Regulation**/*matching interests and experience*)

C: /g/. That's for me!

A: Right. (**Providing Feedback**/*encouragement*)

A: G for Graham (**Instructing**/*modeling*)

A: Right at the end—What are these letters? (**Cognitive Structuring**/*sequencing*)

P: I and t. (**Instructing**/*peer modeling*)

C: Oh, you know what? That last one is an i.

A: Great. (**Providing Feedback**/*encouragement*)

A: We put all these sounds together to read the word. (**Cognitive Structuring**/*rules and logical relationships*)

C: (waits)

A: Spa . . . (**Instructing**/*modeling*)

C: Spaghetti. They're really short letters.

A: You think it's a short word? (**Providing Feedback**/*interpretation of meaning*)

A: Let's count the letters. 1-2-3-4-5-6-7-8-9. Is that short? (**Cognitive Structuring**/*contradictions*)

C: Nine is a long word.

This example illustrates another interaction with a child (C) who needs more intensive levels of support:

A: The first pig built his house out of what? (**Instructing**/*direct questioning*)

C: (no response)

A: Points to object (straw) (**Instructing**/*orienting*)

C: (no response)

A: What's this called? (**Task Regulation**/*making more concrete*)

C: Stick.

A: It's not a stick. It's like a stick, but it's softer. (**Cognitive Structuring**/*rules and logical relationships*)

A: It's straw. The pig made a strawhouse. (**Instructing**/*modeling*)

C: Strawhouse.

A: Little pig made a straw house. (**Instructing**/*modeling*)

A: Feel the straw. (**Task Regulation**/*making more concrete*)

A: What did the little pig make his house out of? (**Instructing**/*direct questioning*)

C: Straw. A house of straw.

Chapter 3

Implementing *Ladders to Literacy*

The main purpose of the *Ladders to Literacy* curriculum is to illustrate how learning about literacy and language is an integral part of daily life at home, at school, and in the community. It provides guidelines and suggestions for teaching a variety of early literacy and language skills across a broad range of situations and tasks (e.g., from quiet book activities to active physical motor games). Activities should be easy for teachers to implement within the context of their daily classroom routines. *Although the activities lend themselves to teaching a broad range of early literacy and language skills, each activity has been assigned to one primary area (print/book awareness, metalinguistic awareness, or oral language), and teachers are recommended to focus on teaching skills in the designated primary area.* Given the range of ages and abilities in inclusive and special education preschool settings, teachers often need to address multiple educational goals within a single activity. Within the primary area (e.g., print/book awareness), recommendations are provided for teaching children with different needs concepts and behaviors that are developmentally appropriate to their individual levels. While reading a storybook, for example, one child can be taught to identify letters, another can sight-read familiar words, and a third can learn to label pictures. For each level, scaffolding or teaching strategies to facilitate the individual goals are suggested.

The physical context in which activities take place is an important factor for the successful implementation of the curriculum. Following are suggestions for arranging the classroom environment to maximize opportunities for children to experience and learn about literacy.

LITERACY-RICH ENVIRONMENT

The physical and social environment exert a strong influence on the development of children (Barker, 1968; Bronfenbrenner, 1979; Piaget, 1971; Vygotsky, 1978). There are many ways in which the environment can be arranged to enhance children's social, emotional, cognitive, and physical development (Weinstein, 1987). Three major principles serve as guidelines for arranging classrooms and child care settings to promote children's development and to create a literacy-rich environment.

1. *The physical environment should foster the child's emotional well-being by providing the child with a sense of comfort and security and by being aesthetically pleasing.* Optimal learning takes place in a setting in which children feel comfortable, safe, and at ease (Weinstein, 1987). The school and classroom environment should be aesthetically pleasing and appealing to the children (Greenman, 1988; Neuman & Roskos, 1993). The classroom should have warm colors and natural lighting (windows) and be directly connected to the natural environment (e.g., indoor plants, animals, outdoor garden). Furniture should be child size and present a variety of textures (e.g., wood, pillows, beanbag chairs). The classroom environment should allow teachers and children to engage comfortably in social and private as well as noisy and quiet activities. The surface should have carpeted and noncarpeted areas so that children can engage in both messy activities (e.g., painting, water play, sand play, clay) in noncarpeted areas and quiet, personal activities (e.g., reading books) in warm, cozy, private areas. The general ambiance should be personalized, reflect the presence of the children, and foster a sense of personal ownership. Children should have spaces for their personal objects, their own cubbies, and mailboxes. Their photographs, drawings, and projects should be hung on the walls.

2. *The physical environment should foster opportunities for integrated learning, social interaction, privacy, and sustained long-term work.* The physical space should be divided in small play and activity areas that offer children opportunities to engage in a variety of social, cognitive, physical, and private activities. Spatial boundaries can be created by using bookshelves, low partitions, furniture, plants, boxes, easels, aquariums, and rugs. Spaces for noisy, social-interactive activities (e.g., dramatic play, block construction) should be grouped together and separated from more quiet and private retreat spaces (e.g., library area, teepees, large boxes, small desk areas) where children can be alone, have quiet conversations, and do individualized work (e.g., reading, manipulatives, art). Areas should be available in which children can continue work on extended projects without having to put things away at the end of each day (Neuman & Roskos, 1993). Figure 1 shows an example of a floor plan for arranging the different areas and furniture in the classroom.

3. *The physical environment should foster opportunities for the development of symbolic expression, including play, language, and literacy.*

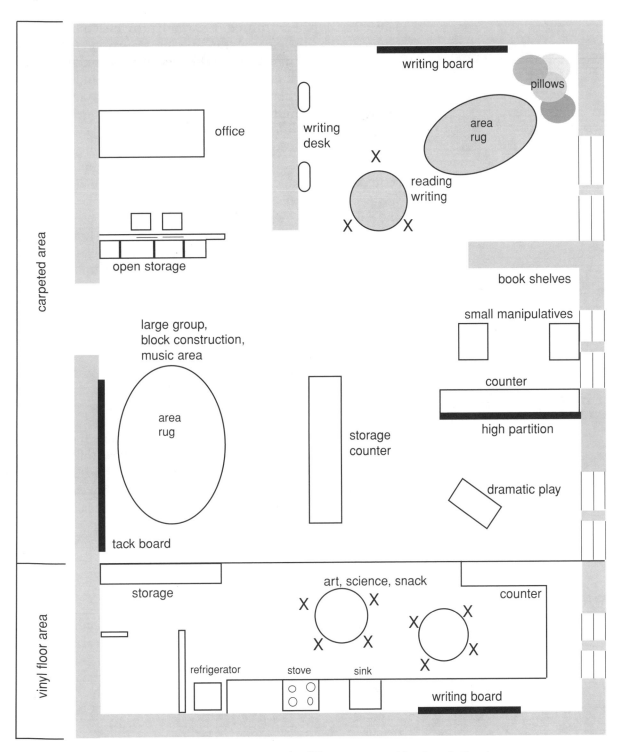

Figure 1.   An example of a floor plan for arranging the different areas and furniture in the classroom.

The classroom environment should provide children with opportunities to learn about literacy (Morrow, 1989). The major achievement of the preschool years is the understanding and use of important symbols such as language and literacy to express oneself, to communicate with others, and to gain knowledge about the world. The classroom environment should provide children with opportunities to learn about literacy. This can be done by using a variety of pictures, symbols, and signs to label areas in the general environment (e.g., play centers, bathroom, exits) and storage locations for objects (e.g., shelves, bins, cupboard drawers) as well as to display directions and rules related to daily classroom routines (e.g., series of pictures that represent the class schedule, a "No Hitting" sign). Other materials may include charts (e.g., weather, attendance, tasks, growth, record keeping, sign-up sheets for activities); news bulletin boards; message boards for personal notes; children's names on personal mailboxes; posters; and, most important, children's own artwork and written products. Special areas in the classroom should be dedicated to activities that foster symbolic expression.

Dramatic Play

The dramatic play area should contain at least a kitchen and a bedroom setting with both realistic toys (e.g., miniature dolls, brushes, cups, spoons) and ambiguous objects that afford more abstract levels of symbolic representation (e.g., blocks, strings, boxes). Literacy props suitable for this area include books, magazines, cookbook recipes, telephone directories, stationery, envelopes, stamps, stickers, pens and crayons, play money, food containers, calendars, and message pads.

Writing Center

The writing center should contain tables, chairs, paper, crayons, index cards (for children's Very Own Words), construction paper, displays of children's writing, envelopes, stamps (for pen pal programs), typewriter, computer, alphabet chart, plastic magnetic letters, and posters displaying sound–symbol associations.

Oral Language Area

The oral language area should encourage children to enact stories with puppets or using flannel board figures. Pictures of interesting topics for discussion (e.g., foreign countries) and of nursery rhyme stories and songs should be displayed. Children should have access to a tape recorder and cassettes.

Art Area

Materials in the art area should encourage children to use a variety of materials for artistic expression, including paint, clay, crayons, marker pens, scissors, glue sticks, yarn, papers, fabrics, and seasonal materials (e.g., leaves, acorns, cotton balls).

Literacy Center

The literacy center should be an important spot that occupies a focal point. The area should be inviting but also private (e.g., partitioned with bookshelves) and allow for five to six children. It should contain a rug, pillows, beanbag chairs, bulletin board, posters, stuffed toys, and puppets. There should be two types of bookshelves: one for stacking books and one for displaying varying feature books. Five to eight books per child are recommended as well as many magazines. Books can be categorized by topic (color stickers work well) and include picture concept books (e.g., that correspond to themes addressed during the year), traditional literature (e.g., *Goldilocks and the Three Bears* [Brett, 1990], *The Three Little Pigs* [Galdone, 1970], nursery rhymes), picture storybooks, realistic literature (e.g., sensitive topics, bedtime, new baby), easy-to-read books (e.g., with repetitive text), fables and folktales (including those from other countries), information books, wordless books, and poetry. Teachers can develop a check-out system and involve children in defining rules.

ACTIVITIES

Components

Each activity includes a purpose statement with a list of behaviors the activity facilitates, a description of the activity procedures and materials, suggestions for specific child objectives and adult assistance, adaptations for specific disabilities, and ideas for home activities and parent involvement.

Purpose Statement

The purpose statement describes the major goals of the activity and how these goals promote the use of literacy and language in daily life settings. It also includes a list of concepts and behaviors across the three major areas of the curriculum (print/book awareness, metalinguistic awareness, and oral language) that the activity develops. These behaviors correspond to items from the *Ladders to Literacy* Preschool Checklist.

Materials and Description of the Activity

Suggestions are provided for organizing materials, setting up the activity, and encouraging child participation.

Adult–Child Interactive Behaviors

The adult–child interactive behavior section describes how, through participation in the same activity, children functioning at diverse levels may learn new concepts and behaviors developmentally appropriate to their individual needs and characteristics. Three groups of learning objectives (these are the task demands) with corresponding teaching strategies (or supports) are outlined: high demand/low support, medium demand/medium support, and low demand/high support. The three levels of task demands consist of skills that correspond to items on the *Ladders to Literacy* Preschool Checklist. These are skills the adult aims to facilitate or teach children during the activity. For example, the three levels of task demands for the Snack/Lunch Menu activity in the print/book awareness section are the following:

- High demand/low support: Children read the menu to find out what will be served for snack/lunch. They will:

    read words and name single letters.

- Medium demand/medium support: Children refer to the menu during snack/lunch and will:

    recognize a few memorized words.

- Low demand/high support: Children will:

    identify foods and objects represented in the pictures.

The skills selected were the behaviors that are the most likely to occur naturally as children participate in a particular activity. As a result, levels of demand may vary from one activity to another. For each level of task demand, specific teaching strategies to support the child's learning of a skill are suggested. Teaching strategies are organized according to levels of assistance from low to high support. In general, the more competent child will require minimal guidance from the adult, whereas other children will need more intensive assistance and higher levels of support. Therefore, low-support strategies are generally the most appropriate for children ready to master tasks presenting at high levels of demand. Children learning tasks with lower demands are more likely to benefit from high-support strategies. For each child participating in the activity, the teacher may determine the most appropriate level of demand based on the child's performance on the *Ladders to Literacy* Preschool Checklist, the individualized education program (IEP)/individualized family service plan (IFSP) goals and objectives, and/or the teacher's recent observations of the child.

For certain activities, multiple skills or goals may be listed within each level so that teachers may select the most appropriate tasks for individual children or address more than one skill for the same child. In the previous example, the high-demand level contains two learning objectives: reading words and naming single letters. When multiple learning objectives are listed for the same level, individual strategies may be applicable to only one of the objectives. In this case, the teacher should select those appropriate for each individual goal. For example, two strategies are suggested for cognitive structuring. One strategy is the following: *Point out distinctive features, similarities, and differences between targeted letter and other letters* ["You said this is a b. Does it look the same as this other b here? Look carefully. Which side of the circle is the stick on?"]. This strategy addresses letter identification. The second strategy is the following: *Provide verbal information about the identity of the word* ["It grows underneath the ground and is orange"]. This latter strategy addresses word recognition.

After determining appropriate levels of task demands for each child, teachers should select two or three teaching strategies to assist the child in accomplishing the task. Figure 2 shows an example of an activity planning form to assist teachers in this task. Begin by using the least intensive support strategy (usually the first listed). If this does not help the child learn the skill, then gradually increase the amount of support.

It is important to remember that children will respond differently to different types of support, with some children benefiting from more direct assistance and others from less direct assistance. Children who are ready to take on high-demand tasks may, at times, need high-support teaching strategies (explicit instructing). In some situations, low-support strategies (open-ended questioning) might be sufficient for children learning low-demand tasks. During the teaching interactions, adults should continually evaluate and revise decisions about appropriate levels of support based on the individual child's responses to prior types of assistance.

Adaptations

Recommendations are provided for adapting materials and activity procedures to facilitate the participation of children with visual, motor, or hearing impairments.

Home Link and Parent Activity

Each activity offers easy-to-implement suggestions for families to enhance the early literacy and language development of their children at home and in community settings. The purpose of these suggestions is to encourage family participation and establish ongoing communication between the home and the school. The suggestions for home activities are simple for teachers to implement, such as sending home samples of children's work or eliciting parent assistance in having children bring special objects from home to share with their peers. Also, we have compiled a special set of Early Literacy Activities for Children and Parents (see Appendix B), which help parents reinforce the concepts and behaviors being taught in

Activity Plan

Activity: _____ Date: _____

Purpose: _____

Description: _____

Levels of participation/child objectives	Levels of support/instructional strategies	Children
High		
Medium		
Low		

Figure 2. An example of an activity planning form.

Ladders to Literacy: A Preschool Activity Book
by Angela Notari-Syverson, Rollanda E. O'Connor, and Patricia F. Vadasy
©1998 Paul H. Brookes Publishing Co., Baltimore

the classroom. Teachers can, for example, include these suggestions in regular parent newsletters; compile them as a special booklet for parents; or make separate copies, on colored paper, to send home. Also, teachers can personalize the activities by adding illustrations or have children draw their own pictures or paste figures or photographs on the copies.

How to Start

All of the activities have been field-tested by teachers working in a variety of inclusive and self-contained child care, preschool, and kindergarten classrooms with children who are at risk, children with disabilities, and typically developing children. The classrooms included children from ethnically and culturally diverse backgrounds (African American, Native American, Asian American, Hispanic, and Arabic). The activities span a range of projects and tasks, from those directly involving language and literacy skills (e.g., looking at books, drawing, reciting nursery rhymes) to those in which language and literacy skills are incorporated as fundamental components (e.g., playing with water, conducting science projects, participating in obstacle courses). Actual implementation of activities will depend on the individual teacher's educational philosophy, regular classroom routines, and material resources. Many activities require minimal preparation and can be conducted daily (e.g., Shared Storybook Reading, Morning/Afternoon Message and News, My First Journal, Nursery Rhymes, Describing the Foods We Eat). Some require more extensive preparation and may be best implemented weekly or monthly (e.g., Science Projects, Clap the Syllables, Musical Instruments, Brainstorming, Let's Say it Another Way). Some activities describe a one-time only project (e.g., Long Jump, Treasure Hunt, Pretend Play: The Store, Interviews) or are ongoing and long term (e.g., Let's Find Out, Museum Exhibit). It is recommended that teachers begin with activities that can be easily included within current classroom routines on a frequent basis and with minimal preparation. For example, if looking at picture books and drawing are already a part of the daily class routine, then it will be easy to implement Shared Storybook Reading or My First Journal. If circle time usually involves singing and musical activities, then Nursery Rhymes and Listening to Songs can be used easily. By beginning with familiar activities, teachers can focus on the facilitation and teaching of behaviors rather than the implementation of procedures. As teachers become more familiar with the instructional strategies, new activities may be added, preferably balancing the activities across the three literacy areas. Activities can be planned to correspond to certain themes and events during the school year (e.g., using My Dream near Martin Luther King Day, using Showtime or Museum Exhibit as an end-of-year event for parents, using Let's Say it Another Way on Cinco de Mayo, using Classroom Post Office for Valentine's Day). Other activities may emerge from unplanned events. An unusually severe snowstorm can lead to a science project on snow. A child's personal experience may lead to a brainstorming session or a special Show and Tell.

Within each section, activities have been sequenced loosely by difficulty. It is not necessary to complete all of the activities in one area before proceeding to another; rather, activities can be selected to enhance ongoing classroom routines and special events. Because the three areas are interrelated, teachers will want to include activities across areas in their weekly planning. We suggest the following implementation sequence:

1. **Begin with Print/Book Awareness:** Shared Storybook Reading; Morning/Afternoon Message and News; My First Journal; **Metalinguistic Awareness:** Sound Representations; Listening to Songs; Nursery Rhymes; **Oral Language:** Show and Tell; Food Talk; Portraits.

2. **By mid-year, introduce Print/Book Awareness:** Snack/Lunch Menu; Making Signs; Many Ways to Write; I Found . . . ; Name Cups; Classroom Post Office; Fill in the Blanks; Making Books; Photography; Science Projects; **Metalinguistic Awareness:** Musical Instruments; Clap the Syllables; Syllable Puzzles; The Rhyming Book; Rhyming Games; Playing with Sounds of Words; Letter Sound of the Week; First Sound Song; **Oral Language:** Talking About Books; Enacting Storybooks; Book Buddy; I See, You See; Treasure Boxes; Water Play; My Dream; Special Words.

3. **During the second half of the year, try Print/Book Awareness:** Following Recipes; Sorting Objects; Blocks; Recording Constructions; Treasure Hunt; Obstacle Course; Long Jump; Landscapes and Maps; Museum Exhibit; **Metalinguistic Awareness:** Sound Isolation; Guess the Word; I'm Thinking of a . . . ; Word to Word Matching Game: First Sound; Play with Miniature Toys and First Sounds; Pretend Play—The Store; Pretend Play—Magic Password; **Oral Language:** What Did You Hear?; Feeling Objects; What Does This Mean?; Let's Say it Another Way!; Interviews; Movie Reviews; Brainstorming; From This to That; Let's Find Out; Showtime.

SECTION II

Print/Book Awareness

Shared Storybook Reading 51
Snack/Lunch Menu 56
Following Recipes 60
Making Signs 64
Many Ways to Write 68
Morning/Afternoon Message and News 72
I Found 76
Name Cups 79
Classroom Post Office 81
Fill in the Blanks 84
Making Books 87
Photography 91
Sorting Objects 94
Blocks 98
Recording Constructions 101
Treasure Hunt 104
Science Projects 107
Obstacle Course 111
Long Jump 114
My First Journal 118
Landscapes and Maps 122
Museum Exhibit 126

During the preschool years, children become aware of print and books, developing concepts of literacy. This knowledge becomes a foundation for much of later school instruction (McCormick & Mason, 1986; Snow & Ninio, 1986). During this time, children develop a model (schema) of what it means to be literate in our culture. Children learn specifically that 1) reading and discussing text can be used as tools to acquire knowledge; 2) reading and writing are ways to communicate with others; and, finally, 3) reading and writing can serve as tools of thought. At the earliest ages (1–3 years), children learn vocabulary from interactions with adults around books (Ninio & Bruner, 1978). When a bit older (2–4 years), children learn more complex linguistic knowledge such as syntax and idiomatic expressions (Snow & Goldfield, 1983). As they become more familiar with storybooks, children begin to learn aspects of narrative structure as well (Heath, Branscombe, & Thomas, 1986; Sulzby, 1985). From picture books, children learn more complex, real-world knowledge (Crain-Thoreson & Dale, 1992). Through these experiences with picture books, children learn to appreciate the enormous potential of literacy as a learning tool. This section provides suggestions for teachers and parents on how to focus on the child's interests while engaging in print-related activities, interactively helping the child acquire knowledge at his or her developmental level. Specific strategies are described on how to target questions to the child's developmental level by monitoring comprehension and remaining flexible and responsive to the child's interests and interpretations. These strategies help teachers to use a single activity to address the diverse needs of a group of children in an inclusive setting. Curriculum activities are designed to assist adults in encouraging children to actively participate in constructing meaning. Adults can do this by asking appropriate questions, making comments, modeling active comprehension processes, and talking about the relation of ideas in books to the child's real-world experiences. The print activities immerse children in authentic literate practice with teachers and other adults acting as readers and scribes. In this way, children learn to use print and books to communicate before they learn to read and write. Children are encouraged to make pictures and then talk about the pictures. The teacher can then write what the child says on the picture. This act of translating a child's meaning into print is a powerful model of literate practice, teaching that meaning can be preserved by writing and recreated by reading.

Children are encouraged to send messages to each other. These messages may be pictures or scribbling. The teacher can ask the child what he or she meant for the message to say and can then transcribe the child's thoughts into print. In this way, one child's message is sent, and another child takes the message to a teacher to be read. When adults constantly model these communicative functions of literacy, children begin to understand the relationship among language, print, and communication (Ferreiro & Teberosky, 1982; McLane & McNamee, 1990). Writing, even more than reading, helps us to think, organize our thoughts, and remember events and ideas (Wells, 1985, 1990). This is the most sophisticated expression of literacy in our culture, and it forms the basis for the more disciplined ways of thinking that are introduced in the upper elementary grades. Writing is essential for scientific thinking in that it helps us to classify, measure, and remember observations. The idea that writing helps us to think, in simplified form, however, can be introduced successfully to preschool children (McCormick, Kerr, Mason, & Gruendel, 1992; Smith, 1994; Wells, 1990). For example, writing can be introduced as a way to sort, measure, and chart activities in the classroom. Teachers can use lists, for example, to keep track of whose turn it is to play with a toy, record the weather, or perform a class job. Children can learn to find their own name and check it when their turn arrives. The teacher or child can make tick marks next to the child's name to keep track of how many times a child has played with certain toys or conducted activities. These tallies integrate ideas about quantity and keeping records, again teaching children very basic notions of scientific ways of thinking. Children's acquisition of print conventions follows a developmental sequence. Children who, for example, do not yet understand that English is a sound-based writing system are not ready to learn sound–symbol correspondences (Byrne, 1992; Dyson, 1984). A fundamental goal of *Ladders to Literacy* is to prepare the child to relate phonological and metalinguistic awareness to symbolic representation, forming a conceptual understanding of how print represents language. By participating in the print/book awareness activities, the child learns 1) symbolic and conventional representations, 2) the conventions of representing language in print, and 3) the sound-based nature of our writing system. These goals are accomplished in the context of authentic literacy activities tailored to each child's developmental level.

- **Symbolic representation**—A major task for the preschool child is to understand the nature of symbols. This aspect of the curriculum has implications for much of later school learning. Children are provided with many materials that encourage representational play. Picture books are used to teach that pictures can represent objects in the environment. For children at a more advanced developmental level, teachers can focus on the relationships among pictures, printed words, and real objects. Teachers are encouraged to comment on pictures while reading to children and to relate the pictures to real objects ["Oh look, here's a picture of a block. And here are some real blocks. Do they look the same or different? How are they the same? How are they different?" "Let's find a picture of a block in another book and see how it's the same or different from these other blocks"]. The teacher can also comment on the relationships between pictures and print ["Here's a picture of a caterpillar. And here's the word for caterpillar. Have you ever seen a real caterpillar? What did it look like?"].

- **Conventions of representing language in print**—Children need to understand the specific conventions of our writing system, and they can begin to learn these conventions in the preschool years. For example, English is read from left to right and from top to bottom. Words are broken and separated with spaces even though there are no such breaks in oral language. Children are encouraged to pretend to write. Even if the writing is scribbling or the spelling is unconventional, teachers can encourage children for their efforts rather than correct errors or exclusively praise (correctness).

- **Sound-based nature of our writing system**—The sound-based nature of our writing system goes together with metalinguistic awareness. As children are immersed in literate activities and exposed to activities that help them to hear and manipulate words and sounds, they become ready to make the connection between print and language. An important goal of this curriculum is to help children discover that a word written in a book is a representation of a spoken word. Later, children become interested in learning that letters stand for individual sounds in the language. As children demonstrate interest, adults can help them spell words when requested, write messages, or label pictures. When children begin to attempt to translate their ideas into print, teachers can introduce all of the formal aspects of our writing system within functional, meaningful contexts.

EARLY LITERACY GOALS AND OBJECTIVES

Each activity presents opportunities for children to learn and practice many print, phonological, and language skills. The activities included in this section, however, were designed to facilitate more specifically the learning of concepts and skills in the area of print/book awareness. The following goals and objectives for each print/book awareness skill are cross-referenced with the activities in this section. More specific definitions of skills and behaviors are provided in the checklist in Appendix A.

Symbolic Representation

- **Play**—Child will use symbols in play.
  Activities: Making Signs; Sorting Objects; Blocks; Landscapes and Maps
- **Pictures**—Child will identify objects, people, and actions represented in pictures.

Activities: Shared Storybook Reading; Snack/Lunch Menu; Following Recipes; Many Ways to Write; I Found . . . ; Classroom Post Office; Making Books; Photography; Sorting Objects; Blocks; Treasure Hunt; Science Projects; Obstacle Course; Landscapes and Maps; Museum Exhibit

- **Graphics**—Child will scribble. Child will name figures after execution. Child will draw recognizable figures.
  Activities: Making Signs; Many Ways to Write; Classroom Post Office; Making Books; Sorting Objects; Blocks; Recording Constructions; Science Projects; Landscapes and Maps; Museum Exhibit

Print

- **Book Conventions**—Child will turn pages. Child will orient book correctly and indicate where the book begins and ends. Child will know that print, not pictures, tells the story. Child will know that text begins at top left corner of page and is read from left to right.
  Activities: Shared Storybook Reading; Following Recipes; Morning/Afternoon Message and News; I Found . . . ; Making Books; Science Projects; Museum Exhibit
- **Awareness of Graphic Symbols**—Child will read environmental print (e.g., logos, road signs, cereal boxes). Child will recognize a few familiar words (e.g., own name, name of friend, familiar words). Child will identify a printed word. Child will read simple words.
  Activities: Shared Storybook Reading; Snack/Lunch Menu; Following Recipes; Making Signs; Many Ways to Write; Morning/Afternoon Message and News; I Found . . . ; Classroom Post Office; Fill in the Blanks; Making Books; Sorting Objects; Blocks; Recording Constructions; Treasure Hunt; Science Projects; Obstacle Course; Long Jump; Landscapes and Maps; Museum Exhibit
- **Letter Identification**—Child will recite part of alphabet. Child will name single letters.
  Activities: Shared Storybook Reading; Snack/Lunch Menu; Making Signs; Many Ways to Write; Morning/Afternoon Message and News; I Found . . . ; Fill in the Blanks; Making Books; Recording Constructions; Treasure Hunt; Science Projects; Obstacle Course; Long Jump; Museum Exhibit
- **Writing**—Child will copy shapes. Child will copy letters. Child will copy a few words (e.g., own name, name of friend, familiar words). Child will write name independently. Child will pretend to write. Child will write a few familiar letters and words. Child will use invented spelling to write messages.
  Activities: Making Signs; Many Ways to Write; Name Cups; Classroom Post Office; Fill in the Blanks; Making Books; Photography; Sorting Objects; Blocks; Recording Constructions; Sci-

ence Projects; Long Jump; Landscapes and Maps; Museum Exhibit

Letter–Sound Correspondence

- **Single Sounds and Letters**—Child will say the most common sound for all letters. Child will select a letter to represent a sound.
  Activities: Shared Storybook Reading; Many Ways to Write; Morning/Afternoon Message and News; I Found . . . ; Name Cups; Classroom Post Office; Making Books; Sorting Objects; Recording Constructions; Treasure Hunt; Obstacle Course; Museum Exhibit
- **Words**—Child will use letter sounds to write words.
  Activities: Many Ways to Write; Morning/Afternoon Message and News; I Found . . . ; Classroom Post Office; Making Books; Sorting Objects; Recording Constructions; Museum Exhibit

SHARED STORYBOOK READING

Main Purpose

To use print as a tool to acquire knowledge

Children learn how to use books as a learning tool. Through story reading with adults, children learn about objects, people, and events in the real world. Cognitive development is facilitated by looking at books that focus on concepts such as colors, numbers, opposites, time, and space. Personal interactions with adults and peers around picture book reading as well as learning about other people and their feelings from books contribute to children's social and emotional development. Through books, children also learn new vocabulary, syntax, and narrative structure.

Materials

Big books (e.g., *I Can Read Colors* [Edge, 1988], *The Opposite Song* [Edge, 1988]), little books, cards with pictures or words that match those of text. *Note:* Big books available through Nellie Edge Resources are ideal for this activity as they come with black-line masters for matching child-size little books.

Description of the Activity

Use big books to read to a large group of children during circle time. Talk about the relevant concepts in the book (e.g., colors, opposites). Call attention to the title, author, and illustrator. Read the story aloud, tracking the print by pointing a finger at each word read. After reading aloud, ask children to recall important points and to find the corresponding part in the text. Draw children's attention to relevant features (e.g., names of colors, words that rhyme, opposites). Use visual aids (separate sheets with isolated print or pictures) to help children focus on specific words. Have children mime or sign when appropriate. Involve children by having them take turns reading to each other or teaching their peers, asking them to label pictures or read words. Encourage children to comment on the pictures and the story and to fill in repetitive words and phrases. Ask the children to predict what might happen next, to provide explanations, and to relate events to their own experiences. Invite children to dramatize the stories. After several shared reading experiences with the same text, give children their own little book—a smaller copy of the big book. While reading the big book, encourage children to turn the pages of their little books, read along with you, and point to the print in their little books that corresponds to selected words in the big book. Send a copy of the little book home for children to share with their families. Encourage children to look at books during the daily, private book reading time in the classroom library area.

This activity develops the following behaviors and concepts that are related to early literacy:

Print/Book Awareness	Symbolic representation—pictures; print—book conventions, awareness of graphic symbols, letter identification; letter–sound correspondence—single sounds and letters
Metalinguistic Awareness	Perception and memory for sounds—words, phrases; phonological skills—rhyming, alliteration
Oral Language	Vocabulary—words and sentences; narrative skills—narrations of fictional story

ADULT–CHILD INTERACTIVE BEHAVIORS

High Demand/Low Support

Children listen to the story and look at their little books. They will:

> read simple words and name single letters

Support Strategies

? Open-ended questioning

Ask for information not portrayed in the illustrations to encourage children to read words.

Cognitive structuring

Show children a short word composed of letter sounds they already know, and encourage children to sound out the letters.

> Let's look at the letters in this word.
> What letters do you see?
> If you say the sounds for those letters, then you can read the word.

Point out distinctive features, similarities, and differences between the targeted letter or word and other letters or words.

> You said this is a b. Does it look the same as this other b here?
> Look carefully. On which side of the circle is the stick?

Holding in memory

Have children look for letters to match a target; keep touching the target to provide the visual model as the children search for matches.

> Let's look for more fs on this page.

Task regulation

Visually isolate a letter or word from the rest of the text with high-lighting or underlining. Increase the children's interest in the task by having them select a word or letter to highlight and read. Increase meaningfulness of the task by selecting a word or letter that relates to a main character or event of the story. Ask children to name letters in their names or other letters they have already learned.

| Instructing | Model sounding out a few short decodable words, and have children sound them out with you. |

Instructing

Model sounding out a few short decodable words, and have children sound them out with you.

> Let's look at this word. The letters say /d/ /a/ /d/. Dad. Do that with me.

Model by reading the word or letter and then repeat the request.

> This is an m. Show me another m.

Medium Demand/Medium Support

Children listen to the story and look at their little books. They will:

> know that print tells the story and recognize a few memorized words in the text

Support Strategies

Open-ended questioning

Ask for information not portrayed in the illustrations to help children realize that the information is conveyed throughout the text.

> What is the fox thinking? We can't see that in the picture. What tells us what he is thinking?

Cognitive structuring

Provide verbal information that helps identify the word.

Task regulation

Simplify the task by selecting the first or last word on the page for the children to identify. Highlight or underline specific words for children to read.

Instructing

Ask children to identify words that are in the classroom environment (e.g., on posters and labels). Read the word, and have the children imitate. Provide visual cues by accompanying the word with a corresponding picture or object.

> This word tells us what this is a picture of.

Low Demand/High Support

Children listen to the story and look at little books. They will:

> identify objects represented in pictures and handle books correctly by turning pages, orienting the book in the right direction, and knowing where the book begins and ends

Support Strategies

Open-ended questioning

Encourage children to describe what they see.

> What do you see in this picture?

Stone Soup

Cognitive structuring	Provide verbal information that helps identify the object (e.g., a dinosaur).
	It's a strange, big animal.
Holding in memory	Remind children to turn the pages of their little books as you turn the pages of the big book.
Task regulation	Increase interest by having children choose pictures to name. Increase the meaningfulness of the task by selecting a picture representing a main character or event of the story or an object or event that relates children's own experiences.
Instructing	Ask children directly to name pictures.
	What's this?
	Label the picture, and have the children imitate. Model turning pages slowly, and tell children directly to turn the pages of their little books. Ask children to show where the book begins and where it ends.

Comments/Adaptations

Comments	Alternative reading materials include newspapers and magazines with photographs; and children's diaries, notebooks, and messages.

Adaptations   For children with visual impairments, prepare relief picture sequences or little books that correspond to the story being read. Select important words that appear in the story (e.g., names of main characters), translate them into braille, and give them to children to hold and feel during story reading. Use props. (Also, see list of tactile picture books in braille in Appendix D.) For children with hearing impairments, use sign language to communicate main events and characters of the story. Make sure pictures are visible to children.

More Ideas   Send home little books; send home videotaped storybook readings for parents to view at home.

Home Link   Parent Activities: Getting to Know Books; Going Places—The Library; Print in the Home; Storybook Reading Routines

SNACK/LUNCH MENU

Main Purpose   To use print as a communication tool

Children learn that print is a tool to communicate with others. This activity prepares children to understand that print contains information about objects and is used pragmatically to allow readers to make choices, such as when reading a menu in a restaurant.

Materials   Cards with words and pictures or large sheet on flipchart; snack foods

Description of the Activity   Set up cards with labels and pictures or photographs of the day's snack, lunch foods, or special treats on the table before you present the actual foods. Ask the children to identify words and pictures in order to anticipate the snack and make choices as appropriate. During the meal, ask the children to associate specific items with their corresponding labels or pictures. Encourage discussion about from where foods come or how certain food is made ["How do you think we make muffins?" "Where do bananas grow?"]. Encourage children to describe foods, to recognize the larger categories in which they belong (e.g., fruits, vegetables), and to express likes and dislikes about foods. Parents may occasionally bring in special treats or foods for birthdays or holidays. Provide parents with a model menu with words/pictures, and ask the parents to make a menu for the foods they bring to class. Keep these menus in a notebook for children to use during play times.

This activity develops the following behaviors and concepts that are related to early literacy:

Print/Book Awareness   Symbolic representation—pictures; print—awareness of graphic symbols, letter identification

Metalinguistic Awareness   Perception and memory for sounds—words, phonemes; phonological skills—alliteration, segmentation

Oral Language   Vocabulary—words and sentences; literate discourse—conversations, categorical organization, decontextualization

ADULT–CHILD INTERACTIVE BEHAVIORS

High Demand/Low Support

Children read the menu to find out what will be served for snack/lunch. They will:

    read simple words and name single letters

Support Strategies

| ? | Open-ended questioning | Show the written menu to the children before the food is presented; ask children to predict which foods will be served by reading words on the written menu; emphasize how the written menu allows them to predict which foods will be served. |

> What are we having today?

Ask children to choose a food or drink to talk about by reading words on the menu.

> Which food shall we talk about today?

| | Cognitive structuring | Show how the letters in the printed word correspond to the sounds in the spoken word; touch under each letter as you sound out the word. |

> Apple. Here's how I know this word is apple. It starts with a, and that says /aaa/. Here's p and it says /p/. Aaap. Now see the l? That says /lll/. Now we have aaapll—apple.

Point out distinctive features, similarities, and differences between the targeted letter or word and other letters or words.

> Look. Here's spaghetti and here's sauce. How do these words start? Can you tell which word is spaghetti?

Provide verbal information about food.

> It's a fruit that monkeys like to eat.

| | Task regulation | Have children touch under individual letters as they sound out the word. Increase familiarity of the task by asking children to name individual letters in the children's names and other words with which they are familiar. |

> Yes, you read banana. Tell me the name of a letter in the word banana.

Highlight or underline specific letters.

| | Instructing | Provide names of new letters, and have children look for a same letter in another word. |

> This is a b. Can you find another b?

Medium Demand/Medium Support

Children refer to the menu during snack. They will:

> recognize familiar words

Support Strategies

	Cognitive structuring	Show children how to use first sound cues.

Cognitive structuring

Show children how to use first sound cues.

See the b? That tells me the word starts with a b. /B/.

Provide verbal information that helps identify the food.

It's yellow.

Task regulation

Ask children to identify words for foods that they like or dislike based on pictures. Have children highlight or underline specific words to read. Provide children with choices.

Does this word say melon or spaghetti?

Instructing

Read the word, and have the children imitate. Provide visual cues by accompanying the word with a corresponding picture or object.

This word tells us what this is a picture of.

Low Demand/High Support

Children will:

identify objects and foods represented in pictures

Support Strategies

Open-ended questioning

Show children the menu with pictures, and ask them to guess the foods that will be served.

What will we eat today?

Task regulation	Increase interest by having children choose pictures to name. Have children label pictures in the presence of the actual food or drink.
Instructing	Orient children's attention to a picture.

Look at what we are having today for snack.

Ask children directly to name pictures.

What's this?

Label the picture, and have the children imitate.

Comments/Adaptations

Adaptations For children with visual impairments, apply a bead of glue around the contour of drawings, or paste figures cut out in thick cardboard so that they can feel the shape of the objects. Print names of the objects in braille. Use props.

More Ideas If the school provides a lunch menu, then ask volunteers to illustrate commonly served foods. These labeled illustrations can also be used by the children to develop concepts of food categories.

Home Link Parent Activity: Send home copies of menus for children to describe to their parents.

FOLLOWING RECIPES

Main Purpose

To use print as a tool of thought

Children learn that print can be used to label and identify objects, to record and remember sequences of steps, and to guide individual and collective actions. This activity focuses on the function of written recipes and object labels. The teacher should repeatedly refer to these two forms of print to show the children how print may serve as an organizational framework for individual and collective activities.

Materials

Ingredients; containers; utensils; recipe, written in large print on a big sheet of paper (each step of the recipe can be written in a different color and accompanied by a picture representing objects and actions involved in the step)

Description of the Activity

Arrange the ingredients for making favorite foods (e.g., cornbread, guacamole, gelatin) or other products (e.g., playdough) on a table. Explain the activity, referring to the recipe written on a large sheet, which should be displayed vertically close to the table. Ask the children to identify each ingredient, and write the names of the ingredients on labels attached to the corresponding objects. Have the children prepare the foods, and assist them, as necessary, in following the recipe. Once the activity is completed, encourage the children to reconstruct the sequence of actions involved in preparing the recipe. This activity can be easily linked to others, such as science projects and learning about other cultures. Making guacamole, for example, provides an opportunity to discuss Mexican culture and learn Spanish words. Also, the pit from the avocado can be used to start a plant and to watch it grow. Facilitate language by having children discuss aspects of the activity, label objects, and talk about the foods. Encourage children to think of words that rhyme with the ingredients (e.g., flour rhymes with power) and the colors (e.g., red rhymes with Fred).

This activity develops the following behaviors and concepts that are related to early literacy:

Print/Book Awareness

Symbolic representation—pictures; print—awareness of graphic symbols, letter identification

Metalinguistic Awareness

Perception and memory for sounds—words, phrases; phonological skills—rhyming

Oral Language

Vocabulary—words and sentences; literate discourse—categorical organization, decontextualization

ADULT–CHILD INTERACTIVE BEHAVIORS

High Demand/Low Support

Children follow and refer to the written recipe with little guidance from the adult. They will:

> read simple words and follow print conventions of reading from top to bottom, left to right

Support Strategies

? Open-ended questioning

Ask children to describe the activity using the written recipe as reference.

> How are we going to make the dough?
> Which ingredients will we need?

Ask children to make predictions based on the information in the written recipe.

> What do you think will happen when you mix the flour and the water?

Have children make cause-and-effect inferences.

> Why is the dough green now?

■	Cognitive structuring	Have children focus on specific parts of the written information by sequencing actions while pointing to each individual step on the recipe.

> What should we do first?

◑	Holding in memory	Remind children to refer to the written recipe and pictures to guide their actions.

> What does the recipe tell us to do next?·

Medium Demand/Medium Support

Children refer to the written recipe and participate in the entire process with some guidance from adults and peers. They will:

> recognize familiar words and know that the printed word provides the information

Support Strategies

■	Cognitive structuring	Explain how print provides the information.

> I can find out what to add next by looking at this word.

◗	Task regulation	Make the task more concrete by having children describe what they are doing and associate actions and objects with words on the written recipe.

> Here's some water. Can you find the word water on the recipe?

Highlight or underline specific words for children to read. Isolate the portion of the recipe that contains the correct word by covering part of the recipe with a blank sheet of paper. Show children one line of the recipe, and ask them to find a word.

> This line says 2 cups of water. Can you find water? Can you find the number 2?

Provide choices.

> Is this word water or salt?

ⓘ	Instructing	Provide a model (e.g., a written label on a card), and ask the children to match it with the corresponding word in the recipe.

Low Demand/High Support

Children participate in one or two actions (e.g., mixing flour and water, pouring water). They refer to the recipe. They will:

> identify pictures of objects and actions

Support Strategies

Task regulation

Comment on children's actions, and ask them to identify the corresponding picture of an action or an object on the recipe.

> You're pouring water. Can you show me a picture of that?

Instructing

Label the picture, and ask children to repeat.

Comments/Adaptations

Ideas for Recipes

Playdough; gelatin; cornbread; banana bread; guacamole; tacos; cookies (*Note:* Recipes can be entered into the computer and printed out to give each child his or her own copy, and sequences of actions can be organized as flowcharts.)

Adaptations

For children with visual impairments, prepare cut-outs of the ingredients that children can explore tactilely, and print names of ingredients in braille. Use Velcro fasteners or tape to facilitate the participation of children with motor impairments who can easily tape the cut-outs onto the recipe sheet.

Link with Oral Language

Later in the day or week, ask children to recall and retell this experience. Write the steps they remember, and encourage children to consider the sequence of steps and other words that describe what they did.

More Ideas

Ask parents to send ideas for simple recipes, especially for dishes that are culturally diverse. Compile a cookbook of favorite foods children have made in class and distribute to parents.

Home Link

Parent Activity: Recipes

Reference Materials

Katzen, M., & Henderson, A. (1994). *Pretend soup and other real recipes: A cookbook for preschoolers and up.* Berkeley, CA: Tricycle Press.

MAKING SIGNS

Main Purpose	To use print as a tool of thought
	Children develop knowledge about words and print and sound–symbol correspondences as they make signs to incorporate into their play and daily activities.
Materials	Tag board; construction paper; writing materials; stand-up sign holders
Description of the Activity	Help the children make signs (e.g., stop, go around, slow, open, closed, exit) they can use as part of their construction activities (e.g., building an airport, a railway station, and a town) in the classroom building center. As children determine the need for new signs, assist them as needed in creating meaningful signs. Signs can also be made to signal daily routines and label play and storage areas as well as to guide behaviors (e.g., a quiet sign).
	This activity develops the following behaviors and concepts that are related to early literacy:
Print/Book Awareness	Print—awareness of graphic symbols, letter identification, writing
Metalinguistic Awareness	Perception and memory for sounds—words, phrases; phonological skills—blending
Oral Language	Vocabulary—words and sentences; literate discourse—categorical organization

ADULT–CHILD INTERACTIVE BEHAVIORS

High Demand/Low Support

Children make or select signs on their own that reflect the context of their current activity. They will:

> draw or write and read the signs they construct

Support Strategies

? **Open-ended questioning**	Ask children to tell what they intend to represent or communicate with the sign.
	> What can you put on this sign to let people know that this is the restaurant?

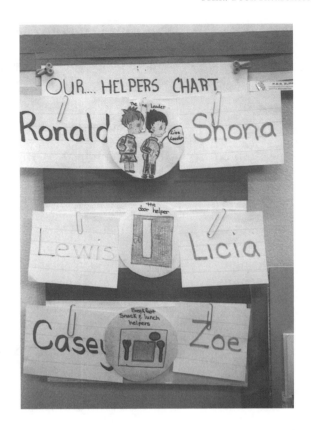

Providing feedback	Encourage and praise children's attempts at drawing, scribbling, or writing. Ask children to talk about their signs, and judge whether other children can understand it.

Providing feedback

Encourage and praise children's attempts at drawing, scribbling, or writing. Ask children to talk about their signs, and judge whether other children can understand it.

> Do you think Marco will understand that this says Monkey House?

Communicate your reading of the sign.

> This looks like a car to me. What could you add to make it look more like a boat?

Encourage children to talk aloud as they draw different parts of the sign.

Cognitive structuring

Help children break down the task into smaller steps.

> Which letter comes first?

Instructing

Encourage children to read by asking questions about their signs.

> What does your sign say?
> Which town is this?
> What do we need to do here?
> What's in this drawer?

Medium Demand/Medium Support

Children construct signs with the help of the adult. They will:

recognize words on the signs they construct

Support Strategies

? Open-ended questioning

Observe children as they play, and ask which signs might be needed.

I see you're making two buildings. Do you need signs to tell people what they are? What shall we write? Now, what does this tell us?

Holding in memory

Help children read the sign by reminding them of their original proposal.

Remember, you said we needed a sign for the grocery store.

Low Demand/High Support

Children will:

read environmental print

Support Strategies

Cognitive structuring

Observe the children's play, and suggest making a sign; help them make the sign; have children place the sign and read it at appropriate opportunities during the activity.

Maybe we need a sign here to stop the train so that children can cross the tracks safely. Shall we make a stop sign for the train? The train is coming. What does the sign say?

Instructing

Draw the children's attention to the object or action the sign represents.

This sign is right by the airplane.

Model first, then ask the children to read the sign.

Comments/Adaptations

Comments

Signs can also be prepared for other activities such as the obstacle course, science projects, recipes, and sorting objects. For example, signs for weather charts and for wind vanes (i.e., N, S, E, W) can be made for science projects.

Adaptations

Make signs with the text in relief for children with visual impairments.

More Ideas   Children can also choose and print simple graphic images using the computer.

Home Link   Parent Activity: Print in the World

MANY WAYS TO WRITE

Main Purpose

To use print as a communication tool

Children practice communicating information with different types of symbols. They learn that messages take many forms by writing and reading the same message in different formats (e.g., pictures, labels, sentences in both print and cursive).

Materials

Flipchart; markers; pens; chalk; chalkboard or eraser board

Description of the Activity

Propose a project that involves the communication of some message, and use different graphic symbols (e.g., drawing, print and cursive) to signify the same idea or object. As part of the morning message, communicate your feelings by drawing a happy face and adding a few features to identify it as your face. Explain to the children what your morning message means ["This message says, (teacher name) is happy. Here's another way to write this message"]. Print your name beneath the picture and read the message ["This message says, (teacher name) is happy"]. Then write the same words in cursive writing ["Sometimes adults also write messages that look like this. Now it says . . . "]. Pause for children to read with you. Send children to tables with writing and drawing materials. Help them begin their own messages by drawing pictures and adding letters or labels. Invite the children to regroup in a circle. Have children show each other or adults their message, and read it for them.

This activity develops the following behaviors and concepts that are related to early literacy:

Print/Book Awareness

Symbolic representation—pictures, graphics; print—awareness of graphic symbols, letter identification, writing; letter–sound correspondence—single sounds and letters, words

Metalinguistic Awareness

Perception and memory for sounds—words, phrases; phonological skills—segmentation

Oral Language

Vocabulary—words and sentences; literate discourse—categorical organization, decontextualization

ADULT–CHILD INTERACTIVE BEHAVIORS

High Demand/Low Support

Children will:

draw recognizable pictures and use invented spelling and letter sounds to write words and messages

Support Strategies

? Open-ended questioning	Ask children what they would like to write, and have them read back what they have written.
Cognitive structuring	Show children how to sound out words.

Show children how to sound out words.

> Dad. /D/ /a/ /d/. /D/ is the letter d, /a/ is the letter a, and /d/ is the letter d again.

Help children sequence sounds and letters.

> Cat. What sound comes first?

Providing feedback

Encourage and praise children's attempts at drawing, writing, and reading. Have children talk aloud as they draw and write messages, words, and letters.

> I'm drawing two circles for the eyes, then a mouth . . .
> I'm writing shaggy . . . .

Holding in memory

Remind them of the message they told you they were writing. Name and sound out letters children have written to help them complete words.

> Mom. You wrote an m and an o. /M/ /o/.

Task regulation

Help the children identify a specific purpose for the message.

> Would you like to write a letter to someone?

Provide verbal clues. For example, associate letters with familiar words.

> /M/. That's the same sound that starts your name. /M/ for Maria. What letter is that?

Instructing

Have children dictate short sentences; write some words and letters for them, and ask them to read them back. Write words and letters to label a picture, and have children copy.

> You've drawn a lion, and lion starts with l. L looks like this.

Medium Demand/Medium Support

Children will:

> draw and name figures, write their names, and pretend to write messages

Support Strategies

? Open-ended questioning

Ask children what they would like to write, have them write or draw a picture that tells about that, and have them read the mes-

sage from the picture and other graphic cues (e.g., scribbles, letters) on the page.

Providing feedback

Encourage and praise children's attempts at drawing, writing, and reading. Remind children that there are many good ways to write messages. Ask children to describe their drawings, and use this information to write a message for them. Encourage children to talk aloud as they draw and pretend to write.

Cognitive structuring

Help children sequence sounds and letters in their names.

Sam. What sound comes first?

Task regulation

Suggest a specific purpose for the message.

How about writing a birthday message to Maya?
Read your message to Jesse.

Relate the task to the children's experience.

Write something about our visit to the park.

Instructing | Ask children to dictate a message. Begin writing or drawing, and then encourage children's participation by having them add or copy drawings, scribbles, or letters. Pair children with peers who are more advanced in the necessary skills to serve as models. Write children's names for them to copy. Ask children to explain their drawing.

Low Demand/High Support

Children will:

> scribble, name figures, and copy shapes

Support Strategies

Open-ended questioning | Ask children what they would like to draw and whether they would they like to describe their drawing.

Task regulation | Provide a purpose for drawing.

> Can you draw us your favorite food?
> Draw a picture to take home to show Daddy.

Relate the drawing to the children's experience.

> Draw an animal we saw at the zoo yesterday.

Instructing | Help children get started by asking them to identify an object for you to draw, and then encourage them to complete the drawing. Give specific suggestions of what to draw.

> How about drawing your mom?

Talk about children's drawings, and ask them to name their pictures. Draw shapes for children to copy (e.g., circles).

Comments/Adaptations

Comment | Make placemats for mealtimes, and decorate them with pictures, words, and children's names. Use computers to generate words in different font styles. Introduce pictographs from other cultures. Introduce ideographic alphabets (e.g., Chinese).

Adaptations | For children with motor impairments, prepare cut-out figures and name tags for them to paste. For children with visual impairments, use braille and figures that can be tactilely explored (e.g., cut-out shapes, drawings with glue applied to contour).

Home Link | Parent Activities: Draw a Picture; Scribbling

MORNING/AFTERNOON MESSAGE AND NEWS

Main Purpose

To use print as a communication tool

Children learn that print is a tool to communicate with others. Thoughts and messages can be translated into print and preserved for others to read and reread. Children are made aware of the process of translating meaningful oral language into print.

Materials

Paper; blackboard; markers; chalk; flannel board; felt letters

Description of the Activity

Write a message each day during the large-group circle, while the children are watching. The content of the message can be generated by one or more children, by adults, or by both children and adults. Children can volunteer information they would like to share with the rest of the class, or you can elicit comments on specific topics (e.g., important events in the community, weekend experiences, a favorite book or activity). You can also ask more specific questions (e.g., what the weather is like, what children liked best about school that day) or use the message for planning by describing the daily schedule and activities or an important event that will take place in the classroom that day. Write the message on a large sheet of paper or chalkboard, or use magnetic boards or letters. Add pictures and objects. Draw children's attention to the process of translating oral language into print, and discuss the advantages of recording a written message and news. Repeat readings of the message, and have children retell the message to one another ["Jamie, tell Sarah what we are going to do today"]. Help children read along by pointing with your finger at each word read. Encourage children to read the message along with the adult, and discuss the message or the news. Encourage children to make evaluations and express opinions ["What did you think of the muffins we baked today?"], to investigate causes and effects ["Did you enjoy the trip to the train station?"], to solve problems ["Why didn't it work?" "What could we have done differently?"], and to make predictions ["What are you planning to do this weekend?"].

This activity develops the following behaviors and concepts that are related to early literacy:

Print/Book Awareness

Print—book conventions, awareness of graphic symbols, letter identification; letter–sound correspondence—single sounds and letters, words

Metalinguistic Awareness

Perception and memory for sounds—words, phrases; phonological skills—alliteration, segmentation

Oral Language

Vocabulary—words and sentences; narrative skills—narrations of real events; literate discourse—categorical organization, decontextualization

ADULT–CHILD INTERACTIVE BEHAVIORS

High Demand/Low Support

Children offer ideas and dictate coherent narratives. They participate in writing the message by helping to spell selected words. They will:

> name individual letters, identify corresponding sounds, select letters to represent sounds, and use letter sounds to write words

Support Strategies

? Open-ended questioning

Ask children to volunteer to spell a word that they dictated.

> Yesterday we had snow. How do we write snow?

Providing feedback

Encourage children to self-evaluate and correct responses by asking them for clarifications.

> Why did you say that we need a t in milk?

Cognitive structuring

Have children identify one letter or sound at a time.

> How do we write cat? What's the first letter?

Help children make distinctions and comparisons of relevant features of letters and sounds.

> How do we write a b? On which side of the circle is the stick? How do we write a d?

Task regulation

Stretch (e.g., Ssss-sunday) or iterate (e.g., T-t-t-today) sounds to help children identify them. Provide choices.

> Does cat start with a c or an s?

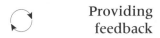 Instructing

Ask children to help spell words by identifying single letters and sounds.

> The first sound in snow is /s/. Which letter is that?

Read one sentence at a time, pointing to each word. Then ask children to read that sentence with you as you point to the individual words.

Medium Demand/Medium Support

Children participate in writing the message by adding comments. They will:

> identify a printed word and recognize some of the words in the message

Support Strategies

? **Open-ended questioning**

Ask children if they would like to add anything to the message.

> Nathan said that it's cloudy today. What else?

Write the additional comments, and ask children to read a word.

Cognitive structuring

Demonstrate the one-to-one correspondence between a child's utterances and the printed words by pointing to each word while reading it aloud.

> Beth said, "I went sledding in the park." And here are the words, *I went sledding in the park.*

Provide strategies for how to identify a printed word.

> Each word is separated from other words by empty spaces.

Task regulation

Circle or highlight with a color marker a word proposed by the child, and ask the child to read it. Circle or highlight names of children in the class or add them at the end of the message as authors, and ask children to identify them. Provide visual cues by drawing a picture or showing an object that corresponds to the chosen word.

  Instructing

Point out important words before reading with the children.

> This sentence was about Bro's trip to the hospital. Let's read the word Bro together.

Model reading the word.

Low Demand/High Support

Children attend to the writing of a message. They will:

> know that the print tells the message

Support Strategies

  Instructing

Draw children's attention to the link between the oral dictation of the message and the print by pointing to the text while reading the message. Ask them to show that print conveys the message.

> Where does it tell us what we are going to do today?

Circle names of children in the class, and model associating printed and spoken names with classmates represented in the message.

Comments/Adaptations

Comments

The message can also be written on the computer, and individual copies can be printed out for each child.

Adaptations

Messages can be translated into braille for children with visual impairments or into a sequence of drawings or pictures for children who have hearing impairments and who are not able to read yet.

Home Link

Parent Activities: Diaries; Scribbling; Writing Messages

I FOUND . . .

Main Purpose To use print as a tool of thought

Children use what they know about letters and words to make sense of written messages. They practice identifying features of print.

Materials Previous day's message of the day; color markers

Description of the Activity Display the large message the class wrote together from the day before. Ask for volunteers to find something familiar in the writing, such as a child's name, a letter, a word, or a punctuation mark. Children will select a variety of features depending on their sophistication with print and memory of the previous day's message.

This activity develops the following behaviors and concepts that are related to early literacy:

Print/Book Awareness Symbolic representation—pictures; print—awareness of graphic symbols, letter identification; letter–sound correspondence—single sounds and letters, words

Metalinguistic Awareness Perception and memory for sounds—words, phrases; phonological skills—alliteration, segmentation

Oral Language Vocabulary—words and sentences; narrative skills—narrations of real events

ADULT–CHILD INTERACTIVE BEHAVIORS

High Demand/Low Support

Children attempt to read all or part of the text. They will:

> read words and name letters and follow print conventions of reading from top to bottom and from left to right

Support Strategies

Cognitive structuring Help children make distinctions and comparisons of relevant features of letters and sounds.

> That letter looks a lot like a d. It has a circle and a stick. Look where the stick is on this letter. See how it comes first? A stick and a ball. That's a b.

| Providing feedback | Encourage children's attempts by accepting their rendition of the message. Then read the message back to them, and fingerpoint words as you read it aloud. |

| Holding in memory | Remind children about the directionality of print.
Remember, we start to read at the top of the page.
We read from left to right. |

| Task regulation | Have children select and circle individual words and letters they choose to read to isolate them from the rest of the text. |

| Instructing | Provide a model.
David circled a t. Can you find another t? |

Medium Demand/Medium Support

Children identify key words, such as children's or teachers' names or destinations for trips or letters in their names. They will:

recognize memorized words

Support Strategies

| Providing feedback | Point out words children recognized correctly.
Yes, there's Barney, just like you read. |

| Task regulation | Have children choose a word and circle or highlight it with a color marker before reading it. |

| Instructing | Ask the child to identify a specific word.
Show me your name.
Model reading the word. Provide a model.
Joshua circled his name. We wrote his name twice. Can you find his name?
Begin to read parts of the printed message that also are illustrated by pictures. |

Low Demand/High Support

Children read a message by identifying drawings and contextual cues. They will:

identify objects and events represented in pictures

Support Strategies

Providing
feedback

Encourage children's attempts by accepting their rendition of the message.

Instructing

Orient children's attention to the drawings and other contextual cues.

> Look, there's a cloud here.
> What do you think this message says?

Ask the child to identify the drawings.

Comments/Adaptations

Comments

Alternative Activities for Smaller Groups—Make sure that each child contributed at least one sentence to the previous day's message. Break down the message in sentence strips. Give each child a strip, and have children put the strips together to re-create the entire message. As each child places the strip, help him or her read his or her news.

Adaptations

Use colors to help differentiate words and letters. Use color to highlight a special letter throughout the message. Discuss the sound of the letter and how the sound is used in words.

More Ideas

Send home a copy of the message for children to share with their parents.

Home Link

Parent Activities: Magnetic Letters; That's My Name!

NAME CUPS

Main Purpose	To learn the conventions of representing language in print

Children learn the connection between print and language by discovering that a written word represents a spoken word. They learn that letters stand for individual sounds that are contained in a specific sequence to spell words.

Materials	Individual cups; cut-out letters
Description of the Activity	Place cut-out letters of each child's name in a cup, and have the children put them in order to form their names. Letters to form other words can also be introduced.

This activity develops the following behaviors and concepts that are related to early literacy:

Print/Book Awareness	Print—book conventions, awareness of graphic symbols, letter identification, writing; letter–sound correspondence—single sounds and letters
Metalinguistic Awareness	Perception and memory for sounds—words, phonemes; phonological skills—blending, segmentation
Oral Language	Vocabulary—words and sentences

ADULT–CHILD INTERACTIVE BEHAVIORS

High Demand/Low Support

Children form their names and other familiar words. They will:
> write a few familiar words and name single letters and the corresponding sounds

Support Strategies

	Cognitive structuring	Help children identify single letters and place them in the correct sequence.
	Providing feedback	Read the words children have formed to help them identify incorrect spellings.
	Instructing	Provide a model for children to copy.

Medium Demand/Medium Support

Children will:

write their names correctly using the cut-out letters

Support Strategies

Instructing

Provide a model for spelling a name by arranging the cut-out letters. Then mix the letters and have children recompose their names. Print each child's name for children to use as models for composing with the cut-out letters. Begin by composing the first two letters, and have the children continue.

Low Demand/High Support

Children will:

recognize their name in print

Support Strategies

Instructing

Compose children's names, and ask them to read the word. Model, and ask them to imitate.

Comments/Adaptations

Adaptations

Translate into braille or prepare letter(s) in relief or in three-dimensional form (e.g., magnetic letters) that can be easily explored tactilely for children with visual impairments.

Home Link

Parent Activity: That's My Name

CLASSROOM POST OFFICE

Main Purpose	To use written messages as a communication tool

Children learn to use words to construct a written message that others will read. They use words and pictures to describe events and experiences in their lives and share them with others.

Materials Paper; crayons; markers

Description of the Activity At an appropriate time during the school day, gather the children together to decide on a message they would like to send to their peers in another classroom. Let the children choose the content of the message. If needed, offer topic suggestions (e.g., descriptions of an activity conducted during school; questions about peers; comments about the weather, seasons, animals, books, and television shows). Have the children dictate a short message and draw pictures to illustrate. Select one or two children to serve as mail carriers to deliver the message to the other class. The teacher in the receiving classroom should show and read the message to the children and display the message prominently. Encourage children to comment and ask questions about the messages. Children may also send individual messages and drawings to special pen pals. Use special occasions such as Valentine's Day, Halloween, birthdays, and other holidays to encourage writing to friends.

This activity develops the following behaviors and concepts that are related to early literacy:

Print/Book Awareness Symbolic representation—pictures, graphics; print—awareness of graphic symbols, writing; letter–sound correspondence—single sounds and letters, words

Metalinguistic Awareness Perception and memory for sounds—phrases; phonological skills— blending, segmentation

Oral Language Vocabulary—words and sentences; narrative skills—narrations of real events; literate discourse—conversations

ADULT–CHILD INTERACTIVE BEHAVIORS

High Demand/Low Support

Children write a message to send to a friend. They will:
    use invented spelling and letter sounds to write words

Support Strategies

? Open-ended questioning

Help children choose and plan their message.

> Who would you like to write to?
>
> What would you like to say?

Draw children's attention to the importance of taking into account the receiver's perspective with respect to both the content of the message and its form. Help children place themselves in the other person's perspective.

> What do you think they would be interested to know about from among the things we did today?

Providing feedback

Praise children's attempts at writing, and make supportive comments about the message conveyed. Request clarifications when messages are unclear.

> What does this mean?

Cognitive structuring

Show children how to sound out words.

> Dad. /D/ /a/ /d/. /D/ is the letter d, /a/ is the letter a, and /d/ is the letter d again.

Help children sequence sounds and letters.

> Love. What sound comes first?

Task regulation

Encourage children to segment the words they want to write to help them spell phonetically.

Medium Demand/Medium Support

Children will:

> pretend to write a message and write a few familiar letters and words

Support Strategies

? Open-ended questioning

Help the children focus on a specific message.

> What would you like to tell your friend next door about what you did at Grandma's house?

Providing feedback

Praise children's attempts at writing, and make supportive comments about the message conveyed.

Cognitive structuring

Help children use segmenting to sequence letters correctly.

> Mom. Listen to the first sound. /M/.

◆	Task regulation	Provide a specific purpose for the message, such as making a Valentine's Day card for peers and family. Encourage children to make use of environmental print in the classroom.

> You want to write about a dinosaur. Is that word in our classroom? Can you copy the word from the poster?

ℹ	Instructing	Print models of words children request so that they can copy them. Pair children with more advanced peers.

Low Demand/High Support

Children will:

> draw a picture to communicate a message and write their names

Support Strategies

?	Open-ended questioning	Help children decide on what to draw by asking them questions.

> What animals did you see at the zoo?

↻	Providing feedback	Praise children's attempts at drawing, and make supportive comments.

◆	Task regulation	Provide choices.

> Would you like to draw something you saw on our field trip to the train station yesterday or something Jennie showed us during circle time this morning?

Provide objects for children to use as models.

ℹ	Instructing	Provide the children models of their names to copy. Draw an outline for the children to color. Prepare pictures for children to paste, and add a label to the picture.

Comments/Adaptations

Adaptations	Messages can be dictated and recorded on an audiotape for children with visual or motor impairments. Children can also generate their messages using the computer.
More Ideas	Have children design cards for their parents for special school events and other occasions. Mail cards and letters to children's homes.
Home Link	Parent Activities: Diaries; Magnetic Letters; Writing Messages

FILL IN THE BLANKS

Main Purpose	To use print as a communication tool

The structure of repetitive language encourages success when children start to read. In this activity, the teacher provides the repetitive format, and children practice writing and reading their own compositions.

Materials	Writing supplies; a phrase, in large type, to be completed by children
Description of the Activity	Ask children questions that require simple responses ["My name is . . . ," "I like . . . "]. Write their responses as children take turns answering the questions. The group then reads the children's responses together as you fingerpoint to the words. Children take turns reading the responses of other students.
Sample Activities	*A Pet:* I have a pet. You bet! I have a [blank]. *My Friend:* My name is [blank]. My friend's name is [blank]. We like to [blank]. *I Can Name:* I can name words that start with [blank]: [blank, blank, blank]. *I Like:* My name is [blank]. I like [blank].

This activity develops the following behaviors and concepts that are related to early literacy:

Print/Book Awareness	Print—awareness of graphic symbols, letter identification, writing
Metalinguistic Awareness	Phonological skills—blending, segmentation
Oral Language	Vocabulary—words and sentences; literate discourse—decontextualization

ADULT–CHILD INTERACTIVE BEHAVIORS

High Demand/Low Support

Children write their own responses. They will:
> use invented spelling and letter sounds to write words

Support Strategies

Providing feedback	Encourage and praise children's attempts at writing and invented spelling. Ask questions to help children clarify their writing.

Cognitive structuring	Show children how to sound out words.

Pet. /P/ /e/ /t/. /P/ is the letter p, /e/ is the letter e, and /t/ is the letter t.

Help children sound out and sequence individual letters to form words.

Task regulation	Encourage children to segment the words they want to write to help them spell phonetically.

Instructing	Demonstrate how to fill in the blanks.

I'll do the first one. My name is Joanna. I'll write Joanna in the first blank.
I like cupcakes, so I'll write cupcakes here.

Provide models of words for children to copy.

Medium Demand/Medium Support

Children dictate their responses to an adult who fills in the blanks. Children read back their responses. They will:

recognize a few familiar letters and words

Support Strategies

Holding in memory	Remind children of the questions.

Remember, here we wrote what your favorite food is.

Task regulation	Assist children by reading the initial text, and have the children complete the sentence.

We like to play with the [blank].

Instructing	Read the first part of the word.

Ma . . . ? (Maria)

Fill in the blanks with the child, and provide models.

This says, "My favorite color is red." We wrote red here. What did we write here?

Low Demand/High Support

Children and adults fill in the blanks together; the adult writes children's responses. Children will:

recognize their name in print

Support Strategies

⊙	Holding in memory	Remind children of the task.

        Remember, we wrote your name here.

Task regulation — Assist by reading the initial text, and have children complete the sentence.

        My name is . . . ?

Instructing — Read the first part of the word.

        Aa . . . ? (Aaron)

Provide a model.

Comments/Adaptations

Adaptations For children who are nonverbal, prepare pictures from which they can choose. This activity can also be done on a computer.

More Ideas Send home copies of their compositions for children to share with their parents. Compile all children's compositions into a classroom book.

Home Link Parent Activity: My Very Own Book

MAKING BOOKS

Main Purpose To use print as a communication tool

Children learn to link oral language and print. The translation of oral language into print enables the transmission of ideas beyond the immediate context. Making books of children's writing also reinforces the value of print as a tool for preserving thoughts and sharing ideas.

Materials Paper; paint; paintbrushes; crayons; markers; pictures; glue

Description of the Activity Have children write and illustrate their own books. Big books for the classroom library can be made as a group project. Children select a theme; and adults assist in developing a storyline, identifying specific illustrations, and assigning tasks. Puppets or felt board figures can be used to act out a story. At times, the teacher may suggest a topic in which children demonstrate interest or which is relevant to their experiences (e.g., families; favorite foods, animals, or toys; emotional reactions to birth of a sibling or to neighborhood violence). Children can paint, draw, or paste pictures. The Fill in the Blanks activity provides a good source for big books. Gather a classroom set of responses for one activity (e.g., *A Pet . . . , I Like . . .* ; see p. 84), and make a class book cover (Pets in Room 18). Read the book to the class during storytime, and add it to the classroom library for children to read to each other or alone. Children can also work in small groups or individually to make books.

This activity develops the following behaviors and concepts that are related to early literacy:

Print/Book Awareness Symbolic representation—pictures, graphics; print—book conventions, awareness of graphic symbols, letter identification, writing; letter–sound correspondence—single sounds and letters, words

Metalinguistic Awareness Perception and memory for sounds—words; phonological skills—rhyming, segmentation

Oral Language Vocabulary—words and sentences; narrative skills—narrations of real events, narrations of fictional story

ADULT–CHILD INTERACTIVE BEHAVIORS

High Demand/Low Support

Children write or dictate text and read completed books independently. They will:

name letters and corresponding sounds and use invented spelling and letter sounds to write words

Support Strategies

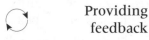

Open-ended questioning

Help children elaborate ideas and plan a story.

What do you want to write about?
What will happen?

Help children plan formats and use of different graphics and print (e.g., drawings, photographs, dictated text, scribbles, own words, letters). Help children select specific words and letters they can attempt to write themselves.

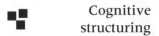

Providing feedback

Encourage and praise children's attempts at writing and invented spellings.

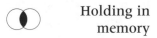

Cognitive structuring

Help children break down words into individual letters and sounds.

What's the first letter in tiger?

Holding in memory

Summarize events children have dictated to help them continue the story. Spell or read aloud parts of words or letters children have written.

Remember here how you wrote /b/.
Dog. You wrote /d/ and /o/.

Task regulation

Propose a story that relates to an event familiar to the child.

Let's write a story about your visit to the doctor.

Have children read aloud words and identify letter names and sounds they wrote themselves. Emphasize the sound of the letter in words by stretching ["ssspider"] or iterating the sound ["b-b-b-bear"].

Instructing

Model writing words and letters for the child to copy or imitate.

Medium Demand/Medium Support

Children participate with the adult and peers in identifying topics, dictating events, and adding drawings and letters; later they look at completed books independently. They will:

write a few familiar letters and words and know that print tells the story and that text begins at the top left corner of the page and reads from left to right

Support Strategies

?	Open-ended questioning	Help children identify a topic for the book or an idea about which to dictate or draw.

> What should we write here about the frog?

	Cognitive structuring	Have children identify one letter or sound at a time.

> How do we write cat? What's the first letter?

Help children make distinctions and comparisons of relevant features of letters and sounds.

> How do we write a b. On which side of the circle is the stick? And what about the d?

While writing children's dictations, emphasize the link between words the children say and the printed text, read dictations back aloud, and point to corresponding words.

	Holding in memory	Remind children of the directionality of print.

	Task regulation	Provide choices.

> Does cat start with a c or an s?

	Instructing	Read print, and show direction of text with finger. Ask children to show where the text begins and the direction of the text.

> Where do we start to read?
> Where do we go from there?

Pair children with peers more advanced in the necessary skills as models. Model writing words and letters for the child to copy or imitate.

Low Demand/High Support

Children participate with the adult and peers in making the book by drawing and naming figures and scribbles and then later looking at completed books with an adult or a peer with more advanced skills. They will:

> draw and name figures and handle books correctly by turning pages, orienting the book in the right direction, and knowing where the book begins and ends

Support Strategies

?	Open-ended questioning	Ask children what they would like to draw.

Providing feedback	Encourage children's attempts at drawing and scribbling. Help them interpret their drawings and scribbles.
	That looks like a sun to me. What do you think?

Cognitive structuring	Help children learn book conventions about sequencing actions.
	Which is the first page? Which is the next page?

Instructing	Ask children specific questions about where the book and text begin and end. Draw outlines for the child to color. Model turning pages. Give directions.
	Find the page with Mrs. Raccoon's house.
	Turn to the next page.

Comments/Adaptations

Comments	Songbooks with pictures and culturally diverse tunes can be made for musical instrument activities. Make a recipe book of foods made in class or described by children. Include recipes of ethnic meals children eat at home.
Home Link	Parent Activity: My Very Own Book

PHOTOGRAPHY

Main Purpose	To use familiar images and symbols as tools of thought

Children learn that two-dimensional images represent real objects and people and that these images can document events that happened in the past. They use photographic records to stimulate reflective thinking and language.

Materials

Camera; paper; binder

Description of the Activity

Take photographs of children engaged in various activities or of interesting objects seen in the classroom or during a field trip. Later, show the photographs to the children. Encourage them to identify objects and to remember and describe events. Create albums by mounting the photographs on paper and writing brief descriptions of the pictures. Laminate them and put them in a binder to which the children can have easy access.

This activity develops the following behaviors and concepts that are related to early literacy:

Print/Book Awareness

Symbolic representation—pictures; print—writing

Metalinguistic Awareness

Perception and memory for sounds—words

Oral Language

Vocabulary—words and sentences; narrative skills—narrations of real events; literate discourse—conversations, decontextualization

ADULT–CHILD INTERACTIVE BEHAVIORS

High Demand/Low Support

Children make comments and relate events about objects and events in photographs. They will:

> use invented spelling and letter sounds to write words and messages

Support Strategies

? Open-ended questioning

Ask children questions about events represented in the photographs to help them choose what to write.

> What were you doing here?
> Why was Susan laughing?
> Was it fun?
> Was it big enough?

91

	Providing feedback	Encourage and praise children's attempts at writing and invented spelling.
	Cognitive structuring	Help children break down words into individual letters and sounds. What's the first letter in the word Mom? Spell out words, and have children write or read individual letters.
	Holding in memory	Spell or read aloud parts of words or letters children have written. Remember how you wrote /m/ before?
	Instructing	Model by writing words.

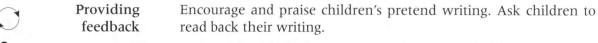

Medium Demand/Medium Support

Children describe the objects and events represented in the photographs. They will:

> pretend to write about them and write a few familiar letters and words

Support Strategies

	Open-ended questioning	Encourage children to formulate a message to pretend to write. What happened here? Why were you laughing in this picture?
	Providing feedback	Encourage and praise children's pretend writing. Ask children to read back their writing.
	Instructing	Describe some aspect of objects or actions in the photograph, and encourage children to add their comments. You're counting apples, and what else? Begin writing, and then ask children to continue. Your turn to write. Orient children's attention by pointing to specific objects or actions in the photograph. What's this? Look! What are you doing here? Write letters and words for children to copy.

Low Demand/High Support

Children will:

> recognize objects, people, and events represented in the photographs

Support Strategies

?	Open-ended questioning	Ask children to comment on the photographs. Tell me what you see here.
◐	Holding in memory	Remind children of the event the photographs document. Remember, we went to the zoo yesterday afternoon.
❧	Task regulation	Offer choices. Is this Mom or Grandma? Make the task more concrete by showing children the real object or miming the real event depicted in the photograph.
👤	Instructing	Ask direct questions. What's this? Label, and have children repeat.

Comments/Adaptations

Comments	This activity is best conducted with small groups of children as it requires individualized attention.
Link with Oral Language	Ask children to evaluate experiences ["What was the most fun that day?" "Where shall we go first next time we go to the zoo?"] and to consider relations and sequences among events ["How old were you then?" "Which one of these photographs came first?"].
Adaptations	Use a tape recorder to record sounds during field trips (e.g., animal noises at the zoo) for children with visual impairments.
More Ideas	Suggest that parents use family photograph albums to encourage children to relate events in the past.
Home Link	Parent Activities: Art Portfolios; Going Places—The Zoo

SORTING OBJECTS

Main Purpose

To use print as a tool of thought

Children learn that print can be used to organize experiences and categorize objects and events.

Materials

Interesting objects such as shells, seeds, nuts, rocks, buttons, toy dinosaurs and other animals, foreign coins, and so forth; containers such as boxes of different colors, trays, bags, jars, and so forth; crayons; markers; paper/sticker labels; glue

Description of the Activity

Gather an assortment of objects. Talk to children about how they might put them in groups. Ask children which categories they want to use to sort the objects ["How are you going to put together the seeds that belong together?"]. Provide hints ["Do we have a lot of colored seeds? A lot of seeds that have different shapes?" "Which shells are you going to put in this box?"]. Have children look for similarities in objects (e.g., shells, seeds, toy dinosaurs) and put those objects they think belong together into groups by color, size, or texture. Children should be encouraged to use their own criteria for grouping (e.g., favorite and nonfavorite objects). Ask children to provide reasons for their classifications ["Why did you put these shells together?"]. Have the children put the objects in colorful boxes or other containers. Children can print labels with the names of categories, criteria for classification, and other characteristics of the objects. Pictures and other symbols may also be prepared. Diversify the activity by introducing pretend play. Have children draw houses and yards for different groups of animals or garages and hangars for cars and airplanes, respectively. Draw children's attention to the function of the label ["What does this tell us?"]. Integrate classification and labeling into daily classroom routines. For example, have children sort classroom objects (e.g., different types of objects that go on different shelves or in different boxes or drawers) and prepare labels.

This activity develops the following behaviors and concepts that are related to early literacy:

Print/Book Awareness

Symbolic representation—pictures, graphics; print—awareness of graphic symbols, writing; letter–sound correspondence—single sounds and letters, words

Metalinguistic Awareness

Perception and memory for sounds—words; phonological skills—segmentation

Oral Language

Vocabulary—words and sentences; literate discourse—categorical organization, interpretive/analytic discourse

ADULT–CHILD INTERACTIVE BEHAVIORS

High Demand/Low Support

Children sort objects into categories. They will:

use invented spelling and knowledge of letter sounds to write words

Support Strategies

? Open-ended questioning

Have children identify categories and write labels, and help them determine categories by asking them to provide reasons for their classification.

Why did you put these rocks together?

Providing feedback

Encourage and praise children's attempts at writing and invented spelling. Encourage children to think aloud as they write labels.

Tell me how you write "big."

Cognitive structuring

Assist children in grouping objects and determining labels by drawing their attention to similarities and differences among objects.

How are these seeds alike?

Help children break down words into individual letters and sounds.

Look at the first letter. What sound does it make?

Spell out words, and have children write or read individual letters.

Holding in memory

Spell or read aloud parts of words or letters children have written.

Big. You wrote b. What comes next?

Instructing

Provide models of words for children to copy.

Medium Demand/Medium Support

Children group together objects according to their own personal categories (e.g., rocks that go together because they all are from the child's backyard). Write children's categories on labels and have them read back the labels. They will:

recognize memorized words

Support Strategies

Cognitive structuring

Assist children in grouping objects by drawing their attention to similarities among objects and reading the written label to find the answer.

How are these rocks alike? We wrote it here.

Holding in memory

Help children recognize written words on labels by reminding them of their definitions and categories.

> Remember, you said these go together because they are big rocks.

Task regulation

Provide children with a specific purpose for reading labels by having them group additional objects.

> Here's another green seed. In which box does it go?
> On which shelf does the rhino go?

Add visual, contextual cues and drawings to written labels (e.g., place a banana by a yellow color card and an apple by a red color card, place a picture of a seed and a rock by the corresponding labels). Provide choices.

> Does this word spell big or little?

Instructing

Ask direct questions to help children define categories to write on the labels.

> What color is this?

Assist children in grouping objects by giving them directions.

> Let's put all of the red bears together and write the word red on this jar. Put this red bear in the correct jar. Can you find more red bears?

Say the first sound of the word to help children guess what the label says. Model reading the label, and have children repeat.

Low Demand/High Support

Children explore and play with objects. They will:

> draw pictures and identify objects in pictures

Support Strategies

Task regulation

Draw pictures of objects or give children photographs, and have children sort objects by matching them with pictures or other visual representations (e.g., place all leaves on a picture of a leaf, place all rocks on a picture of a rock).

Instructing

Ask children to label pictures.

> What's this?

Comments/Adaptations

Adaptations

Use braille for drawings or pictures with relief outlines for children with visual impairments.

More Ideas   Have children take home containers with labels to sort and classify objects they have at home (e.g., cups or boxes to sort colored crayons).

Home Link   Parent Activities: Going Places—The Museum; Going Places—The Zoo

BLOCKS

Main Purpose

To use print and symbols as tools of thought

Children learn how graphic symbols (e.g., drawings, words, signs) can be used to guide actions.

Materials

Large and small blocks; cardboard boxes; paper; masking tape; markers; Popsicle sticks; miniature toys (e.g., animals, people, cars, trucks, traffic signs)

Description of the Activity

Have children build a variety of buildings, objects, and landscapes with large and small blocks. Use drawings, photographs, and small models to guide their construction. Provide photographs of farms with farmhouses, yards, and fences; and have children build these features. Encourage children to plan before they build ["Where will you put the house?"]. Have children compare their constructions with the model ["Does the road you built go to the same house as the one on the photo?"]. Relate projects to children's experiences. After a field trip to the zoo, for example, have children draw animals, cut them out, and display them on a large bulletin board. Help them arrange the animals in different areas and cages as they would be arranged in a zoo. Children then can build a zoo with blocks using the display as a model. Help make written labels and signs of such things as the names of animals and entry and exit signs ["Do not feed the animals!"]. Encourage children to collaborate on the same project, and facilitate peer interaction. Encourage dramatic play and oral language.

This activity develops the following behaviors and concepts that are related to early literacy:

Print/Book Awareness

Symbolic representation—pictures, graphics; print—awareness of graphic symbols, writing

Metalinguistic Awareness

Perception and memory for sounds—words

Oral Language

Vocabulary—words and sentences; narrative skills—narrations of real events; literate discourse—conversations

ADULT–CHILD INTERACTIVE BEHAVIORS

High Demand/Low Support

Following a theme, children build constructions using blocks, drawings, photographs, and small models as guidelines. Children prepare labels (e.g., library, art museum) and signs (e.g., danger, entry). They will:

use invented spelling and letter sounds to write words

Support Strategies

? **Open-ended questioning**

Ask children what they would like to build, suggest that they use the drawings or models to plan for how they would build it and what they would need, and have them compare their constructions with the original drawing or model. Encourage them to write labels.

How could we know that it's a fire station?

Providing feedback

Compliment children for their constructions; and encourage their attempts at drawing, writing, and invented spelling.

Cognitive structuring

Help children break down words into individual letters and sounds.

What's the first letter in danger?

Spell out words, and have children write or read individual letters.

Instructing

Guide children's construction by preparing relevant materials (e.g., prepare a paper road, outline the room or building borders by putting color tape on the floor, prepare labels to serve as models for children to copy).

Medium Demand/Medium Support

Children participate in the construction. They will:

read simple words

Support Strategies

? **Open-ended questioning**

Participate in children's play, and encourage children to read signs to provide explanations for actions.

Why do you think I made the horse go into this building?

Cognitive structuring

Help children sequence sounds.

What's the sound of the first letter? What comes next?

Holding in memory

Remind children to read labels to direct their actions as they play.

Instructing

Ask children to read labels.

What does this say?

Say the first sound to help children guess what the label says.

High Support/Low Demand

Children build simple structures by stacking blocks. They will:

read environmental print (e.g., stop signs) and use symbolic actions with miniature toys

Support Strategies

Open-ended questioning

Participate in children's play, and encourage children to read environmental signs to provide explanations for actions.

Why did the car stop here?

Encourage representational play by asking children to describe their constructions and their play.

What could this building be?
What is the horse saying?

Providing feedback

Comment on and describe children's pretend play.

Instructing

Ask children to read signs.

What does this say?

Model representational play with toys. Give verbal directions to elicit symbolic play.

We need a fence for the horses.
Make a line with the blocks. Make the horse jump over the fence.

Ask the child to identify pictures.

What kind of building is this?

Comments/Adaptations

Comments

Children can use the computer to prepare signs and labels. Talk and show children pictures of buildings from different parts of the world (e.g., pagoda, adobe, log home, tent) as well as different environments (e.g., jungle, desert, forest).

Home Link

Parent Activity: Print in the Home

RECORDING CONSTRUCTIONS

Main Purpose   To use print as a tool of thought

Children learn that writing and drawing can be used to record information.

Materials   Paper; writing materials; individual notebooks

Description of the Activity   Children often build things during the preschool day that need to be taken apart during clean-up time. For this activity, children attempt to capture their construction in pictures and words. After children build something with blocks or Legos or other material, encourage them to try to draw a picture of the construction prior to taking it apart. Assist the children in labeling the picture with meaningful letters or a few words to help the children remember the construction. If available, use photographs or videotapes of construction.

This activity develops the following behaviors and concepts that are related to early literacy:

Print/Book Awareness   Symbolic representation—graphics; print—awareness of graphic symbols, letter identification, writing; letter–sound correspondence—single sounds and letters, words

Metalinguistic Awareness   Phonological skills—segmentation

Oral Language   Vocabulary—words and sentences; literate discourse—decontextualization

ADULT–CHILD INTERACTIVE BEHAVIORS

High Demand/Low Support

Children draw, label, and write the name of the construction on a sheet of paper or in a special notebook. They will:

> draw recognizable figures and use invented spelling and letter sounds to write words

Support Strategies

?   **Open-ended questioning**   Compliment children on their constructions; and encourage their attempts at drawing, writing, and invented spelling. Encourage children to talk aloud to help guide and revise their drawings and writings.

> Tell me how you are drawing the tower.

Cognitive structuring

Help children break down words into individual letters and sounds.

> What's the first letter in the word barn?

Encourage children to make comparisons between the three-dimensional object and their drawing.

> The tower is higher than the car. Which is taller in your drawing?

Help children pick out relevant aspects to record, and suggest strategies for accurate drawing.

> How high is your castle? First count the blocks. Do the blocks tell you how high you should draw it in your picture?

 Holding in memory

Remind children of the purpose for drawing.

> I can see you put a lot of effort into making your castle so high. Let's draw a picture of it before you put the blocks away so that we'll always remember what it looks like.

 Instructing

Model by sketching along with the children, talking through the drawing process.

> First I'm drawing the blocks that make up the bottom layer. Now I'm making it higher.
> See how the color changes to yellow for the top row.

Medium Demand/Medium Support

Children attempt to draw a picture of a real construction. They will:

> name the figure after execution, write their names, and copy letters

Support Strategies

 Open-ended questioning

Encourage and praise children's attempts at drawing, writing, and inventing spelling.

 Holding in memory

Remind children of the purpose for drawing and writing.

> You built a big barn for the cows. Let's draw a picture of it before you put the blocks away, so you can show Mom what it looks like. Write your name so we know you did it.

Instructing

Give verbal suggestions to help children draw.

> How about if you draw the door here?

Write down children's names and labels for the picture, and have them copy. Ask children to tell what their drawing represents.

Low Demand/High Support

Children will:

> label figures drawn by the adult and add their own scribbles

Support Strategies

?   Open-ended questioning   Ask children to describe the drawing and to give you advice on what to draw and how to draw it.

> What should I draw now?
> How high should I draw the window?
> Where shall I put the chimney?

i   Instructing   Ask questions about the drawing.

> What's this?

Comments/Adaptations

Adaptations   Help children with visual impairments record a verbal description of their construction on an audiotape. Take photographs for children with motor impairments.

Home Link   Parent Activity: Let's Draw the Building You Made!

TREASURE HUNT

Main Purpose

To use print and symbols as tools to gain knowledge

Children learn that graphic symbols and written words can be used to gain information about procedures and activities required to attain a goal.

Materials

Cards with written words, graphic symbols, and pictures; interesting objects, such as food, stickers, small toys, and books

Description of the Activity

Organize a treasure hunt during which children search for objects (e.g., stickers, small toys or books, foods) in small teams using a set of cards with pictures (e.g., photographs of objects and locations), graphic signs (e.g., sign for the bathroom), and words to guide their hunt. Provide each team with its own itinerary to avoid confusion. Cards can indicate various locations in which children can find additional directions. In your directions you can use cards containing all three types of symbolic representations or cards with photographs/pictures only.

This activity develops the following behaviors and concepts that are related to early literacy:

Print/Book Awareness

Symbolic representation—pictures, graphics; print—awareness of graphic symbols, letter identification

Metalinguistic Awareness

Perception and memory for sounds—words

Oral Language

Vocabulary—words and sentences; literate discourse—conversations

ADULT–CHILD INTERACTIVE BEHAVIORS

High Demand/Low Support

Children participate in the treasure hunt and independently conduct the search by deciphering words, graphic symbols, and pictures on the cards. They will:

> read simple words and identify letters and letter sounds

Support Strategies

? **Open-ended questioning**

Ask questions that encourage children to refer to the written and graphic information on the cards.

How do you know where to go next?
Why did you look under the sink?
Where do you think it might be?

| | Cognitive structuring | Help children read words by sounding out letters one at a time. |

| | Task regulation | Narrow the task by providing clues. |

> This word looks like the title of the book we read this morning in circle.

| | Instructing | Say the first sound of the word to help children guess what the label says. Model reading words and identifying letters. Ask direct questions. |

> What does this word say?
> What's the name of this letter?

Medium Demand/Medium Support

Children participate in the treasure hunt and are able to interpret cards with the help of more advanced peers. They will:

recognize a few memorized words

Support Strategies

| | Open-ended questioning | Ask questions that encourage children to refer to the graphic information on the cards. |

> Where can you find out where to look next?
> What does this card tell you?

| | Task regulation | Narrow the task by providing clues. |

> This sign shows something that goes up (a staircase).

Give children choices.

> Does this word tell you to go to the book area or to the chalkboard?

| | Instructing | Pair children with a peer with more advanced skills. Ask direct questions. |

> What does this say?

Low Demand/High Support

Children participate in the treasure hunt with peers. They will:

identify objects, people, and actions represented by the pictures on the cards

Support Strategies

Task regulation

Give children choices.

Does your card show a picture of a book or a table?

Instructing

Ask a peer with more advanced skills to model and guide children to the location represented in the picture. Ask children to identify pictures and associate them with the actual object or location. Model, and give directions.

This is a barn. Go look in our animal barn.

Comments/Adaptations

Adaptations

For children with visual impairments, prepare cards in braille or with relief pictures and signs or pair them with a peer who can read or interpret clues for them. Make sure objects and clues are placed in easily attainable areas for children with motor impairments.

Home Link

Have children take home their treasure to show their parents together with a fill-in-the-blank note or card ["I found a (blank) in my treasure hunt today"].

SCIENCE PROJECTS

Main Purpose To use print as a tool of thought

Literacy skills are fundamental in scientific activities. Children must read and write to gain and communicate knowledge. Labeling objects and events and recording observations and data are important aspects of scientific experimentation.

Materials Materials for specific science project; notebooks; markers; pencils; posters; paper; books; charts

Description of the Activity When planning science projects (e.g., planting seeds, studying animals), integrate literacy activities as part of the project. For example, introduce the project by reading books about the topic. Show relevant pictures, and hang related posters in the science area. Have children make drawings. Prepare big charts on which children can record relevant daily data (e.g., colors, heights, lengths, weights, shapes). Use notebooks and bulletin boards on which children can write or draw observations and exchange messages on the progress of the project or experiment. Encourage children to categorize objects and events at both basic (e.g., bean, carrot) and superordinate (e.g., vegetable) levels. Expose children to simple scientific terms, and encourage them to seek definitions of new words. Involve children in planning the project. Before and during the project, facilitate a large-group discussion about the project. Have children make predictions, formulate hypotheses, relate events, evaluate, and provide explanations and clarifications. Guide children to compare the different features of the groups and to notice similarities and differences and changes over time. If necessary, ask them direct questions ["What color was it before?"]. At the end of the project, have the children use the data and observations recorded to summarize and evaluate the experiment. Have the children dictate a brief report based on their observations to go in a notebook. Make a poster or design an exhibit to share information with classmates, the children's families, and children in other classrooms.

This activity develops the following behaviors and concepts that are related to early literacy:

Print/Book Awareness Symbolic representation—picture, graphics; print—book conventions, awareness of graphic symbols, letter identification, writing

Metalinguistic Awareness Perception and memory for sounds—words

| Oral Language | Vocabulary—words and sentences; narrative skills—narrations of real events; literate discourse—decontextualization |

ADULT–CHILD INTERACTIVE BEHAVIORS

High Demand/Low Support

Children prepare lists (e.g., things needed to grow plants), make labels (e.g., writing the names of different plants they are growing), record numbers, mark dates and heights, and list events (e.g., rain, snow). Children will:

use letter sounds to write and read simple words

Support Strategies

| | Open-ended questioning | Ask children to identify relevant information to record. |

What should we write on the list?
What do we need to know about this?
How can we keep track of how it's growing?

Ask children to describe objects and events by referring to written information.

How much taller is our sunflower?

| | Providing feedback | Encourage and praise children's attempts at writing or at invented spelling. |

| | Cognitive structuring | Help children read and write words by having them sound out letters one at a time or segment a spoken word into sounds. |

What's the first sound in sun?

| | Holding in memory | Remind children of the purpose of recording information. |

Remember, we need to write down how many cups of water it took to fill up this can so that we can decide whether the bottle is bigger or smaller than the can.

| | Instructing | Sound out words, and point to each letter as you say the sound. Model reading and writing new words and letters. Demonstrate the recording system. |

Here are all the days of the week.
We measured the rainfall Monday and wrote the amount here.
Where shall we write today's measurement?

Medium Demand/Medium Support

Children draw simple graphic symbols, signs, and pictures to describe or record events and their observations on charts and graphs. They will:

> draw recognizable figures and write and recognize a few familiar words and letters

Support Strategies

? **Open-ended questioning**

Ask children to identify relevant objects or events to draw and label.

> Which pictures will we need if we want to record the weather?

Providing feedback

Encourage and praise children's attempts at drawing, writing, and reading. Help children evaluate their drawings.

> Did you draw all of the parts, or is something missing?

Cognitive structuring

Help children identify relevant features to record by pointing out categories and relations.

> We'll need to know which are sunflower seeds and which are corn seeds.
> The green jar is bigger.

Explain how pictures and signs are used to record and report information.

> Every day we write our names on the attendance chart so we know who came to school each day. Tell me the name of someone who is here today.

Holding in memory

Remind children of the purpose of recording objects and events.

> We need to draw what the tadpole looks like now to help us remember what it looked like before it became a frog.

Task regulation

Provide choices.

> Look at my ruler. Is that 2 inches or 6 inches?

Instructing

Give children suggestions for drawings.

> Let's draw a sun, a cloud, and rain.

Say the first sound in a word to help children guess the label.

> This word starts with /sss/.

Write labels, and have children copy letters and words. Model reading the words on the labels.

Low Demand/High Support

Children use pictures and signs to report information. They will:

> identify objects and actions represented in drawings and pictures

Support Strategies

Cognitive structuring

Explain how pictures and signs are used to record and report information.

> Every day we record the weather on our calendar. Look outside the window. Choose the picture that tells us what the weather is like.

Task regulation

Have children choose from drawings and pictures.

> Here's a picture of the sun, and here's a picture of a cloud. What is the weather like today?

Instructing

Ask children to find out specific information.

> In which pot did we plant the sunflower?
> What was the weather like yesterday?

Orient the children to relevant information.

> Look. These lines show us how far the turtle walked.

Comments/Adaptations

Comments

Prepare sequence cards before the activity. Have children draw before and after sketches (e.g., melting ice, growing seeds in potato heads). Use different colors to differentiate states. Photograph or videotape the results. The computer can be used to generate graphs and bar charts.

Adaptation

Children with visual impairments can record observations on an audiotape.

More Ideas

Planting seeds and charting growth; recording weather observations with weather chart; making potato heads with grass-seed hair; melting ice with salt and adding paint to fill cracks; measuring the amount of liquid in containers of different shapes and sizes (use measuring cups with colored tape to mark levels); freezing objects in water; measuring shadows; looking with a magnifying glass or through a prism

Home Link

Parent Activity: Measuring

OBSTACLE COURSE

Main Purpose To use print and symbols as tools for communication

Children learn that symbols and print contain information about objects and their uses and can also guide actions and behaviors and give directions.

Materials Gross motor equipment; paper; markers

Description of the Activity Set up an obstacle course in which children can practice a variety of motor skills (e.g., walking, running, balancing, crawling, climbing). Prepare written labels and instructions with pictures, signs, and words for each part of the course. For example, by the steps post a sign for "Steps" and the direction "Go Up" accompanied by an upward arrow and a drawing of a person climbing up steps. Before the children begin the course, show them each part of the course, and have them read or interpret the symbols and signs. Talk about how words and pictures tell us about objects and give us directions.

This activity develops the following behaviors and concepts that are related to early literacy:

Print/Book Awareness Symbolic representation—pictures; print—awareness of graphic symbols, letter identification; letter–sound correspondence—single sounds and letters

Metalinguistic Awareness Perception and memory for sounds—words, phrases; phonological skills—segmentation

Oral Language Vocabulary—words and sentences

ADULT–CHILD INTERACTIVE BEHAVIORS

High Support/Low Demand

Children participate in the course and follow rules and directions by reading labels, signs, and symbols. They will:

> read simple words and say the most common sound for letters

Support Strategies

? **Open-ended questioning** Encourage children to read signs by asking questions about rules and directions related to the course.

> What do you do after you come down the slide?
> What do you do with the rope?

Holding in memory

Remind children to read signs to find out how to go through the course.

 Task regulation

Sound out letters individually. Stress specific letters by stretching or iterating the sound.

> D-d-d-down.

 Instructing

Ask children to identify letters and sounds in a meaningful context.

> Right! This says "Down." What sound does d make?

Model reading words and sounding letters.

Medium Demand/Medium Support

Children participate in the course and follow rules and directions by reading familiar labels, signs, and symbols. They will:

> recognize memorized words and name single letters

Support Strategies

 Cognitive structuring

Provide children with clues.

> This sticker is on the ball. It must tell us something to do with the ball.

 Holding in memory

Remind children to read signs to find out how to go through the course.

 Task regulation

Provide choices.

> Does this word say "Jump," or does it say "Crawl"?

Instructing

Ask direct questions to encourage children to read the signs.

> What does this sign tell you to do?

Help children interpret signs and symbols by orienting their attention to important features.

> In what direction do we go if we climb the steps?

Encourage children to use contextual cues or observe their peers to help recognize words and signs.

> Look what Mara is doing.
> What did Ramona say this word is?

Model reading words and interpreting signs.

Low Demand/High Support

Children will:

> read environmental print and identify objects and actions in pictures

Support Strategies

Task regulation	Provide choices.
	Does the arrow go up or down?
	Does this sign say stop or go?

Instructing

Orient children's attention to the signs.

Look at the arrow. Where does it tell us to go?

Ask direct questions.

What's the boy doing in this picture?

Provide models.

This picture shows running.

Comments/Adaptations

Comments

This activity requires the help of several adults or older peers. Station them along the course to assist the younger children in understanding and following the signs.

Adaptations

Prepare relief pictures and braille signs for children with visual impairments. Make sure the course is accessible for children with motor impairments.

Home Link

Parent Activities: Diaries; Making Signs

LONG JUMP

Main Purpose   To use print as a tool of thought

Children learn that printed symbols can be used to plan and organize events, make measurements, and serve as a record for making decisions.

Materials   Sand pit; paper; masking tape; markers

Description of the Activity   Have children take turns running from a starting point and jumping into a sand pit. Involve children in planning the event. Help children develop rules for deciding on the order of participation and for measuring and recording the jump. Use tape to mark the starting line. Use another piece of tape that you mark with measurement symbols. Place the measurement tape along the sand pit to measure the length of the jump. On a large sheet of paper, list children's names in the order in which each child will jump. Record by each child's name the length of the jumps. Make a bar graph of the results, and encourage children to compare the length of their jumps. Use a variety of symbols (e.g., numbers, letters, pictures, signs) for this activity. For example, place a picture of an arrow at the starting line in the direction of the runway. Use clear visual markers to indicate the track and the starting points for running and jumping. Let children have practice jumps. If necessary, provide verbal cues ["Run! Run! Run! Jump now!"], or accompany the child by running along for part of the way. Children can be assigned different responsibilities: jumping, measuring the jump, recording the measurements, or monitoring the order of participation.

This activity develops the following behaviors and concepts that are related to early literacy:

Print/Book Awareness   Print—awareness of graphic symbols, letter identification, writing; letter–sound correspondence—words

Metalinguistic Awareness   Perception and memory for sounds—words; phonological skills—segmentation

Oral Language   Vocabulary—words and sentences

From Forman, G. (1993). Multiple symbolization in the Long Jump Project. In C. Edwards, L. Gandini, & G. Forman (Eds.), *The hundred languages of children* (pp. 171–188). Norwood, NJ: Ablex Publishing; adapted by permission.

ADULT–CHILD INTERACTIVE BEHAVIORS

High Demand/Low Support

Children participate in the event at various levels (e.g., in the planning, the competition, the measuring, the scoring). They read and write names, numbers, and other words related to the event. They will:

> read simple words and use letter sounds to write words

Support Strategies

?	Open-ended questioning	Encourage children to participate in the planning process, and identify reasons and methods for recording events.

> What are the important things we will need to write down?
> How will we know whose turn it is to jump?
> How will we decide who jumped the farthest?

	Cognitive structuring	Encourage children to refer to the written information to establish categories and sequences and to examine relationships.

> Let's group jumpers into long jumpers and short jumpers.
> In which order are we jumping?
> Whose jump was the longest?
> Does running fast help to jump longer? Let's look at the results to find out.

Show how the letters in the printed word correspond to the sounds in the spoken word by touching under each letter as you sound out the word.

> Start. Here's how I know this word is start. It starts with s, and that says /sss/. Here's t and it says /t/. Ssst.

Help children sequence sounds and letters as they write.

> Andy. What's the first sound? /Aaa/. What letter is that? What sound comes next?

	Task regulation	Have children touch under individual letters as they sound out the word. Highlight or circle specific words for children to read.
	Instructing	Say the first sound to help children guess the word.

> This word starts with /sss/.

Medium Demand/Medium Support

Children participate in the jump, read the numbers on the measurement tape, and refer to the printed list of names to find out the order of participation. They will:

> recognize a few memorized words and name single letters

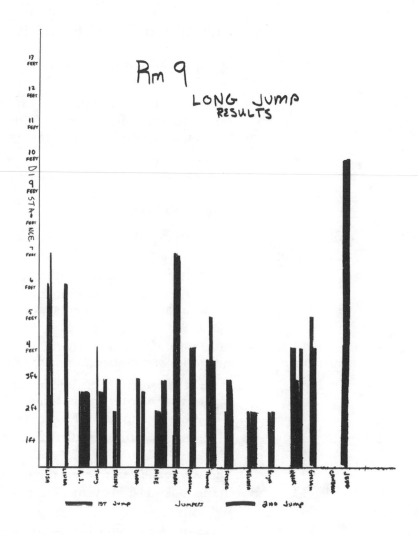

Support Strategies

Cognitive
structuring

Show children how to use a list of names to determine fair turns.

> Let's find your name in this list. Look, you jump after Brian.
> See, Brian's name is just before yours, and your name is
> right after Brian's.

Task
regulation

Ask meaningful questions that encourage children to refer to written words and symbols for answers.

> Whose turn is it next?
> How long was Mara's jump?

Ask children to read their own name when it's their turn and to
read the length of their own jump. Ask children to identify letters
in familiar words and in the context of meaningful tasks.

> Whose run is next? Andy's. Can you find a letter d in Andy?
> Can you find the letter f in the word finish?

Instructing

Say the first letter to help children guess the word.

This name starts with a b.

Model reading names, numbers, and letters; and ask children to repeat.

Low Demand/High Support

Children participate in the jump and follow the rules by reading symbols and environmental print. They recognize the meaning of the starting line and arrows indicating directions. They will:

read environmental print and identify objects and actions in pictures

Support Strategies

Instructing

Ask children to interpret the signs before they act.

What does this sign tell you to do?

Provide verbal cues.

You have to run to the sand pit from here.

Model appropriate actions (e.g., run, jump).

Comments/Adaptations

Comment

This activity is best conducted with small groups, as young children have difficulty waiting a long time for a turn.

Adaptations

Children with motor impairments can assume a major role in the planning and in the scoring of this activity.

Home Link

Send home a copy of the chart of the Long Jump results.

MY FIRST JOURNAL

Main Purpose

To use print as a tool of thought

By creating a graphic and written record of their own thoughts, ideas, and experiences, children learn to express, understand, and organize their emotions and thoughts.

Materials

Individual notebooks; crayons; pencils; markers; pictures; photographs

Description of the Activity

Provide children with their own individual notebooks to record experiences, ideas, and feelings during the school year. Set aside specific times during the day for children to draw or write in their notebooks. Children may choose to share their journal with their classmates during the group times.

This activity develops the following behaviors and concepts that are related to early literacy:

Print/Book Awareness

Symbolic representation—pictures, graphics; print—book conventions, awareness of graphic symbols, letter identification, writing; letter-sound correspondence—words

Metalinguistic Awareness

Perception and memory for sounds—words; phonological skills—blending, segmentation

Oral Language

Vocabulary—words and sentences; narrative skills—narrations of real events, narrations of fictional story; literate discourse—conversations, decontextualization, interpretive/analytic discourse

ADULT–CHILD INTERACTIVE BEHAVIORS

High Demand/Low Support

Children draw pictures, dictate a structured narrative, and write words and messages. They will:

> pretend to write messages and use invented spelling and letter sounds to write words and messages

Support Strategies

Open-ended questioning

Assist children in organizing their text.

> What do you want to write about?

| | Providing feedback | Encourage and praise children's attempts at writing or invented spelling. Have children talk aloud as they draw and write messages, words, and letters. |

Encourage and praise children's attempts at writing or invented spelling. Have children talk aloud as they draw and write messages, words, and letters.

Providing feedback

> Tell me what you are writing.

Cognitive structuring

Help children read and write words by having them segment words into sounds and sound out letters one at a time.

Instructing

Sound out words, and point to each letter as you say the sound. Model reading and writing new words and letters.

Medium Demand/Medium Support

Children draw pictures, dictate simple sentences, and write a few memorized words and letters. They will:

> draw recognizable figures and write a few familiar words and letters

Support Strategies

Open-ended questioning

Encourage children to draw pictures and dictate sentences by helping them identify a topic.

> How about writing about your favorite science project?
> What did you see today on your way to school?

Ask open-ended questions about children's drawings.

> What's happening here?

Providing feedback

Encourage and praise children's attempts at drawing and writing. Have children talk aloud as they draw and write words and letters.

> Tell me what you are drawing.

Comment on children's drawings to help them elaborate their drawings.

> You're drawing a face. A face has eyes, a nose, and a mouth.
> You're drawing a bus, but it looks like it's sitting still on the street. What else do you need to add so that it can move?

Task regulation

After children draw their pictures, ask them to tell you what they drew, and suggest they write the name of their picture.

> I see your lion. Can you add some letters to label your picture?

Suggest choices for letters.

> Bus. Which letter goes better with bus: b or f?

Instructing

Show children how to write a word or letter to label a drawing.

You've drawn a lion, and lion starts with an l. Do you see an l on the wall? It looks like this.

Select labels from children's dictations, and model how to write the words.

Low Demand/High Support

Children will:

scribble and name figures after execution and identify objects, people, and events in pictures

Support Strategies

? | **Open-ended questioning** | Encourage children to draw pictures by helping them identify a topic.
| | Tell us about your favorite pet.
| | Ask open-ended questions about children's drawings.
| | What's happening here?

↻ | **Providing feedback** | Encourage and praise children's attempts at drawing. Have children talk aloud about their drawing.

◖ | **Task regulation** | Prepare photographs and pictures of significant objects or events, and have children paste and identify them.

Instructing

Ask children what they would like for you to draw, and ask them to identify your drawings.

Comments/Adaptations

Comments

Children with visual impairments may paste objects (e.g., shells, leaves) or keep a journal in the form of a personal audiotape.

Home Link

Parent Activities: Diaries; My Very Own Book

LANDSCAPES AND MAPS

Main Purpose

To use print as a tool to acquire knowledge

Children learn how graphic symbols, drawings, words, and signs can be used to represent space (e.g., classrooms; familiar landscapes, towns, and countries).

Materials

Large or small blocks; paper; crayons; paint; boxes; cloth; sandbox

Description of the Activity

Have children work as a group to create familiar large-scale landscapes, such as mountains, lakes, rivers, bridges, and buildings; use large blocks to build houses, blue cloth or paper to form rivers and lakes, or a box to represent a mountain. Landscapes can also be created by playing with sand in the sandbox. For smaller scale landscapes, have children draw maps or build playdough models of the classroom, school, home, or neighborhood. Use print to label various landmarks: a lake, the zoo, streets, school, traffic signs, and directions. Representations can be three dimensional (using boxes), can be drawn on large sheets of paper, or can be cutouts pasted as a mural on the wall. Encourage children to enact pretend play scenes using the landscapes as contexts (e.g., adventures at sea, animals in the jungle). Have children re-create landscapes and maps of places they visited on field trips (e.g., the port, train station, library, market, zoo). Encourage the children to recall events related to the outing. Other themes to propose may be "My Dream House" or "My Dream City." Encourage children to collaborate on the same project, and facilitate peer interaction. This activity may require adult guidance and advance preparation of materials (e.g., maps, objects representing various landmarks). A project can be implemented over multiple sessions. For example, during the first session, children can paint a big lake, then during following sessions, they can add islands and bridges and build boats and lakeside buildings.

This activity develops the following behaviors and concepts that are related to early literacy:

Print/Book Awareness

Symbolic representation—pictures, graphics; print—awareness of graphic symbols, writing; letter–sound correspondence—words

Metalinguistic Awareness

Perception and memory for sounds—words; phonological skills—segmentation

Oral Language

Vocabulary—words and sentences; narrative skills—narrations of real events

ADULT–CHILD INTERACTIVE BEHAVIORS

High Demand/Low Support

Children use specific themes, build landscapes, and enact imaginary stories. They write words to label buildings, roads, and other aspects of the landscape. They will:

> use invented spelling and letter sounds to write words and messages

Support Strategies

? | **Open-ended questioning** | Help children in planning.
> What areas of the zoo do you want to draw in your model?
> Who will build what? Where? Let's make a list.

Encourage them to label areas and constructions.
> How will you know which door is the entrance?

Providing feedback | Encourage and praise children's attempts at drawing, writing, or invented spelling. Have children evaluate the correctness of their model or map and the need for additional labels.
> Is the duck pond that close to the alligator river?
> How do we know which is which?

Cognitive structuring | Help children write words by having them sound out letters one at a time.

Task regulation | Sound out and dictate letters individually.

Instructing | Model writing new words and letters.

Medium Demand/Medium Support

Children participate with their peers in building or drawing a landscape by focusing on specific areas within the larger context (e.g., a table on a map of a classroom, a flag to put on a boat in the lake, an animal to define an area of the zoo). They will:

> draw recognizable figures

Support Strategies

? | **Open-ended questioning** | Ask children what they would like to draw on the map.

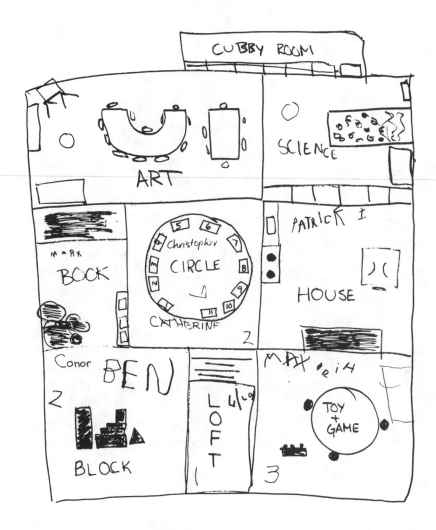

| | Providing feedback | Encourage and praise children's attempts at drawing. Have children describe their drawings to help them identify ways to make the drawings more accurate. |

Providing feedback

Encourage and praise children's attempts at drawing. Have children describe their drawings to help them identify ways to make the drawings more accurate.

Task regulation

Have children draw models or maps of their immediate environment (e.g., school, home).

Instructing

Pair children with peers who are more advanced in these skills. Draw children's attention to relevant features.

Look at how big the lake is and at how small the boat is.

Offer verbal suggestions to help children make the drawing more recognizable.

Can you make the river longer?

Provide visual models for children to copy (e.g., real objects, photographs, drawings).

Low Demand/High Support

Children will:

> identify objects, people, and actions represented in pictures and drawings

Support Strategies

Task regulation   Ask children to identify objects represented in pictures that are in their immediate environment (e.g., in the classroom).

Instructing   Prepare a model of the larger landscape ahead of time (e.g., a big sheet of paper representing the school building and grounds), and have children locate specific areas (e.g., classrooms, gym, library).

> Where's the gym?
> Show me the library.

Model responses, and have children imitate.

Comments/Adaptations

Comments   This project can be extended over a long period of time. Completed projects can be the subject of a museum exhibit. Place real maps on classroom walls for children to see. Use them to locate places to which children might have traveled. An easier version of this activity is to have children create simple maps based on stories from children's books such as *Spot's First Walk* (Hill, 1981). As suggested by Maxim (1997), children can illustrate Spot's friends and arrange their illustrations on the floor or on a wall to create a sequence map of Spot's travels.

More Ideas   Send home a copy or a photograph of the child's project.

Home Link   Parent Activity: Mapping the Territory

MUSEUM EXHIBIT

Main Purpose	To use print and symbols as tools to acquire knowledge
	Children learn that print and other forms of symbolic representation (e.g., drawings, photographs, miniature objects) provide access to knowledge about objects, people, and events that are detached from the immediate context in time and space.
Materials	Objects, pictures, and photographs; paper; crayons; markers
Description of the Activity	Design a specific space in the classroom as the museum or exhibition area. Work with different groups of children to create special exhibits (e.g., other countries and cultures, science topics, transportation, the neighborhood field trip destinations). Involve children in planning exhibit topics; and generate a calendar of events by making a written list of topics, dates, and exhibit committee members to hang in the classroom. Make invitations for families and children from other classrooms. Plan so each child is part of an exhibit committee at least once during the school year. Involve families by asking them to help their children gather special exhibit materials.
	This activity develops the following behaviors and concepts that are related to early literacy:
Print/Book Awareness	Symbolic representation—pictures, graphics; print—book conventions, awareness of graphic symbols, letter identification, writing; letter–sound correspondence—single sounds and letters, words
Metalinguistic Awareness	Perception and memory for sounds—words
Oral Awareness	Vocabulary—words and sentences; literate discourse—decontextualization

ADULT–CHILD INTERACTIVE BEHAVIORS

High Demand/Low Support

Children participate in preparing written descriptions about exhibits and making labels. They will:

> pretend to write, using invented spelling and letter sounds to write words and messages

Support Strategies

? **Open-ended questioning**	Encourage children to prepare written descriptions about the selected topic.

What do you think is important for people to know about these shellfish?

How does this instrument work?

	Providing feedback	Encourage and praise children's attempts at writing and invented spelling.
	Cognitive structuring	Help children read and write words by having them sound out letters one at a time.
	Instructing	Sound out words, and point to each letter as you say the sound. Model reading and writing new words and letters.

Medium Demand/Medium Support

Children provide information about objects in the exhibit, dictate to the adult, and draw recognizable pictures to include as exhibits or as part of the descriptive text. They will:

> draw recognizable figures and recognize familiar words and letters

Support Strategies

?	Open-ended questioning	Help children decide what to draw.

> What would you like to draw to help people know more about Mexico?

Encourage children to refer to the written labels to obtain information.

> What does this tell us about the Eskimo?

	Providing feedback	Encourage and praise children's attempts at drawing. Have them describe their drawings to help them identify ways to make the drawing more accurate.
	Task regulation	After children draw their pictures, ask them to tell what they drew. Suggest they write the name of their picture.

> I see your shark. Can you write some letters to label your picture?

Suggest choices for letters.

> Fish. Which letter goes better with fish: t or f?

	Instructing	Pair children with peers who are more advanced in the necessary skills. Show children how to write a word or letter to label a drawing.

> You've drawn a moon, and moon starts with m. Do you see an m on the wall? It looks like this.

Ask children to read a familiar word they dictated. Ask children directly to label their drawing.

> What did you draw?

Offer verbal suggestions to help children make the drawing more recognizable.·

> Let's put some fins on your fish.

Provide visual models for children to copy (e.g., real objects, photographs, drawings).

Low Demand/High Support

Children will:

> scribble and name figures after execution and identify objects, people, and events in pictures

Support Strategies

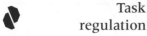

Providing feedback

Encourage and praise children's attempts at drawing.

Task regulation

Ask children to draw a specific object to include as part of the exhibit or the descriptive text.

> These are photographs of all the big fish we saw at the aquarium. Can you draw a picture of your favorite big fish?

Prepare photographs and pictures of objects in the exhibit for children to identify and paste on descriptive labels. Have children color outlines.

Instructing

Ask children to label their drawings. Ask children to identify drawings that are part of the exhibit or the descriptive text. Name objects, and have children repeat.

Comments/Adaptations

Comments

Use products from Let's Find Out activity as topics for exhibit. Children can use computers to prepare texts and graphics.

More Ideas

Have children design an invitation for their parents and friends to come and visit the exhibit.

Home Link

Parent Activity: Going Places—The Museum

EARLY LITERACY OBSERVATION FORM

Child's name: _____

Print/Book Awareness:

1. Things about my play   2. Drawing and writing   3. What I know about print/books

Date	What I did or said

Ladders to Literacy: A Preschool Activity Book
by Angela Notari-Syverson, Rollanda E. O'Connor, and Patricia F. Vadasy
©1998 Paul H. Brookes Publishing Co., Baltimore

PRINT/BOOK AWARENESS CHECKLIST
Behaviors observed

Name: _____

Scoring: Dates: _____ _____ _____

2 = Consistently/independently   1 = Sometimes/partly   0 = Not yet   Activity: _____ _____ _____

Notes:

A = Assumed   NO = No opportunity   R = Report   H = Help   M = Modifications

I. SYMBOLIC REPRESENTATION
Play
    A. Uses symbols in play _____( )_____( )_____( )

Pictures
    B. Identifies objects, people, and actions represented in pictures _____( )_____( )_____( )

Graphics
    C. Scribbles _____( )_____( )_____( )
    D. Names figures after execution _____( )_____( )_____( )
    E. Draws recognizable figures _____( )_____( )_____( )

II. PRINT
Book Conventions
    A. Turns pages _____( )_____( )_____( )
    B. Orients book correctly, knows where book begins and ends _____( )_____( )_____( )
    C. Knows that print, not pictures, tells the story _____( )_____( )_____( )
    D. Knows that text begins at top left corner of page, is read from left to right _____( )_____( )_____( )

Awareness of Graphic Symbols
    E. Reads environmental print (e.g., words, logos, road signs, cereal boxes) _____( )_____( )_____( )
    F. Recognizes a few memorized words in print (e.g., name) _____( )_____( )_____( )
    G. Identifies a printed word _____( )_____( )_____( )
    H. Reads simple words _____( )_____( )_____( )

Letter Identification
    I. Recites part of alphabet _____( )_____( )_____( )
    J. Names single letters _____( )_____( )_____( )

_____
continued

Ladders to Literacy: A Preschool Activity Book
by Angela Notari-Syverson, Rollanda E. O'Connor, and Patricia F. Vadasy
©1998 Paul H. Brookes Publishing Co., Baltimore

Name: _____

Writing

K.	Copies shapes	_____( )_____( )_____( )
L.	Copies letters	_____( )_____( )_____( )
M.	Copies a few words (e.g., name)	_____( )_____( )_____( )
N.	Pretends to write	_____( )_____( )_____( )
O.	Writes name independently	_____( )_____( )_____( )
P.	Writes a few familiar letters and words	_____( )_____( )_____( )
Q.	Uses invented spelling (related letters) to write messages	_____( )_____( )_____( )

III. LETTER–SOUND CORRESPONDENCE

Single Sounds and Letters

A.	Says most common sound for each letter	_____( )_____( )_____( )
B.	Selects a letter to represent a sound	_____( )_____( )_____( )

Words

C.	Uses letter sounds to write words	_____( )_____( )_____( )

Ladders to Literacy: A Preschool Activity Book
by Angela Notari-Syverson, Rollanda E. O'Connor, and Patricia F. Vadasy
©1998 Paul H. Brookes Publishing Co., Baltimore

SCAFFOLDING STRATEGIES CHECKLIST

Child's name: _____

Date: _____   _____   _____

Activity: _____   _____   _____

Circle strategies used during activity:	Used	Did it help?	Used	Did it help?	Used	Did it help?
Open-ended questioning descriptions predictions and planning explanations relating to the child's experience	☐Y ☐N	☐Y ☐N	☐Y ☐N	☐Y ☐N	☐Y ☐N	☐Y ☐N
Providing feedback encouragements evaluations thinking aloud clarification requests interpretation of meaning acknowledgments and information talk	☐Y ☐N	☐Y ☐N	☐Y ☐N	☐Y ☐N	☐Y ☐N	☐Y ☐N
Cognitive structuring rules and logical relationships sequencing contradictions	☐Y ☐N	☐Y ☐N	☐Y ☐N	☐Y ☐N	☐Y ☐N	☐Y ☐N
Holding in memory restating goals summaries and reminders	☐Y ☐N	☐Y ☐N	☐Y ☐N	☐Y ☐N	☐Y ☐N	☐Y ☐N
Task regulation matching interests rearranging elements and experience reducing alternatives making more concrete	☐Y ☐N	☐Y ☐N	☐Y ☐N	☐Y ☐N	☐Y ☐N	☐Y ☐N
Instructing modeling orienting direct questioning elicitations coparticipation	☐Y ☐N	☐Y ☐N	☐Y ☐N	☐Y ☐N	☐Y ☐N	☐Y ☐N

Ladders to Literacy: A Preschool Activity Book
by Angela Notari-Syverson, Rollanda E. O'Connor, and Patricia F. Vadasy
©1998 Paul H. Brookes Publishing Co., Baltimore

SECTION III

Metalinguistic Awareness

Sound Representations...138
Musical Instruments...141
Rhythmic Activities 144
Listening to Songs 147
Clap the Syllables 150
Syllable Puzzles 153
Nursery Rhymes...156
The Rhyming Book 159
Rhyming Games...162
Playing with the Sounds of Words 165
Sound Isolation 168
Letter Sound of the Week 171
First Sound Song 175
Guess the Word (Blending) 179
I'm Thinking of a . . . (Blending by Category) 181
Word to Word Matching Game: First Sound................................184
Play with Miniature Toys 187
Pretend Play—The Store 190
Pretend Play—Magic Password 193

Children's abilities to understand and manipulate the structural features of language develop gradually (Brady, Gipstein, & Fowler, 1992; Fowler, 1991; Vandervelden & Siegel, 1995). Word play activities teach metalinguistic processes explicitly by making children increasingly aware of the sounds in spoken words. This section's activities guide children, through games and small-group activities, to develop awareness and memory for sounds and to rhyme, segment, and blend sounds together. Because these skills are taught through a game format, the activities are fun for children with and without disabilities and, thus, are appropriate for inclusive preschool settings. The activities teach the following broad sets of skills.

- **Perception and memory for sounds and words**—Children first need to be able to listen to and provide meaning to sounds in their environment. Playing musical instruments, imitating animal sounds, and guessing the objects that are the sources of sounds offer young children many opportunities to learn about sounds. Also playing with the sounds of words encourages children to practice perception, production, word recognition, and memory for words and phonemes, all important foundations for phonological awareness (Fowler, 1991).
- **Word awareness**—Word awareness refers to the recognition that words have structural and linguistic features as well as meaning (Tunmer et al., 1988). The first step is for children to understand that an utterance can be broken down into individual words and that words consist of smaller units, phonemes (Ball, 1993).
- **Rhyming**—Phonological awareness often begins with a child's knowledge of nursery rhymes—the first experience with literacy for many children and also the first opportunity to analyze sounds in words. The rhyme (i.e., the match between the ending sounds of two or more words) is a salient clue that makes it easier for children to remember and recite the nonrhyming portions of the poems. Children who can recite rhymes at the age of 3 tend to become better readers than 3-year-old children who cannot, and the ability to recite rhymes is not dependent on intelligence or cultural background (Maclean et al., 1987). Later in development, when reading instruction begins, children who understand that two words share a common feature (e.g., the sound of the ending part) have an advantage for decoding words within word families (Goswami & Bryant, 1992). Activities with nursery rhymes are developmentally appropriate for a range of children with differing ability levels, from about 3 years of age through the primary grades. These activities can be conducted in whole class settings; in small groups; and/or individually by teachers, teacher assistants, and parents. For example, children can rhyme with the names of foods they eat during snacktime

or recite rhymes while waiting for the bus. Rhymes can also initiate conversation, build vocabulary, or be incorporated into art activities.

- **Alliteration**—Alliterating, or recognizing or producing words with common initial sounds, requires a sensitivity to speech units smaller than words and syllables (Ball, 1993). Children as young as 3 are able to recognize words that start with a same sound, and measures of alliteration are related to early reading (Maclean et al., 1987).

- **Blending**—Blending is an oral activity; however, it is also an essential part of early reading instruction. To decode a word independently, children must be able to say the sound of each letter in a word and blend those sounds together (S + a + m = Sam). Oral blending of onset-rime (/m/ + /at/ = /mat/) has been taught to 4-year-old children in a Head Start preschool (Slocum et al., 1993) and to 4-, 5-, and 6-year-old preschool children with disabilities (O'Connor et al., 1993). Many typically developing kindergarten children are able to blend sounds without explicit training (Torgeson, Wagner, & Rashotte, 1994; Yopp, 1988); however, most second-grade children with reading disabilities still have difficulty with oral blending (Vellutino & Scanlon, 1987). Researchers have suggested that instruction in oral blending before children begin reading instruction could make the difficult task of decoding words easier (Haddock, 1976; Lewkowicz, 1980). All of the experiences mentioned previously are introduced in this section through play. For example, the teacher may use puppets (e.g., the teacher talks through a turtle, which only knows how to say words slowly; the children become turtle interpreters) or guessing games ["Let's see if I can fool you. Who knows what I'm trying to say? Re-cess"].

- **Segmentation**—Segmenting, or saying all of the sounds in spoken words separately, is considered a compound skill because a child must hold the word in memory *and* isolate a portion of the word in order to correctly segment it. A child who can segment words finds it easier to use orthographic codes in reading and to acquire spelling rules (Ball & Blachman, 1991; Juel, 1988). Separating words into syllables provides early practice in identifying speech units smaller than whole words. Breaking words into syllables is an easier task than splitting individual syllables into phonemes (Fox & Routh, 1975; Treiman & Zukowski, 1996) and may provide the necessary foundation for the isolation of phonemes in segmentation (Lundberg et al., 1988). Children are developmentally able to segment spoken words much earlier than they can learn to read, often by the age of 3 or 4. The ability to hear and see words in syllables makes decoding longer words easier for beginning readers and is a strategy that continues to be useful through adulthood (Adams, 1990). In this section, syllable segmentation is treated as an oral game: children listen and/or say the word and count its syllables without seeing the word in print (banana = ba-na-na = 3 syllables). The approach to syllable segmentation easily accommodates a range of abilities within a group of young children and begins with small- and large-group clapping games, with procedures for individual practice as necessary. Whereas some children clap or jump to the syllables in a word, other children may hold up fingers or say the number of syllables they hear. Syllable counting can be included easily in other activities throughout the preschool day by using the names of objects around the room, snack foods, children's names, and longer words in the stories teachers read to children. Later in development, most children can be easily taught to say the first sound. Teachers can then use this skill as the foundation for more difficult segmenting tasks involving segmentation of words into three or four phonemes (e.g., m-a-n).

EARLY LITERACY GOALS AND OBJECTIVES

The following goals and objectives for each metalinguistic awareness skill are cross-referenced with the activities in this section. More specific definitions of skills and behaviors are provided in Appendix A.

Perception and Memory for Sounds

- **Environmental sounds**—Child will use sounds to represent objects and animals. Child will identify the source of sounds.
  Activities: Sound Representations; Musical Instruments; Listening to Songs; Clap the Syllables; Playing with the Sounds of Words; Play with Miniature Toys; Pretend Play—Magic Password
- **Words**—Child will repeat short words. Child will repeat multisyllabic words.
  Activities: Musical Instruments; Rhythmic Activities; Listening to Songs; Clap the Syllables; Nursery Rhymes; The Rhyming Book; Rhyming Games; Play with Miniature Toys
- **Phrases**—Child will repeat phrases (e.g., repetitive lines in familiar stories).
  Activities: Musical Instruments; Rhythmic Activities; Listening to Songs; Nursery Rhymes; The Rhyming Book
- **Phonemes**—Child will repeat single phonemes after a short delay (1–2 seconds). Child will repeat two to three phonemes after a short delay (1–2 seconds). Child will discriminate between two phonemes (e.g., same/different).
  Activities: Sound Representations; Musical Instruments; Listening to Songs; Playing with the Sounds of Words; Play with Miniature Toys

Word Awareness

- **Words**—Child will identify a word from a spoken sentence. Child will identify the longer word out of two spoken words. Child will play with the pronunciation of a word.
  Activities: Listening to Songs; Nursery Rhymes; Playing with the Sounds of Words; Guess the Word (Blending); I'm Thinking of a . . . ; Pretend Play—Magic Password

Phonological Skills

- **Rhyming**—Child will say common rhymes along with teacher or peers. Child will fill in last word in rhymes. Child will recite common rhymes independently. Child will recognize that pairs of words do or do not rhyme. Child will say a rhyming word to a target word.
  Activities: Listening to Songs; Nursery Rhymes; The Rhyming Book; Rhyming Games; Pretend Play—Magic Password
- **Alliteration**—Child will recognize words that start with a same sound. Child will say words that start with a same sound as another word.
  Activities: Letter Sound of the Week; First Sound Song; Word to Word Matching Game: First Sound
- **Blending**—Child will blend syllables into words. Child will blend words with sounds pronounced in onset-rime format (e.g., m-ake). Child will blend three to four phonemes into words (e.g., s-a-t; m-a-n).
  Activities: Musical Instruments; Rhythmic Activities; Clap the Syllables; Syllable Puzzles; Guess the Word (Blending); Word to Word Matching Game: First Sound; Pretend Play—The Store; Pretend Play—Magic Password
- **Segmentation**—Child will segment words into syllables. Child will identify first sound in words. Child will separate words into onset-rime. Child will segment one-syllable words into three to four phonemes.
  Activities: Musical Instruments; Rhythmic Activities; Clap the Syllables; Syllable Puzzles; Letter Sound of the Week; First Sound Song; Word to Word Matching Game: First Sound; Play with Miniature Toys

SOUND REPRESENTATIONS

Main Purpose

To develop awareness of sound and the relationship between sound and meaning

Children experiment with sounds and use sounds to represent objects (e.g., animals, vehicles).

Materials

Toy animals and vehicles; pictures; books about animals or objects that make sounds (e.g., *Polar Bear, Polar Bear, What Do You Hear?* [Martin & Carle, 1991]); dramatic play props (chosen depending on pretend play to be encouraged)

Description of the Activity

During storytime, pretend play, or songtime, encourage children to make onomatopoeic sounds to represent animals (e.g., arf-arf, meow), toy vehicles (e.g., beep, varoom), and other events (e.g., an explosion, a waterfall, wind). Look at books with animal or object sounds. Have children guess which sounds go with the animals or objects ["What does a cat say?" "Boom! What could have made this sound?"]. Introduce new onomatopoeia, and encourage children to invent their own. Have children repeat new sounds and segment these sounds into two to three phonemes. Ask children to say their own sounds ["What sound do you say, Lisa?"], and include them in songs ["Lisa said 'Fala.' Let's all sing the fala song"].

This activity develops the following behaviors and concepts that are related to early literacy:

Print/Book Awareness

Symbolic representation—pictures; print—book conventions; letter–sound correspondence—single sounds and letters

Metalinguistic Awareness

Perception and memory for sounds—environmental sounds, words, phonemes; word awareness—words

Oral Language

Vocabulary—words and sentences; literate discourse—conversations

ADULT–CHILD INTERACTIVE BEHAVIORS

High Demand/Low Support

Children will:

use sounds to represent objects and animals and invent their own, repeat sequences of at least three phonemes, and play with the pronunciation of words

Support Strategies

?   Open-ended questioning

Encourage children to invent sounds and play with the pronunciation of words.

> The cat says "meow." What else could he say if he lived on Mars and spoke another language?

Cognitive structuring

Help children sequence phonemes.

> Which sound came first?

Task regulation

Decrease memory demands by saying the initial phoneme.

> /S/ /a/ /m/. S . . . ?

Instructing

Ask children to repeat a series of three phonemes.

> This puppet is from Mars. He's saying "Hi" in his language. /A/ /s/ /i/. Can you say "Hi" back to him in his language?

Model playing with sounds and the pronunciation of words, and ask children to add to the list.

> Danny, Fanny, Manny, . . .

Medium Demand/Medium Support

Children will:

> use sounds to represent objects and animals, identify the source of sounds, and repeat sequences of at least two phonemes

Support Strategies

Cognitive structuring

Help children sequence phonemes.

> Which sound did the dinosaur say first?

Task regulation

Present tasks in the context of meaningful, playful activities.

> The dinosaurs lived a long time ago and spoke a funny language. This one says /d/ /e/. Can you speak like the dinosaur?

Decrease memory demands by saying the initial phoneme.

> The cow says /M/ . . .

Present tasks in the context of meaningful, playful activities.

> Meow. Who says "Meow"?

Provide choices.

> Oink. Is that the cat or the pig?

Instructing

Ask children specific questions.

> What sound does the pig make?

Ask children to repeat sounds.

> The donkey says "ee-haw." You say "ee-haw."

Low Demand/High Support

Children will:

> repeat words and sounds with one phoneme

Support Strategies

Task regulation   Present tasks in the context of meaningful, playful activities (e.g., have children play copycat and take turns repeating familiar words and sounds). Sing songs in which children repeat sounds.

> Let's sing "The ghost says 'Boo!'"

Instructing   Model sounds, and ask children to repeat.

> The dog says "Woof!" You say "Woof."

Comments/Adaptations

Comments   Singing (e.g., "Old MacDonald Had a Farm") is a good opportunity to practice this activity. Encourage children to accompany sounds with gestures and actions to help differentiate and sequence sounds.

Home Link   Parent Activity: What Did You Hear?

MUSICAL INSTRUMENTS

Main Purpose To use music to discriminate sounds and segment words

Children learn to produce, discriminate, and manipulate sounds of objects and words.

Materials Drums; cymbals; bells; xylophone; tambourine; triangle; songbooks

Description of the Activity Let the children choose instruments and make sounds with them. This activity helps children discriminate contrasting sounds (e.g., high, low; loud, soft). If necessary, help the children to produce loud and soft sounds as well as to notice which instruments make high and low sounds. Encourage children to make comments about the music and instruments. Select songbooks with pictures, and encourage children to sing and chant. Show the children how to segment multisyllable words by using the instruments to emphasize each syllable (e.g., by producing one drumbeat for each syllable). Select or make pictures and written labels for instruments that can be placed in the location used to store the instruments. Introduce children to instruments and songs from a variety of cultures (e.g., balalaika, sitar). If instruments are too complicated for the children to play, then the adult can play, and the children can sing along and comment on sounds, melody, tempo, rhythm, and pitch. Have children learn or create verses to go with the music, and write them down on a large sheet or in a songbook.

This activity develops the following behaviors and concepts that are related to early literacy:

Print/Book Awareness Symbolic representation—pictures; print—awareness of graphic symbols, letter identification

Metalinguistic Awareness Perception and memory for sounds—words, phrases, phonemes; word awareness—words; phonological skills—segmentation

Oral Language Vocabulary—words and sentences

ADULT–CHILD INTERACTIVE BEHAVIORS

High Demand/Low Support

Children play instruments, sing songs, and discuss sounds and instruments. They will:

> discriminate between different phonemes and segment words into syllables and phonemes

Support Strategies

? Open-ended questioning

Encourage children to segment words of their choice.

> Let's sing and play the music slowly. Which word would you like to sing slowly?

⊹ Cognitive structuring

Highlight the relationships among instruments, actions, and sounds.

> The harder you hit the drum, the louder you made the sound. How did the big bell sound compared with the little bell?

Have children group together instruments that make similar sounds. As children segment a word, have them count the number of separate syllables or phonemes.

> How many parts are there in the word butterfly?

◗ Task regulation

Have children segment words into syllables or phonemes as they play an instrument (e.g., beat a drum). Begin with segmenting familiar words such as children's own names.

ℹ Instructing

Model (e.g., beat the drum five times and segment hip-po-po-ta-mus, and have children repeat or say the word along with you). Model using visual cues (e.g., raise a finger for each phoneme).

Medium Demand/Medium Support

Children play instruments and learn their names. They will:

> identify the source of sounds and repeat unusual, multisyllable words

Support Strategies

? Open-ended questioning

Encourage discussion about instruments, music, and related cultural aspects using new and unusual words.

> Native Americans play drums at their powwows. Has anyone been to a powwow?

Encourage children to plan together what kind of song or melody they want to play (e.g., happy, sad, slow, fast, loud, soft), and have them make predictions.

> How should we play to make the song sound happy?

ℹ Instructing

Show children a few instruments along with their names and sounds, and then ask children direct questions.

> What's the name of this instrument?
> Which instrument made this sound?

Model unusual names, and have children imitate.

> Can you say "Balalaika"? What about "accordion"?

Low Demand/High Support

Children play simple instruments and listen to sounds. They will:

repeat common words

Support Strategies

Instructing

Model names of instruments, and have children imitate.

Can you say "drum"?

Ask children direct questions.

What's this?

Comments/Adaptations

Comments

Use songbooks made by the class. Incorporate words from other languages. Use rhyming activities that go with music. Use instruments from different cultures, such as maracas, Tibetan bells, gongs, gourds, drums, flutes, and conch shells.

Adaptations

For children with hearing impairments, use amplified, vibrating musical instruments (e.g., big drums).

Home Link

Parent Activity: Let's Dance!

RHYTHMIC ACTIVITIES

Main Purpose
To develop awareness of sounds and the ability to separate sounds from their meanings

Children learn to explore rhythm by moving their bodies to music. Exploration of rhythm helps children become sensitive to the temporal quality or duration of sounds. Children also learn to manipulate sounds in words independently of their meanings.

Materials
Drum; sticks; pictures; piano; books; other rhythm instruments

Description of the Activity
Have children move their bodies to different rhythms and music. Beat a drum, clap hands, or play the piano to different beats (e.g., even, uneven), tempos (e.g., fast, slow), intensities (e.g., soft, loud), frequencies (e.g., high, low), and durations (e.g., long, short). Have the children move to the music and respond with their bodies to different rhythms. Begin with slow, regular, even beats to which children can clap their hands. Introduce uneven beats later, with variations in intensity and tempo. Encourage children to sing and chant along. Introduce blending and segmenting of sentences and multisyllable words by clapping hands, banging the drum, or hopping or jumping to individual syllables. Relate movement to children's personal experiences ["Let's move slowly and pretend we are walking in heavy snow"]. Propose a theme or an imaginary story for the children to mime. Pretend, for example, that the children are slowly climbing up a mountain and then running down fast. Pretend that children are different animals (e.g., a heavy, slow elephant; a light butterfly). Use pictures or books to help children focus on the theme. Encourage children to plan ahead ["Which animal will you be when the music gets real loud?"]. Discuss how different music can affect feelings (e.g., sad, happy, sleepy). During and after the activities, ask the children to explain what they thought the music was about, how the music made them feel, and why they moved in a certain way. Encourage imaginative thinking and dramatic play.

This activity develops the following behaviors and concepts that are related to early literacy:

Print/Book Awareness
Symbolic representation—play

Metalinguistic Awareness
Perception and memory for sounds—words, phrases; phonological skills—blending, segmentation

Oral Language
Literate discourse—conversations, decontextualization, interpretive/analytic discourse

144

ADULT–CHILD INTERACTIVE BEHAVIORS

High Demand/Low Support

Children move to the different rhythms of the music, playing imaginary roles and developing pretend play scenes. They will:

> segment words into syllables

Support Strategies

?	Open-ended questioning	Have children choose to be an object or animal that moves slowly or in a fragmented manner, and have them segment words into syllables. Think of an animal that hops or jumps and can say words in little bits. Which animal would you like to be?
	Task regulation	Have children segment words into syllables and hop or clap to each syllable. Begin with segmenting familiar words such as children's own names.
	Instructing	Model word segmentation, and have the children repeat or say word segmentation along with you. How many parts are there to the word butterfly? But-ter-fly! Use visual and auditory cues (e.g., hop, clap hands) while modeling.

Medium Demand/Medium Support

Children play pretend roles and move to the different rhythms of the music. They will:

> blend syllables into words

Support Strategies

?	Open-ended questioning	Ask children to choose an animal or an object that moves fast, and have children say words fast.
	Task regulation	Play slow music when presenting the segmented word and fast music when asking children to blend the word (e.g., ba-na-na [to slow music]; banana, banana [to fast music]).
	Instructing	Draw children's attention to what to listen for. Is this music fast or slow? Raise your hands when the music changes.

Say words segmented into syllables, and ask children to say the word fast. Model the blended word, and have children repeat.

Low Demand/High Support

Children move to the different rhythms of the music. They will:

repeat common words and phrases

Support Strategies

 Open-ended questioning

Ask children how the music makes them feel like moving.

 Providing feedback

Describe the music and children's actions and movements.

The music is fast, and you are hopping up and down just like a little rabbit!

Task regulation

Provide choices.

This music is fast and soft. Do you want to run or walk?

Ask children to repeat words and sentences to a peer.

Tell Jamal, "Run fast!"
Tell Josie, "I'm jumping up and down!"

Instructing

Give directions.

When Nathan plays the drum quickly, everyone run fast!

Ask direct questions.

How are you going to run?

Ask children to imitate words and sentences.

Can you say "tiptoe"?

Comments/Adaptations

Comments

Introduce this activity after children have become familiar with the musical instruments, as they will tend to focus first on the instruments rather than on the beat and rhythms. The Clap the Syllables activity can be incorporated within this activity. An easier version of this activity is to play Musical Chairs or other similar games during which children move when the music plays and stop when the music stops.

Home Link

Parent Activity: Let's Dance!

LISTENING TO SONGS

Main Purpose

To develop listening skills and memory for sounds

Children develop listening skills by attending to verbal and non-verbal sounds. Children need to listen in order to learn and produce words and sounds. Especially important is the ability to focus on relevant sounds and words and screen out other auditory stimuli.

Materials

Tapes of songs (e.g., "Can You Sound Just Like Me?"; "Finger Play" and "Ready Set" by Red Grammer; "Letter Sounds" by Hap Palmer; multicultural children's songs sung by Ella Jenkins); tape recorder

Description of the Activity

Have children listen to songs that require them to imitate sounds (e.g., "Can You Sound Just Like Me?"), to make gestures with their hands (e.g., "Finger Play"), and to move their whole bodies (e.g., "Ready Set"). Show children the cover of the tape, with the name of the song and the singer. After listening to the songs, encourage children to talk about the content and actions. Ask them to describe what they like and dislike about the music, movements, and other aspects of the activity. Expose children to music and songs from different cultures. Talk about the background of the song and music. Include photographs and props (e.g., pictures representing other cultures, musical instruments used in the songs). Have children bring favorite recordings from home. Include nursery rhymes and rhyming songs, and draw attention to words that rhyme.

This activity develops the following behaviors and concepts that are related to early literacy:

Print/Book Awareness

Symbolic representation—pictures; print—awareness of graphic symbols, letter identification

Metalinguistic Awareness

Perception and memory for sounds—words, phrases, phonemes; phonological skills—rhyming

Oral Language

Literate discourse—conversations, decontextualization, interpretive/analytic discourse

ADULT–CHILD INTERACTIVE BEHAVIORS

High Demand/Low Support

Children listen to the songs and actively participate by making gestures and moving their bodies. They will:

>   recite familiar rhymes and rhyming songs independently and identify a word from the songs or rhymes

Support Strategies

| ? | Open-ended questioning | Ask children to volunteer to say a rhyme or song of their choice. |

? Open-ended questioning — Ask children to volunteer to say a rhyme or song of their choice.
> Which song would you like to sing?

Ask children to select one word from the song or rhyme.

Cognitive structuring — Explain what a word is.
> We use words to talk about things. One word tells us one thing. We put words together to make sentences.

Then ask children to say one word from the song or rhyme.

Task regulation — Display posters and pictures representing characters and events in the song or rhyme for children to refer to as they recite the song or rhyme. Recite parts of the rhyme or song and have children fill in.

Medium Demand/Medium Support

Children listen to and participate in the songs. They will:

> say common rhymes along with peers and repeat phrases and lines in songs and rhymes

Support Strategies

Open-ended questioning — Ask children to choose phrases to repeat from the song or rhyme.
> What does this song say?

Task regulation — Focus children's attention to the activity by telling them they will need to "put on their listening ears" to cue them into focusing their attention on listening to the song. Ask them to tell you when they feel ready. Provide the initial words.
> The itsy-bitsy spider . . .

Instructing — Highlight and model parts of songs and rhymes for them to repeat.

Low Demand/High Support

Children listen to and participate in some of the actions and gestures. They will:

> repeat common words

Support Strategies

Task regulation — Have children repeat words in fingerplay songs that are associated with gestures.

Instructing   Ask children direct questions.

> The itsy-bitsy spider went up the water spout. Who went up the water spout?

Ask children to imitate.

> This song is about six little ducks. Can you say "Duck"?

Comments/Adaptations

Comments   Encourage children to change words to familiar songs and make up their own verses.

Adaptations   Use sign language, pictures, and props to assist children with hearing impairments.

More Ideas   Ask parents to send to school cassette tapes of songs they enjoy at home, especially those of different cultures. Tape songs in school, and send them home to parents.

Home Link   Parent Activity: Sing a Song

CLAP THE SYLLABLES

Main Purpose
To understand that words can be conceptualized as a collection of parts

The child recognizes that words can be subdivided at the syllable level. This activity introduces children to differentiating the sound of words from their meaning. Children come to view words as collections of sounds apart from their meaning.

Materials
Drums or other musical instruments; paper; crayons

Description of the Activity
During circle time, begin the activity by modeling the clapping behavior and encouraging taking turns. Go around the circle. Say each child's name, then say the name in syllables, clapping for each beat. Encourage children to clap the beat with you ["Andrew! Andrew"]. Lead children in clapping twice. After the first few times, children should join you in clapping syllables. You can extend the activity in several ways. Call out the names of objects in the classroom ["Table"]. Have the children repeat the word, clapping the syllables along with you. Encourage children to take turns calling out the name of an object in the classroom, then have all of the children repeat the child's word, clapping the syllables. Instead of clapping, you can use musical instruments such as drums, tambourines, or xylophones. Also pictures and labels with names can be used as visual support.

This activity develops the following behaviors and concepts that are related to early literacy:

Print/Book Awareness
Symbolic representation—pictures; print—awareness of graphic symbols

Metalinguistic Awareness
Perception and memory for sounds—words; phonological skills—blending, segmentation

Oral Language
Vocabulary—words and sentences

ADULT–CHILD INTERACTIVE BEHAVIORS

High Demand/Low Support

Children will:

segment words into syllables by clapping and saying words in syllables

Support Strategies

Cognitive structuring

Explain how to segment words.

> Table has two beats. Ta-ble. Do you hear the two beats in table? Ta-ble.

Model saying words in syllables, and have children count the number of syllables before clapping themselves.

> Hippopotamus. Count the parts. Hip-po-po-ta-mus! How many parts did you count?

Task regulation

Have children segment familiar words, such as their names or objects present in their classroom.

> Say Kelley in two parts.
> Say banana in little parts.

Have children choose words to segment. Have children segment two-syllable words.

> Table. Say it slow.

Have children segment compound words (e.g., caterpillar, spaceship). Say the first one or two syllables, and then have children add the syllables that follow.

> Elephant. I say el-e. You say -phant.

Instructing

As you model saying words in syllables, have children clap to the syllables. Model saying words in syllables, and have children repeat the word in syllables.

> Vol-ca-no. Say volcano like that.

Medium Support/Medium Demand

Children will:

> blend syllables into words and repeat words segmented into syllables

Support Strategies

Task regulation

Have children blend familiar words such as their names or objects present in their classroom.

> Lin-da. What word is that?

Use two-syllable words.

> Win-dow. Say it fast.

Instructing

Model blending the word, and then repeat the task with a new word. Say a word segmented into syllables, and have the child repeat.

> Pump-kin. Say these two sounds: pump-kin.

Physically guide children by holding them in your lap, taking their hands, and gently clapping to the syllables.

Low Demand/High Support

Children will:

> repeat multisyllabic words

Support Strategies

Task regulation   To elicit children's interest say unusually long words that are likely to be novel and unfamiliar (e.g., kookaburra, extraordinary, enormous). Enunciate words slowly.

Instructing   Have children repeat words that peers have blended or segmented.

> What word did Ly say?

Comments/Adaptations

Comments   This activity can be incorporated into the rhythmic activities. This activity can also be used for segmenting sentences into words and segmenting compound words. Children can use movements and actions other than clapping (e.g., jumping, placing a block in a container for each segment, tapping the table with their hand). Children can also be asked to segment or repeat words while looking at books with unusual multisyllable words (e.g., *Many Luscious Lollipops* [Heller, 1989]).

More Ideas   Audiotape activity, and send tape to parents.

Home Link   Parent Activity: Let's Dance!

SYLLABLE PUZZLES

Main Purpose

To understand that words can be conceptualized as a collection of parts

Children learn concepts about words and to manipulate sounds by segmenting, blending, and substituting syllables.

Materials

Objects; pictures

Description of the Activity

Have children draw or prepare in advance pictures of objects with names that are multisyllable words (e.g., volcano, dinosaur, helicopter) or a compound word (e.g., butterfly). Cut pictures into a number of parts corresponding to the number of syllables or word parts (e.g., a picture of an elephant is cut into three pieces). The children take apart and put together the images as they segment or blend the word ["el-e-phant"]. Make puzzles of different lengths so that longer words have longer puzzles (e.g., an 8-inch long alligator puzzle, a 4-inch long spider puzzle).

This activity develops the following behaviors and concepts that are related to early literacy:

Print/Book Awareness

Symbolic representation—pictures

Metalinguistic Awareness

Perception and memory for sounds—words; phonological skills—blending, segmentation

Oral Language

Vocabulary—words and sentences

ADULT–CHILD INTERACTIVE BEHAVIORS

High Demand/Low Support

Children put puzzle pieces together correctly. They will:
  segment syllables and play with the pronunciation of words

Support Strategies

?

Open-ended questioning

After modeling a segmented word, ask children to make new words by changing just a little part of the word.

> Ti-ger. That's two parts. Let's change the first part and make a new word. Mi-ger!

Cognitive structuring

To help children segment words, suggest that they count puzzle pieces to identify the corresponding numbers of syllables in words. Help children identify segmented words and blended words by

153

associating segmentation with saying the word slowly and blending with saying the word fast.

Task regulation

Encourage children to use pictures as visual supports by having them touch individual puzzle pieces as they pronounce individual syllables and pull puzzles apart as they segment words. Have children practice segmenting and blending the same word.

> Coconut. Say it fast. Now say it slow.

Begin the segmenting by enunciating the first syllable, and have children add the others.

> Ze. . . . What comes next? That's right. Zebra!

Instructing

Encourage children to observe and listen to more skilled peers. Model segmenting the word, and then repeat the task with a new word and corresponding puzzle. Model changing the pronunciation of words, and have children make up their own.

> Alphabet. Alphazet. You make another word.
> Crackerjack. Crackertack. You make a new word.

Medium Demand/Medium Support

Children put puzzle pieces together. They will:

> blend syllables into words and identify the longer of two spoken words

Support Strategies

Cognitive structuring

Demonstrate the relationship between the length of the puzzle and the length of the word.

> Look, here's table and here's tablecloth. (Add a puzzle piece for cloth.) See how the word gets longer?

Task regulation

Say words segmented into parts, and have children use pictures to identify the word.

> Vol-ca-no. What word did I say? Look at the picture.

Encourage children to use puzzles as visual cues to compare short words (e.g., two-piece puzzle) with longer words (e.g., three- or four-piece puzzles). Exaggerate differences between shorter and longer words by saying the shorter word faster and the longer word slower.

 Instructing   Model blending the word, and then repeat the task with a new word and corresponding puzzle. Model blending the word, and ask children to repeat.

> El-e-phant. Elephant. Now, you say it fast.

When modeling segmented and blended words, exaggerate the difference by pronouncing the segmented word very slowly and the blended word much faster.

Low Demand/High Support

Children put puzzle pieces together and will:

> repeat multisyllabic words

Support Strategies

 Instructing   Have children repeat words that peers have blended or segmented.

> What word did Shosone say?

Model, and have children repeat.

> That's a dinosaur. Tell Amy what that is.

Comments/Adaptations

Adaptations   Use brightly colored images in relief figures made of thick cardboard for children with visual impairments.

Home Link   Send home a syllable puzzle.

ze-bra

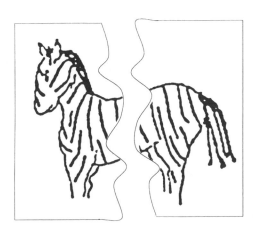

NURSERY RHYMES

Main Purpose	To develop awareness of the sounds of words

Nursery rhymes give children the opportunity to become aware of the sounds in words. By learning to recite nursery rhymes, children develop listening and auditory memory skills and learn about rhyme.

Materials	Picture sequence of story in nursery rhyme; text with rhyming words highlighted; crayons
Description of the Activity	During small-group activities, show children pictures that illustrate well-known nursery rhymes, accompanied by text. Use different pictures that illustrate the sequence of events in the rhyme. Recite the rhyme; and proceed to sequence the pictures, eliciting the participation of the children. Encourage each child to learn to recite parts of the nursery rhyme. Draw the children's attention to the words that rhyme, and write the words on the chalkboard. Focus the children's attention on the match between the ending sounds of two or more words that rhyme. Give children pictures that illustrate the rhyme to color and keep. Encourage discussion about the content or story of the nursery rhyme.

This activity develops the following behaviors and concepts that are related to early literacy:

Print/Book Awareness	Symbolic representation—pictures; print—awareness of graphic symbols
Metalinguistic Awareness	Perception and memory for sounds—words, phrases; phonological skills—rhyming
Oral Language	Vocabulary—words and sentences; narrative skills—narrations of fictional story; literate discourse—decontextualization

ADULT–CHILD INTERACTIVE BEHAVIORS

High Demand/Low Support

Children will:

recite the whole nursery rhyme independently and say new rhyming words

Support Strategies

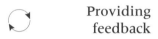 Open-ended questioning

Have children choose a rhyme to recite to their peers. Encourage children to talk about the story told by the rhyme and to comment about related personal experiences.

> What's this rhyme about?
> Do you look at stars at night? Can we see stars during the day?

Ask children to choose two rhyming words from the rhyme and to add a new one of their own.

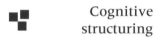 Providing feedback

Have children repeat their rhyming words or repeat back to them their answers, and ask children to reevaluate if their words rhyme.

> Wall. Horse. Do these two words sound the same?

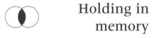 Cognitive structuring

Explain the concept of rhyme.

> Words that rhyme end with the same sound. Funny. Bunny. Both end with -unny. They rhyme.

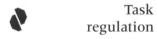 Holding in memory

Provide visual cues in the form of posters, pictures, or books that illustrate the nursery rhyme story.

Task regulation

Say two words that rhyme and emphasize the parts of the words that sound alike, asking children to identify the parts that sound the same. Have children pick the odd word or the two words that sound the same from three words of which only two rhyme.

> High, sky, twinkle. Which is the odd word? Which two sound the same?

Medium Demand/Medium Support

Children will:

> recite the whole nursery rhyme along with peers and recognize pairs of words that do or do not rhyme

Support Strategies

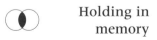 Open-ended questioning

Have children choose a rhyme to recite with their peers. Ask children questions about the story.

> What did the spider do?

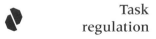 Holding in memory

Provide visual cues in the form of posters, pictures, or books that illustrate the nursery rhyme story.

Task regulation

Pair a word chosen by the children from the rhyme with another word, and ask children to identify whether the words rhyme.

Mouse, house. Do these words sound the same?

Pair nonrhyming words that sound very different.

Clock, rhinoceros. Do these words rhyme?

Provide pictures that are similar (e.g., same color) for rhyming and dissimilar (e.g., different colors) for nonrhyming words (e.g., a brown pear and a brown bear, a red cat and a blue house).

Instructing   Model pairs of words that rhyme, and have children repeat.

Low Demand/High Support

Children will:

repeat phrases and fill in last words in rhymes

Support Strategies

Task regulation   Give children choices of rhymes.

Shall we say "Hickory Dickory Dock" or "Hey Diddle Diddle"?

Have children fill in the final rhyme in a rhyming couplet.

Humpty-Dumpty sat on a wall. Humpty-Dumpty had a great . . .

Instructing   Draw children's attention to specific illustrations related to lines or words in the rhyme. For example, point to a picture of the wall when having children fill in the final rhyme.

Humpty-Dumpty sat on a . . .

Call on children individually to ensure their participation in the recital.

Andy, say it along with us.

Model, and have children repeat lines.

Comments/Adaptations

Comments   Flannel board figures and real props can be used as well as pictures.

Adaptations   Use sign language, pictures, and props to assist children with hearing impairments.

More Ideas   Ask a librarian to help select picture books with rhymes, and enjoy these books with children. Send home copies of rhymes with pictures for children to learn with their parents. Tape record children as they recite the rhymes. Let children borrow the tape to play at home.

Home Link   Parent Activity: Nursery Rhymes

THE RHYMING BOOK

Main Purpose   To develop memory for words and rhyming skills

Children learn to listen to and repeat words and phrases and become aware of words that rhyme.

Materials   Blank books; notebooks; pictures; crayons

Description of the Activity   Make the rhyming book together with the children. These books can consist of collections of pictures of words that rhyme (e.g., a book of words that rhyme with "cat") or of a story or song with rhyming verses. The following is an example for a rhyming songbook, which can be illustrated by the children and used on a regular basis ["I went to a party . . ."]. Children choose words that rhyme from pictures contained in the book or separate pictures and objects that are available. Also, children can propose their own words. Ask the children to insert the first rhyming word, for example, snail ["I went to a party. I asked my (snail). He wanted to bring something. So we took a look in his rhyming book. To see what he could bring! The (snail) brought the . . ."]. Ask the children to choose a second rhyming word, for example, whale ["And we all went to the party! We danced all night. 'Til they turned out the light! . . . And we had to go home in the morning!"].[1]

This activity develops the following behaviors and concepts that are related to early literacy:

Print/Book Awareness   Symbolic representation—pictures, graphics; print—book conventions, awareness of graphic symbols

Metalinguistic Awareness   Perception and memory for sounds—words; phonological skills—rhyming

Oral Language   Vocabulary—words and sentences

ADULT–CHILD INTERACTIVE BEHAVIORS

High Demand/Low Support

Children participate in making the books by drawing pictures and creating verses. They will:

propose new words that rhyme

---

[1]The authors thank Valerie Cohen for her contribution to the development of this activity.

159

Support Strategies

?	Open-ended questioning	Ask children to help make up songs and text by proposing pairs of words that rhyme.

Who shall we ask to go to the party?
What did the cat bring?

Ask children to add other rhyming words.

The snail brought the whale. What else?

Providing feedback	Have children repeat their answers, or repeat the answers back to them, and ask children to reevaluate if the words rhyme.

Dog. Bat. Do these two words sound the same?

Cognitive structuring	Explain the concept of rhyme.

Words that rhyme end with the same sound. Bake. Lake. Both end with -ake. They rhyme.

Holding in memory	Remind children that words need to rhyme or sound the same.

The dog has to bring something or somebody that has a name that sounds like dog.

Task regulation	Emphasize the part of words that rhymes.

Cat. Hat. These words end with -at. Do they sound the same or different? Do they rhyme?

Show the children a picture of the object with which their word must rhyme.

Medium Demand/Medium Support

Children participate in making the book by choosing pictures. They will:

recognize that pairs of words do or do not rhyme

Support Strategies

?	Open-ended questioning	Ask children to suggest characters they want to invite to the party, and then ask if the word rhymes with the word in the song.

The dog brought a hog. Dog. Hog. Do they rhyme?

Task regulation	Pair nonrhyming words that sound very different.

Dog. Alligator. Do these words rhyme?

Provide pictures of the same color for rhyming words and different colors for nonrhyming words.

| | Instructing | Model pairs of words that rhyme, and have children repeat. |

Low Demand/High Support

Children will:

> say the rhyming song along with their peers and repeat words and phrases

Support Strategies

| | Instructing | Draw children's attention to specific illustrations. |

> Look at this picture.

Call on individual children to ensure their participation in the recital.

> Tom, say it along with us.

Model words and lines, and have children repeat.

Comments/Adaptations

Home Link   Send a rhyming book home for each child.

RHYMING GAMES

Main Purpose	To recognize that some words share common sounds

The child learns that words are made up of sounds that can be disassociated from the entire word. Rhyming has been identified as one of the earliest competencies that demonstrates phonological awareness. It is a skill that may help children to isolate the smaller sounds in words.

Materials	Laminated pictures of rhyming word pairs; rhyming puzzles; rhyming mazes
Description of the Activity	Take some laminated pictures displaying rhyming words and spread them out on the floor, beginning with one pair of pictures and gradually expanding the set. To help children find rhyming mates, each pair of rhyming pictures can have matching jagged, puzzle-like edges. Ask the children to match the rhyming pair, say the rhyming words represented by the pictures, and fit the pairs together. As children become competent with picture rhymes, add words to the pictures to label them. Rhyming mazes can also be prepared to help children match rhyming words. For example, a maze may have a snake trying to find its way to eat a cake or a mouse going to its house. Encourage children to ask questions and talk about the pictures.

This activity develops the following behaviors and concepts that are related to early literacy:

Print/Book Awareness	Symbolic representation—pictures; print—awareness of graphic symbols
Metalinguistic Awareness	Perception and memory for sounds—words; phonological skills—rhyming
Oral Language	Vocabulary—words and sentences

ADULT–CHILD INTERACTIVE BEHAVIORS

High Demand/Low Support

Children independently match rhyming pictures and identify rhyming word pairs. They will:

> say a rhyming word to a target word

Support Strategies

? **Open-ended questioning**	Ask children to produce new rhymes, using either real or nonsense words.

You put the boy with the toy. What else goes with these two words?

	Providing feedback	Repeat back to children their answers, and ask children to reevaluate whether the words rhyme.

You put box with chair. Do these two words sound the same?

Encourage children to repeat names of objects aloud to determine whether the words rhyme.

	Task regulation	Select three pictures of objects (two of which rhyme), and have children pick the odd word or the two words that rhyme.

Cat. Truck. Hat. Which two pictures go together? Which one doesn't fit?

Medium Demand/Medium Support

Children will:

recognize pairs of words that do or do not rhyme

Support Strategies

	Cognitive structuring	Explain the concept of rhyme.

Words that rhyme end with the same sound. Snake. Cake. Both end with -ake. They rhyme.

	Task regulation	Pair a picture chosen by the children with another picture, and ask children to determine if the words rhyme.

Pear. Bear. Do these words sound the same?

Pair pictures of nonrhyming words that sound very different.

Cat. Dump truck. Do these pictures go together?

	Instructing	Model by matching correct pictures, draw children's attention to the reason for matching, and have them repeat pairs of words that rhyme.

Cat. Hat. They go together because they rhyme. Say cat, hat. Do they rhyme?

Low Demand/High Support

Children label pictures and will:

repeat short words

Support Strategies

	Instructing	Model, and have children name pictures to peers.

You have a cake and a snake. Tell José what you have.

Model matching correct pictures, and have children repeat the pairs of words that rhyme.

The fox goes on the box. Say "fox" and "box."

Comments/Adaptations

Adaptations   Use paste or glue to create relief mazes for children with visual impairments. Write the words or outline them in the paste.

Home Link   Parent Activity: Tell Me a Word that Rhymes with . . . !

PLAYING WITH THE SOUNDS OF WORDS

Main Purpose To facilitate manipulation of the sounds of spoken language

Playing with the sounds of language helps children explore the phonetic structure of words and learn to separate the sound of the word from its meaning.

Materials Storybooks

Description of the Activity During circle time, while reading a story, writing the daily message, singing songs, or doing any other appropriate activity, select words of interest to children. Propose ways to play with the sound of the word by breaking the word into syllables or phonemes and modifying them ["Di-no-saur can become saur-di-no" "N-o can become o-n"]. In addition, have children find ways to make words longer (e.g., snow becomes snowy) and make words shorter (e.g., butterfly becomes butter). Encourage children to repeat words, syllables, and sounds and to invent their own modifications.

This activity develops the following behaviors and concepts that are related to early literacy:

Print/Book Awareness Symbolic representation—pictures, graphics; print—awareness of graphic symbols

Metalinguistic Awareness Perception and memory for sounds—words, phrases, phonemes; word awareness—words

Oral Language Vocabulary—words and sentences

ADULT–CHILD INTERACTIVE BEHAVIORS

High Demand/Low Support

Children will:

> play with the pronunciation of words and discriminate between phonemes

Support Strategies

Open-ended questioning Ask children to make words sound funny or silly, make words longer (e.g., fun to funny, duck to duckling) or shorter (e.g., bunny to bun, snowflake to snow), turn words upside down, and turn words inside out (e.g., run to nur, far to raf).

> How can we make duck longer?

Today is Monday. What's a funny way to change the word Monday?

Ask children to provide sounds that are different and sounds that are the same. Ask children to select a sound to change in a word.

Tree. Which sound in tree shall we change?

Cognitive structuring

Propose rules for changing words and parts of words.

You can change the first sound. Bee. We can change the /b/ to /z/. Bee. Zee.

Caterpillar. You can break it down into two parts and say the second part first. Pillarcater.

Task regulation

Provide choices of sounds in a word for children to change.

Tree. Which sound in tree shall we change? The /tr/ or the /ee/?

Have children discriminate sounds in words they have invented themselves.

Paula said dog. You said kog. /D/ and /k/. Do they sound the same or different?

Instructing

Model changing the pronunciation of words, and have children find their own.

Birthday. Firstday. You find another word.

Ask children to say two sounds, and ask a peer to say whether they are the same or different.

Medium Demand/Medium Support

Children will:

identify the longer word of two spoken words

Support Strategies

Cognitive structuring

Make sure children understand the concepts of long and short, and explain what makes a word long (e.g., has more sounds, takes longer to say).

Task regulation

Have children compare words taken from one of their own utterances. Exaggerate differences between short and long words by saying the shorter word faster and the longer word slower. Have children use visual cues to judge the length of words (e.g., refer to written words).

Low Demand/High Support

Children will:

repeat phrases, words, and single phonemes

Support Strategies

Holding in memory
Begin a familiar phrase or word, and have children complete it.

Task regulation
Present tasks in the context of meaningful, playful activities (e.g., have children play copycat and take turns repeating phrases, words, and phonemes).

Instructing
Model, and have children say or sing along with you.
Let's sing this silly song: Alley, alley, alley!

Comments/Adaptations

Comments
Use colors and cut-up images as visual supports to help differentiate syllables and phonemes. Use gestures and actions to help sequence sounds.

Home Link
Parent Activity: Say it Fast

SOUND ISOLATION

Main Purpose

To encourage children to learn that sounds can be isolated from words

Phonological activities require children to attend to sounds of language, yet many children have little experience uttering sounds in isolation. This activity develops familiarity with the phonemes and smaller-than-word units.

Materials

A collection of songs familiar to children (e.g., "Apples and Bananas" by Raffi, "Letter Sounds" by Hap Palmer).

Description of the Activity

Use any tunes children know (e.g., "Happy Birthday," "I'm a Little Teapot") or familiar rhythms (e.g., knocking patterns). Instead of words and beats, substitute isolated phonemes or meaningless pairs of phonemes. Have the children sing "Lala lala la la" to the tune of "Happy Birthday," and then substitute "Beebee, beebee, bee, bee" and "Tata, tata, ta, ta." When children are able to articulate meaningless phonemes, try starting all of the words in a familiar tune with the same phoneme (e.g., bappy birthday bo bou . . .). Integrate the tasks within a play context. For example, introduce the B puppet man who only says words that start with b. Ask the children to select a "sound of the hour." During that time, start all children's names with that sound (e.g., if /p/ is the sound, then Susan becomes Pusan, Tom becomes Pom, and so forth). The traditional song "Apples and Bananas" sung by Raffi is good for children to listen to and sing along. Each lyric of the song substitutes a new long vowel sound in the words (e.g., apples becomes oples).

This activity develops the following behaviors and concepts that are related to early literacy:

Print/Book Awareness

Symbolic representation—pictures; letter–sound correspondence—single sounds and letters

Metalinguistic Awareness

Perception and memory for sounds—words, phrases, phonemes; word awareness—words; phonological skills—rhyming, segmentation

Oral Language

Vocabulary—words and sentences

ADULT–CHILD INTERACTIVE BEHAVIORS

High Demand/Low Support

Children participate in modifying sounds and words and make suggestions for new words and games. Children will:

play with the pronunciation of words and identify the first sound in words

Support Strategies

?	Open-ended questioning	Ask children to select a sound of the hour, and modify words of their choice by starting them with the selected sound.

> The sound of the hour is /g/. Daniel, you change your word soccer. Right. Now it's goccer!

	Providing feedback	Praise children.

> You made the Barney song really funny when you started all of the words with /h/.

	Cognitive structuring	Make rules explicit to the children.

> We change the first sound only.
> We start all of the words with the same sound.

	Task regulation	Emphasize first sounds by stretching ["Sssss-susan"] or iterating ["T-t-t-tom"]. Have children begin by modifying their own names. Have children modify familiar songs.

Medium Demand/Medium Support

Children will:

> identify a word from the song or rhyme and repeat phrases and sequences of two to three phonemes

Support Strategies

	Task regulation	Ask children to choose a favorite word from a song or a rhyme. Have children sing to a familiar tune by repeating a syllable and substituting one sound (e.g., Lala lala lala, tatatata).

	Instructing	Draw children's attention to the changes in pronunciation of words in the songs and rhymes.

> Okay everyone. Put on your listening ears. Listen carefully to the new words in the songs.

Ask children to tell you when they feel ready. Highlight and model phonemes, words, and parts of songs and rhymes for them to repeat. Ask children to imitate.

> Bappy birthday bo bou.
> The mitsy mitsy mider.

Low Demand/High Support

Children will:

repeat single phonemes and the modified words

Support Strategies

Task regulation

Have children repeat words in favorite and familiar songs. Exaggerate the pronunciation of the new sounds. Begin with having children imitate repetitive sequences of the same syllable.

Dadadada.

Instructing

Highlight and model phonemes, words, and parts of songs and rhymes for them to repeat. Ask children to imitate.

Banini. Can you say Banini?

Comments/Adaptations

Link with Print/ Book Awareness

Post a menu of songs the children know, and have them choose a song from the list. Suggest or have children choose sound to substitute for words.

Home Link

Parent Activity: What Did You Hear?

LETTER SOUND OF THE WEEK

Main Purpose	To isolate and identify first sounds in words
	Children develop awareness of the first sound in words and the letter which accompanies that sound. Children also develop familiarity with phonemes and smaller-than-word units.
Materials	Pictures; isolated letters; drawing materials
Description of the Activity	This activity takes place over several days. Select a letter to study for each week. Focus on the sound of the letter rather than on its name. Day 1: Introduce a letter, and say its most common sound ["Here's S. It says /s/. Let's think of things that start with /s/"]. Begin by identifying children's names that begin with /s/, and then encourage children to find things in the classroom that start with /s/. Day 2: Review S and the sound /s/; invite children to name things that start with /s/, and then use pictures to demonstrate other objects and actions that start with /s/. Include some pictures of objects that do not start with /s/, and encourage children to identify /s/ words. Day 3: Review S and /s/, and invite children to name things that start with /s/. Start a list of /s/ words, and post it prominently. Encourage children to expand the list.

This activity develops the following behaviors and concepts that are related to early literacy:

Print/Book Awareness	Print—letter identification, writing; letter–sound correspondence—single sounds and letters
Metalinguistic Awareness	Perception and memory for sounds—words, phonemes; phonological skills—alliteration, segmentation
Oral Language	Vocabulary—words and sentences

ADULT–CHILD INTERACTIVE BEHAVIORS

High Demand/Low Support

Children will:

> identify the first sound in words and tell a word that starts the same as another

Support Strategies

Cognitive structuring	Make sure children differentiate the letter name (i.e., S) from its sound (i.e., /s/).
	Which letter is this? What sound does it make?

Task regulation

Stress the first sound of several examples of words by stretching ["ssss-snake, Ssss-sally, ssss-salad]" or iterating ["t-t-t-turtle, T-t-t-tommy, t-t-t-tiger"], and have children add words ["What else starts like /s/?"]. Provide visual cues in the form of alphabet letters and pictures of one or more words that start with the letter sound.

Instructing

Tell children to listen for a particular sound before you say words.

> Listen for the /k/ at the beginning of this word: cat. Do you hear the /k/ at the beginning?

Ask children direct questions after teaching.

> Which sound does apple start with?
> Does ssss-snack start with /s/?

Make the first sound obvious by stretching or iterating it; have children repeat, and then elicit identification of the first sound.

> M-m-monday. /M/ is the first sound you say in Mmmm-monday. Say Mmmm-monday. Say the first sound in Monday.

Model lists of words that start with a same sound, and ask children to add a new word.

> Tell me a word that starts the same as these: bear, ball, bell . . .

Medium Demand/Medium Support

Children will:

> discriminate between two phonemes (same or different) and recognize two words that start with the same sound

Support Strategies

Cognitive structuring

Make sure that children understand the concept of same and different by asking them to identify similarities and differences among concrete objects and pictures.

Task regulation

Use words and sounds taken from words in meaningful contexts such as pictures in books or objects in the classroom.

> Sack and sand. /S/ and /s/. Do they sound the same?
> Dog and doll. Do they start the same?

Have children discriminate between phonemes that are clearly different, and exaggerate the sounds (e.g., /s/ versus /t/). Present sounds in the context of words that are clearly similar or different.

> · Here's a boat, and here's another boat. This boat starts with /b/, and this boat starts with /b/. Are they the same or different?
> Cat /k/ and salamander /s/. /K/ and /s/, are they the same or different?

Provide visual cues by accompanying words and sounds with pictures of objects or letters of the alphabet. Have children select the odd word from three words, two of which share a common initial sound.

> Book, hand, and hat. Which sounds different?
> Sea, lake, and sun. Which is the odd word?

Instructing

Model sounds that are similar and sounds that are different by stretching or iterating sounds, and then repeat the question.

> B-b-b-b-bug and p-p-p-puppy. /B/ and /p/. They sound different. /B/ and /p/. Are they the same or different?
> Ssss-sock and ssss-sun. They start with the same sound. Sock and sun. Do they start the same?

Low Demand/High Support

Children will:

> repeat phonemes and words

Support Strategies

Task regulation

Present the task within meaningful contexts (e.g., ask children to repeat a word or a sound to a peer who was not present or attentive). Present words that are familiar to children and phonemes that are easy to pronounce. Provide visual cues, such as signs and pictures, to help children recall sounds and words (e.g., use a picture of a snake to help remember the sound /s/).

Instructing

Ask children to repeat first sounds identified by peers.

> Which sound did Laura say?

Model and ask direct questions.

> This is a tadpole. What did I say this was?

Model sounds and words, and ask children to repeat.

> Right, Rena. Monday starts with /m/. Doug, can you say /m/? Lisa, can you say Monday?

Comments/Adaptations

Comments

Decorate the classroom with graphics of the letter, objects, and pictures of the objects whose names begin with the letter sound of the week.

Home Link

In your newsletter to parents, add a paragraph on which letter the class is learning about at the present time.

We are learning about the letter S and the sound it usually makes at the beginning of words. Please take a few minutes over the next few days to look through pictures or magazines with your child to find at least one picture of a word that starts with S. Encourage your child to cut out the picture(s) and bring it to school. We will mount the picture(s) and add it to our S list.

FIRST SOUND SONG[2]

Main Purpose

To develop phonological memory and sound manipulation

Children learn to remember words, phrases, and sounds and to identify the first sound in words.

Materials

The First Sound Song booklet (see the end of this activity for an example of a First Sound Song)

Description of the Activity

The First Sound Song encourages children to think about the sounds in words. A single sound may be emphasized throughout the whole song, or each verse may focus on a different sound. Make First Sound Song booklets for each child with pictures of animals and objects and initial letters. Sing the First Sound Song to the tune of "Old MacDonald Had a Farm." Have the children learn the verses. Then encourage them to change and propose new words. At the end of a verse, repeat the words and ask children to identify the first sound ["We sang tiger, tree, and train. What sound do these words begin with?"].

This activity develops the following behaviors and concepts that are related to early literacy:

Print/Book Awareness

Symbolic representation—pictures, graphics; print—book conventions, awareness of graphic symbols, letter identification; letter–sound correspondence—single sounds and letters

Metalinguistic Awareness

Perception and memory for sounds—words, phrases, phonemes; phonological skills—alliteration, segmentation

Oral Language

Vocabulary—words and sentences

ADULT–CHILD INTERACTIVE BEHAVIORS

High Demand/Low Support

Children draw pictures and label words that begin with the same first sound to use in the verses of the song. They will:

> identify the first sound in words and tell a word that starts the same as another

---

[2]This activity was developed from a recommendation in Yopp, H. (1992). Developing phonemic awareness in young children. *The Reading Teacher, 45*(9), 696–703.

Support Strategies

?	Open-ended questioning	Ask children to identify words that begin with a particular first sound, and incorporate children's suggestions into the verses of the song.

> What words begin with /t/?

⬛	Cognitive structuring	Make sure children differentiate the letter name (e.g., t) from its sound (e.g., /t/).

> /T/ is the sound of t.

◗	Task regulation	Stress the first sound of words by stretching ["Ssss-silly, Ssss-sam, and ssss-sick"] or iterating ["D-d-daddy, d-d-duck, and d-d-deep"]. Repeat the trio of words several times emphasizing the first sound.

👤	Instructing	Tell children to listen for a particular sound in words before beginning the song.

> Listen for the /t/ at the beginning of the words in the song.

Have a more skilled peer identify the correct first sound. Model, and elicit a response.

> Betty, bear, and bat. /B/ /b/ /b/. What's the sound that starts Betty, bear, and bat?

Model lists of words that start with a same sound, and ask children to add a new word.

> Candy, cat, and can. . . . What's another word that starts the same?

Medium Demand/Medium Support

Children sing along with peers and will:

> discriminate between two phonemes (same or different) and recognize two words that start with the same sound

Support Strategies

⬛	Cognitive structuring	Make sure that children understand the concept of same and different by asking them to identify similarities and differences among concrete objects and pictures.

◗	Task regulation	Have children discriminate between phonemes that are clearly different. When saying the phonemes, exaggerate the pronunciation of the sounds (e.g., /sss/ and /t/-/t/-/t/.). Present sounds in the context of words that are clearly similar or different.

> Two ducks. Duck and duck. /D/ and /d/. Do they sound the same or different?

Tiger and satellite. /T/ and /s/. Are they the same or different?

Have children select the odd word from three words, two of which share a common initial sound.

> Daddy, hat, and duck. Which sounds different?
> Igloo, ice, and crow. Which is the odd word?

Instructing   Model sounds that are similar and sounds that are different, and repeat the question.

> Mommy, man, and milk. /M/, /m/, and /m/. They sound the same. /M/ and /m/. Are they the same or different?

Model words that are the same and different, and repeat the question.

> Daddy and duck, they start the same. Daddy and duck. Do they start the same?
> Rabbit and net, they start with a different sound. Rabbit and net. Do they start the same?

Low Demand/High Support

Children sing along parts of song with peers and will:

> repeat phonemes, words, and phrases

Support Strategies

Task regulation   Provide visual cues by drawing children's attention to the pictures in the book or related objects (e.g., miniature toys, props).

Instructing   Ask children to repeat first sounds following peer model. After having sung the song in group, call on children to take turns in repeating individual lines or words. Model sounds, words, and sentences; and ask children to repeat.

Comments/Adaptations

Comments   Initially, you will lead the song. As children learn to classify pictures by first sound or name objects by first sound, they can "create" a trio of words to use in verses. These words can be posted and identified by several class members before beginning the song. Post the trio of words to use in the verse for the day. Show children the words, call their attention to the similarity among them (i.e., first letter, first sound), and encourage children to "read" the words along with you before and during the song.

First Sound Song example   First verse: ["What's the sound that starts these words: turtle, time, and teeth?" (Wait for a response from the children). "/T/ is the

tiger   tree   train

sound that starts these words: turtle, time, and teeth. With a /t/, /t/ here, and a /t/, /t/ there, here a /t/, there a /t/, everywhere a /t/, /t/. T is the sound that starts these words: turtle, time, and teeth"].

Second verse: ["What's the sound that starts these words: chicken, chin, and cheek?" (Wait for a response from the children.) "/Ch/[3] is the sound that starts these words: chicken, chin, and cheek. With a /ch/, /ch/ here and a /ch/, /ch/ there, here a /ch/, there a /ch/, everywhere a /ch/, /ch/. /Ch/ is the sound that starts these words: chicken, chin, and cheek"].

Third verse: ["What's the sound that starts these words: daddy, duck, and deep?" (Wait for a response from the children). "/D/ is the sound that starts these words: daddy, duck, and deep. With a /d/, /d/ here and a /d/, /d/ there, here a /d/, there a /d/, everywhere a /d/, /d/. /D/ is the sound that starts these words: daddy, duck, and deep"].

Home Link   Send home First Sound booklets.

---

[3]For the purpose of clarity, the authors use the English alphabet symbol /ch/ instead of the international phonetic alphabet sign /tʃ/.

GUESS THE WORD (BLENDING)

Main Purpose	To demonstrate how sounds can be blended into spoken words
	Children learn how to blend initial sounds to form words.
Materials	Picture cards and word cards of simple words
Description of the Activity	Begin by telling the children there is an association between the word you are saying and the pictures you are showing them ["Guess the word I'm saying. It's one of these pictures"]. Pronounce words segmented into phonemes (e.g., c-a-t), onset-rime (e.g., d-og), and syllables (e.g., ti-ger). Begin with words that start with sounds that can be stretched (e.g., s, m, z, f). Spread four pictures across the floor or table ["Ssss-snake"]. When the children guess snake, call on a child to show the picture of a snake with the word snake printed at the bottom. Repeat the game with other pictured words. Gradually introduce pictures with words beginning with stop sounds (e.g., k, t, d, p). Children may have more difficulty with words that cannot be stretched out. This game can also be played with objects and miniature toys.
	This activity develops the following behaviors and concepts that are related to early literacy:
Print/Book Awareness	Symbolic representation—pictures; print—awareness of graphics symbols; letter–sound correspondence—single sounds and letters
Metalinguistic Awareness	Phonological skills—blending
Oral Language	Vocabulary—words and sentences

ADULT–CHILD INTERACTIVE BEHAVIORS

High Demand/Low Support

Children will:

> guess words correctly, blending words with sounds pronounced as two, three, or four phonemes

Support Strategies

Task regulation	Use words with continuous sounds (e.g., ssssaaaam, fffffaaat) rather than stop sounds (e.g., p-e-t, c-a-k-e) so that words can be stretched without breaking between sounds. Use pictures and objects to rep-

179

   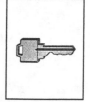

resent the words to be blended. Ask children to name the objects or pictures before guessing the words from separated phonemes.

Instructing   Have children repeat the segmented word before blending it.

Medium Demand/Medium Support

Children guess words correctly. They will:

blend words with sounds pronounced in onset-rime format

Support Strategies

Task regulation   Reduce choices of pictures and objects to two or three. Use words with continuous sounds (e.g., ssssail, mmmmoon, shhhheet, ffffly) rather than stop sounds (e.g., b-oy, c-up, t-op, h-at, p-encil) so that words can be stretched without stopping between sounds. Ask children to name the objects or pictures before guessing the words pronounced in onset-rime format.

Instructing   Have children repeat the segmented word before blending it.

Low Demand/High Support

Children will:

blend syllables into words

Support Strategies

Task regulation   Limit choices of pictures and objects to two or three. Begin with two-syllable words (e.g., rac-coon) or compound words (e.g., butter-fly).

Instructing   Model, then repeat task.

Comments/Adaptations

Adaptations   Use objects and props that children with visual impairments can explore.

Home Link   Parent Activity: Say it Fast

I'M THINKING OF A . . .
(BLENDING BY CATEGORY)

Main Purpose	To demonstrate how sounds can be blended into spoken words
	This activity introduces blending of sounds into words by providing categories to facilitate children's answers.
Materials	None necessary (may use pictures or objects)
Description of the Activity	Encourage children to blend isolated sounds into words by providing categories for children's responses. For this activity, teachers provide a category for children to search (e.g., animals, things with which to write, children in their class, birds, things on which to sit). If letters and their sounds are taught concurrently, teachers can also use first-sound categories ["Things that start with the letter t"] to reinforce beginning sounds and particular letters. Begin by stating the category, which is perhaps linked to a current theme in the classroom ["I'm thinking of an animal. Here's the clue: c-at," "I'm thinking of a flying thing that is not a bird. B-a-t. Can you tell me what this word is?"]. Words can be presented in different formats: segmented into syllables (e.g., mon-key) for the younger children to guess and in an onset-rime format (e.g., c-at, l-ion, m-onkey) for the older children. As children become more skilled, present short words with all phonemes separated ["/D/ /o/ /g/"]. A helpful strategy is to ask the children to repeat the segmented version before they guess an answer. Vary the activity by putting objects into a bag for the children to guess or using pictures cards, which you turn to show the children when they correctly guess the words ["f-l-y, b-ee, but-ter-fly"].
	This activity develops the following behaviors and concepts that are related to early literacy:
Print/Book Awareness	Symbolic representation—pictures
Metalinguistic Awareness	Phonological skills—blending
Oral Language	Literate discourse—categorical organization

ADULT–CHILD INTERACTIVE BEHAVIORS

High Demand/Low Support

Children guess words correctly. They will:
   blend three to four phonemes into words

Support Strategies

Cognitive
structuring

Provide additional clues.

It's a bug. It flies. It stings. It's a w-a-s-p.

Point out contradictions.

The first sound is /p/, so it can't be train.

Task
regulation

Use words with two to three phonemes. Use words with sounds that can be easily stretched instead of segmented (e.g., stretch m-u-g to make it long).

Instructing

Encourage children to repeat the segmented word before guessing.

Medium Demand/Medium Support

Children will:

guess words with sounds pronounced in onset-rime format

Support Strategies

Cognitive
structuring

Review names that go into a category before having children guess words.

Let's think of words that are names of food, such as carrot, jam, and hot dog.

Task
regulation

Begin with two- to three- phoneme words. Use words with initial sounds (onset) that can be easily stretched instead of segmented (e.g., s-eal, not teal). Provide visual cues by letting children choose from pictures or objects, such as mouse, ant, and fish.

Which word am I thinking of? F-ish?

Instructing

Encourage children to repeat the segmented word before guessing. Have children repeat words modeled correctly by peers.

Low Demand/High Support

Children will:

guess words by blending syllables into words

Support Strategies

Task
regulation

Give children a choice of two objects or pictures (e.g., lizard and dinosaur) from which to select.

Which word am I thinking of? Di-no-saur?

Use compound words (e.g., hamburger, sunflower).

Instructing   Give children objects and pictures to classify. Segment names of objects into syllables when you present the objects or pictures. Then have children label them.

> Let's put all of the flowers in the basket and the shapes in the jar. Here's a flower. It's a pop-py. What is it?

Comments/Adaptations

Adaptations   Use objects and props that children with visual impairments can explore.

Home Link   Parent Activity: Say it Fast

WORD TO WORD
MATCHING GAME: FIRST SOUND

Main Purpose

To develop categorization and manipulation of sounds

Children learn to discriminate and identify sounds and words based on the onset sounds.

Materials

A deck of laminated picture cards with several examples of words beginning with each sound represented in the deck.

Description of the Activity

To play this game, children need a stack of cards that have simple pictures of common objects on them. Children match pictures that have names that begin with the same first sound. Lay one card out for all children to see (e.g., table). Ask the children to name the picture and identify the onset sound ["Table. /T/"]. Let each child draw a card, name the new picture (e.g., turtle) and then the previous word (e.g., table), and decide whether they share the same onset ["Table. Turtle. Yes, they start the same"]. Let children take turns drawing cards, and continue the game until all of the cards have been drawn. For the next round of play, you (or a child) pick a new picture card for the others to match. This game can also be played with objects.

This activity develops the following behaviors and concepts that are related to early literacy:

Print/Book Awareness

Symbolic representation—pictures; print—letter identification; letter–sound correspondence—single sounds and letters

Metalinguistic Awareness

Perception and memory for sounds—words, phonemes; phonological skills—alliteration, segmentation

Oral Language

Vocabulary—words and sentences

ADULT–CHILD INTERACTIVE BEHAVIORS

High Demand/Low Support

Children will:

> identify the first sound in words and tell a word that starts with the same sound as another

Support Strategies

Cognitive structuring

Tell children the name of the letter.
> Pig starts with a letter p. What sound does a p make?

Show children other cards with words that begin with the same sound.

> Snake. That goes with these pictures of a seal and a sailboat.

Associate words with those that start with the same onset.

> Turtle. Table and turtle. They start the same. What sound do they start with?

Holding in memory

Remind children of specific onset sounds.

> We are looking for a match for table. /T/, /t/, /t/.

Task regulation

Select cards for the deck that represent only two onsets (e.g., /s/ words and /t/ words). Repeat picture names to children, and stress the first sound by stretching ["Sssssnake. Sssssalad"] or iterating ["T-t-t-turtle, t-t-t-table"]. Provide choices.

> Which word starts with /s/: sun or cat?

Instructing

Participate in the game, draw cards, and model. Ask children direct questions.

> Does tiger start with /t/?

Stretch ["Ssss-slug"] or iterate ["T-t-t-turtle"] the first sound, and have children imitate the stretched or iterated words. Model words that start with the same sound, and have children repeat.

> Box and book. They start with the same sound. Box. Tell me a word that starts the same as box.

Model lists of words that share a common initial sound, and have children add new words.

> Pet, pig, and pop. What else?

Medium Demand/Medium Support

Children will:

> discriminate between two phonemes (same or different) and recognize two words that start with the same sound

Support Strategies

Cognitive structuring

Make sure that children understand the concept of same and different by asking them to identify similarities and differences among real objects and pictures.

Task regulation

Select cards for the deck that represent phonemes that are clearly different (e.g., /k/ versus /s/). Select pictures of words that have clearly similar or different contextual features (e.g., word length, perceptual characteristics).

Here's a table, and here's turtle. /T/ and /t/. Are they the same or different?

Crocodile and bee. /K/ and /b/. Are they the same or different?

Have children select the odd word of three words, two of which share a common initial sound.

Wig, wasp, and mug. Which is the odd word?

 Instructing Model words and sounds that are similar and sounds that are different, and repeat the question.

Bug and squirrel. Bug starts with /b/, and squirrel starts with /s/. Are they the same or different?

Put together two cards with pictures of objects with names that start with the same sound, and have children name the pictures.

Low Demand/High Support

Children will:

repeat phonemes and words

Support Strategies

 Task regulation Present the task within meaningful contexts (e.g., ask children to repeat a word or sound to a peer who was not present or attentive). Provide visual cues (e.g., signs, pictures) to help children recall sounds and words, such as a picture of a snake to help remember the sound /s/.

 Instructing Ask children to repeat first sounds identified by peers.

What sound did Cher say?

Model, and ask direct questions.

This is a goat. What did I say this was?

Model sounds and words, and ask children to repeat.

Right, José, sunflower starts with /s/. Eric, can you say /s/?

Comments/Adaptations

Comments Print words, and highlight first sounds on word cards by coloring them or cutting them apart from the rest of the word.

Adaptations Use objects and props so that children with visual impairments can feel them. Use sign language, and color code letters to assist children with hearing impairments.

Home Link Parent Activity: First Sound

PLAY WITH MINIATURE TOYS

Main Purpose	To develop phonological memory and word manipulation skills
	Children learn how words are composed of individual sounds.
Materials	A box of small toys
Description of the Activity	Organize the children to engage in play with miniature animals and characters. Encourage children to enact play themes (e.g., a visit to the zoo, a night in the jungle) and to talk about the animals and other toys. As children play, seize opportunities to practice phonological skills by identifying first sounds of animals with which children choose to play, blending animal names pronounced in an onset-rime manner, and repeating new words. For example, point to an object a child is playing with and stress the first sound ["B-b-b-bear. Say it with me. B-b-b-bear. /B/ is the first sound in bear. Say the first sound /b/. Bear starts like /b/," "What's this?" (Hold up the boy doll.) "Yes! B-b-b-boy. Say it with me. B-b-b-boy. Say the first sound /b/. Boy starts like /b/," "What's this?" (Hold up a ball, and repeat pattern.)]. Focus on one initial sound until a few of the children are consistently accurate, then switch to a new initial sound ["What's this?" (Hold up a tiger.) "Yes! T-t-t-tiger. Say it with me. T-t-t-tiger. What's the first sound?"]. If a child suggests correct letter names, along with letter sounds, then write the letter on paper for the child to copy.
	This activity develops the following behaviors and concepts that are related to early literacy:
Print/Book Awareness	Symbolic representation—play; print—letter identification
Metalinguistic Awareness	Perception and memory for sounds—words; phonological skills—blending, segmentation
Oral Language	Literate discourse—categorical organization

ADULT–CHILD INTERACTIVE BEHAVIORS

High Demand/Low Support

Children engage in pretend play and will:
    identify the first sound in words

Support Strategies

Cognitive structuring	Define the concept of *first sound*.

Listen to the very first sound you say when you pronounce the word. The first sound is how you start the word.

Task regulation

Ask children to identify first sounds of words or objects of their choice. Stretch or iterate the first sound.

Mmmmonkey. B-b-b-bear.

Limit toys to two or three categories of objects that have names that start with similar first sounds (e.g., monkey, moose, mouse; cow, cat, kangaroo). Ask specific questions to elicit words that begin with the same first sound as a word contained in the questions.

What color is the bear? Yes. Now, what's the first sound in brown?

Instructing

Provide models.

Bear starts with /b/. What's the first sound in bear?

Ask children to repeat first sounds identified by peers.

What did Marco say the first sound in bear was?

Medium Demand/Medium Support

Children engage in pretend play and will:

blend words pronounced in onset-rime format

Support Strategies

Task regulation

Use words with initial sounds (onset) that can be easily stretched instead of segmented. Provide visual cues by giving children a choice of objects, for example, bear, tiger, and cat.

B-ear. Which animal is that?

Instructing

Encourage children to repeat the segmented word before guessing. Model, and have the child repeat the task.

C-ow. That's a cow. C-ow. What's that?

Low Demand/High Support

Children engage in simple symbolic play actions with objects and toys. They will:

repeat short and multisyllabic words

Support Strategies

Task regulation

Present children with novel and unfamiliar toys and objects to elicit their spontaneous requests for object labels.

| Instructing | Model, and ask children to repeat. |
| | This elephant is enormous. Can you say enormous? |

Comments/Adaptations

| Comments | This activity can also be implemented during picture book reading. |
| Home Link | Parent Activity: First Sound |

PRETEND PLAY—THE STORE

Main Purpose

To develop syllable and phoneme manipulation skills

Children learn to conceptualize that words are collections of parts (syllables and phonemes).

Materials

Pretend play items

Description of the Activity

Set up a drug/grocery store pretend play center. Let children take turns at being the owner of the store. The adult plays the customer, who asks for items by pronouncing their names segmented into syllables or phonemes. The children have to guess the items. Explain the concept that words are composed of parts and that the parts can be broken and put back together. Verify that the children understand by asking them to explain the tasks ["I'm going to speak in a funny way. I'm going to break up my words in little bits. What do you have to do to guess the words?"]. Make labels for objects in the store. Ask questions about store items, their composition, and uses. (*Hint:* This activity requires prior experience with blending. Try the Guess the Word and I'm Thinking of a . . . activities before setting up the store area.) Children who have learned to segment can also be customers by requesting store items segmented into syllables or phonemes (e.g., tooth-paste, spa-ghet-ti, m-ilk, j-a-m).

This activity develops the following behaviors and concepts that are related to early literacy:

Print/Book Awareness

Symbolic representation—pictures; print—awareness of graphic symbols

Metalinguistic Awareness

Phonological skills—blending, segmentation

Oral Language

Vocabulary—words and sentences; literate discourse—conversations

ADULT–CHILD INTERACTIVE BEHAVIORS

High Demand/Low Support

Children participate actively in the game as both customer and store owner. They enact sequences of imaginary play acts. They will:

> segment words into onset-rime format and into three to four phonemes

Support Strategies

Cognitive structuring

Help make explicit the onset-rime segmentation process.

> Juice. Say the word in two parts. The first sound first. Then the rest.

Explain the concept of phonemes.

> Words are made up of little bits. We can hear each little bit if we say the word slowly. Say pop very slowly.

Task regulation

Provide visual cues (e.g., give children two coins and have them say first the onset and second the rime when touching each coin). Hold up a hand or finger before children pronounce the onset and then the rime.

> Say a part when my hand goes up.

Say the first part, and have children complete the word.

> Here are some pears. You want to buy a p . . . ?

Instructing

Model, and have children repeat. Have children say the segmented word along with you.

Medium Demand/Medium Support

Children participate in the game by playing roles and using imaginary objects. They will:

> guess segmented words by blending words pronounced in onset-rime format and segment words into syllables

Support Strategies

Open-ended questioning

Ask children questions to help them discover the blending and segmentation processes.

> How did I say the word?

Cognitive structuring

Help make explicit the segmentation and blending processes.

> I said the word in little bits. Now you have to put the little bits all together again.
> I say a word really slowly. You say it fast.

Point out contradictions.

> The first sound is /p/, so it can't be cereal.

Task regulation

Blend the word in a stretched fashion.

> Miiilk.

Instructing

Have children repeat the segmented word before guessing. Model, and emphasize differences between the segmented and the blended words by pronouncing the segmented word very slowly and the blended word much faster.

Low Demand/High Support

Children participate in the game using simple symbolic actions with toys and objects. They will:

> guess segmented words by blending syllables

Support Strategies

Task regulation

Have children blend short familiar words.
> I'd like to buy some but-ter. What do I want?

Begin with compound words.
> Mush-rooms. Say it fast.

Provide choices.
> Sham-poo. Did I ask for shampoo or spaghetti?

Instructing

Have children repeat the segmented word before guessing. Model blending the word, and then repeat the task with a new word.

Comments/Adaptations

Comments

Try enacting similar themes like The Restaurant, The Dry Cleaner, or The Airport.

Home Link

Ask parents to send empty packages for stocking the store shelves, such as small cereal boxes, toothpaste boxes, juice containers, and canned goods.

PRETEND PLAY—MAGIC PASSWORD

Main Purpose	To develop phonological skills: rhyming, syllable, and phoneme blending
	Children learn to rhyme and to conceptualize that words are collections of parts (syllables and phonemes).
Materials	Pretend play items: toy animals, blocks, barn; paper, crayons
Description of the Activity	Have children enact pretend play activities with toy animals, blocks, and other materials. Tell the children that the animals have to guess a magic password to gain access to or to leave a location (e.g., barn, zoo, trap, magic cave). Pretend you are the guardian and the child is the animal. Tell the children that the magic password is a word that rhymes ["You have to say the magic password. Tell me a word that rhymes with dog"] or a word fragmented into syllables (e.g., Pop-si-cle), onset-rime (e.g., k-ey), or phonemes (e.g., b-a-g). When appropriate, show the child the written word ["Can you read this word? Cat. What word rhymes with cat?"]. Make children aware that words are composed of sounds. Some words sound similar whereas others are very different, and words rhyme when they sound similar at the end. Explain the concept that words are composed of parts and that the parts can be separated and put back together. Verify that the children understand by asking them to explain the tasks ["I'm going to speak in a funny way. I'm going to break up my words in little bits. What do you have to do to guess the words?"]. Try to use magic passwords that are meaningful within the context (e.g., "open" to open a make-believe door, "fly" to fly over a mountain, "candy" to give as a gift to you). Encourage children to enact dramatic play episodes, talk about events, tell stories, and draw figures and pictures.
	This activity develops the following behaviors and concepts that are related to early literacy:
Print/Book Awareness	Symbolic representation—play, graphics; print—awareness of graphic symbols, letter identification.
Metalinguistic Awareness	Phonological skills—rhyming, blending, segmentation
Oral Language	Vocabulary—words and sentences; narrative skills—narrations of fictional story

ADULT–CHILD INTERACTIVE BEHAVIORS

High Demand/Low Support

Children participate actively in the game and expand it by introducing variations. They enact sequences of imaginary play acts. They will:

> guess first sounds or segmented words by blending words pronounced in an onset-rime format or in three to four phoneme sequences

Support Strategies

? Open-ended questioning

Ask children questions to help them discover the blending and segmentation processes.

> How did I say the word?

Cognitive structuring

Help make explicit the segmentation and blending processes.

> I said the word in little bits. Now you have to put the little bits all together again.
> Listen to how I say the word. Sometimes I chop it up, and sometimes I stretch it out.
> I say a word really slowly. You say it fast.

Point out contradictions.

> The first sound is /d/, so it can't be open.

Suggest strategies.

> Say only the first bit of the word.
> Don't stop between the sounds when you say the word.

Task regulation

Blend the word in a stretched fashion.

> Dooooooog, mmmaaannn.

Stretch or iterate the first sound.

> Ooooopen, p-p-p-pull.

Instructing

Have children repeat the segmented word before guessing. Model, and emphasize differences between the segmented and the blended words by pronouncing the segmented word very slowly and the blended word much faster.

Medium Demand/Medium Support

Children participate in the game and enact imaginary actions with the toys. They will:

> say a rhyming word to a target word

Support Strategies

Providing feedback

Encourage children to repeat aloud names of objects to see whether words rhyme. Have children repeat or repeat back to them their answers, and ask children to reevaluate whether words rhyme.

> You said dog is the magic password for rock. Dog and rock. Do they sound the same?

Cognitive structuring

Suggest strategies.

> Change the first part only. The last part must stay the same.

Task regulation

Provide choices.

> Which word rhymes with fly: sky or coat?

Instructing

Model, and have children repeat the two words that rhyme.

Low Demand/High Support

Children use simple symbolic actions with toys. They will:

> blend syllables into words

Support Strategies

Task regulation

Have children blend syllables in short familiar words.

> The magic password is can-dy.

Use words that make sense within the context. For example, if a child places an animal in a barn, then say a magic password for the animal to get out (e.g., window). Provide choices.

> Cir-cle. Is the magic word "circle" or "square"?

Provide visual cues by pointing to an object or picture or enacting a corresponding action.

Instructing

Have children repeat the segmented word before guessing. Model blending the word, and then repeat the task with the same word. Model, and have children imitate.

Comments/Adaptations

Comments

This activity can be enacted using other themes and objects (e.g., an obstacle course) when children have to say magic passwords to get through the obstacles.

Home Link

Parent Activity: Magic Password

EARLY LITERACY OBSERVATION FORM

Child's name: _____

Metalinguistic Awareness:

1. What I know about sounds, words, and sentences   2. Nursery rhymes and word play
3. Putting sounds together   4. Finding the first sound   5. Words that sound the same

Date	What I did or said

Ladders to Literacy: A Preschool Activity Book
by Angela Notari-Syverson, Rollanda E. O'Connor, and Patricia F. Vadasy
©1998 Paul H. Brookes Publishing Co., Baltimore

METALINGUISTIC AWARENESS CHECKLIST
Behaviors observed

Name: _____

Scoring: Dates: _____ _____ _____

2 = Consistently/independently   1 = Sometimes/partly   0 = Not yet   Activity: _____ _____ _____

Notes:

A = Assumed   NO = No opportunity   R = Report   H = Help   M = Modifications

I. PERCEPTION AND MEMORY FOR SOUNDS
Environmental Sounds

    A. Uses sounds to represent objects and animals   _____( )_____( )_____( )

    B. Identifies the source of sounds   _____( )_____( )_____( )

Words

    C. Repeats short words   _____( )_____( )_____( )

    D. Repeats multisyllabic words   _____( )_____( )_____( )

Phrases

    E. Repeats phrases (e.g., repetitive lines in familiar songs, nursery rhymes, and stories)   _____( )_____( )_____( )

Phonemes

    F. Repeats single phonemes after a short delay (1–2 seconds)   _____( )_____( )_____( )

    G. Repeats two to three phonemes after short delay (1–2 seconds)   _____( )_____( )_____( )

    H. Discriminates between two phonemes (same/different)   _____( )_____( )_____( )

II. WORD AWARENESS
Words

    A. Identifies a word from a spoken sentence   _____( )_____( )_____( )

    B. Identifies the longer word of two spoken words   _____( )_____( )_____( )

    C. Plays with the pronunciation of a word   _____( )_____( )_____( )

III. PHONOLOGICAL SKILLS
Rhyming

    A. Says common rhymes along with teacher or peers   _____( )_____( )_____( )

    B. Fills in last word in rhyme   _____( )_____( )_____( )

    C. Recites common rhymes independently   _____( )_____( )_____( )

    D. Recognizes that pairs of words do or do not rhyme   _____( )_____( )_____( )

    E. Says a rhyming word for a target word   _____( )_____( )_____( )

continued

Ladders to Literacy: A Preschool Activity Book
by Angela Notari-Syverson, Rollanda E. O'Connor, and Patricia F. Vadasy
©1998 Paul H. Brookes Publishing Co., Baltimore

METALINGUISTIC AWARENESS CHECKLIST
(continued)

Name: _____

Alliteration

    F. Recognizes words that start with the same sound   _____( )_____( )_____( )

    G. Says a word that starts with the same sound as another word _____( )_____( )_____( )

Blending

    H. Blends syllables into words   _____( )_____( )_____( )

    I. Blends words with sounds pronounced in onset-rime
format (e.g., m-ake)   _____( )_____( )_____( )

    J. Blends three to four phonemes into words (e.g., s-a-t, m-a-n) _____( )_____( )_____( )

Segmentation

    K. Segments words into syllables (e.g., clapping, saying words
in syllables)   _____( )_____( )_____( )

    L. Identifies first sound in words   _____( )_____( )_____( )

    M. Separates words into onset-rime   _____( )_____( )_____( )

    N. Segments one-syllable words into three to four phonemes _____( )_____( )_____( )

Ladders to Literacy: A Preschool Activity Book
by Angela Notari-Syverson, Rollanda E. O'Connor, and Patricia F. Vadasy
©1998 Paul H. Brookes Publishing Co., Baltimore

SCAFFOLDING STRATEGIES CHECKLIST

Child's name: _____

Date: _____   _____   _____

Activity: _____   _____   _____

Circle strategies used during activity:	Used	Did it help?	Used	Did it help?	Used	Did it help?
Open-ended questioning descriptions predictions and planning explanations relating to the child's experience	□Y □N	□Y □N	□Y □N	□Y □N	□Y □N	□Y □N
Providing feedback encouragements evaluations thinking aloud clarification requests interpretation of meaning acknowledgments and information talk	□Y □N	□Y □N	□Y □N	□Y □N	□Y □N	□Y □N
Cognitive structuring rules and logical relationships sequencing contradictions	□Y □N	□Y □N	□Y □N	□Y □N	□Y □N	□Y □N
Holding in memory restating goals summaries and reminders	□Y □N	□Y □N	□Y □N	□Y □N	□Y □N	□Y □N
Task regulation matching interests and experience rearranging elements making more concrete reducing alternatives	□Y □N	□Y □N	□Y □N	□Y □N	□Y □N	□Y □N
Instructing modeling orienting direct questioning elicitations coparticipation	□Y □N	□Y □N	□Y □N	□Y □N	□Y □N	□Y □N

Ladders to Literacy: A Preschool Activity Book
by Angela Notari-Syverson, Rollanda E. O'Connor, and Patricia F. Vadasy
©1998 Paul H. Brookes Publishing Co., Baltimore

SECTION IV

Oral Language

Show and Tell 206
Food Talk 210
Talking About Books 213
Enacting Storybooks 218
Book Buddy 222
Portraits 225
What Did You Hear? 228
Feeling Objects 231
I See, You See 234
Treasure Boxes 237
Water Play: Floating Objects 240
My Dream 243
Special Words 246
What Does This Mean? 250
Let's Say it Another Way! 253
Interviews 256
Movie Reviews 259
Brainstorming 263
From This to That 267
Let's Find Out! 271
Showtime 276

Language and literacy develop simultaneously and in an interrelated manner. Oral and sign language, pictures, and written language all are forms of symbolic representations used to signify, create, and communicate meanings. This section emphasizes this constant interplay among meaning, language, and representation. For example, children need something to talk about in order for language development to take place, and pictures and print can be used as means to get information. This section uses many kinds of literate events as opportunities for children to develop their oral language skills. Several aspects of language development have been linked to early exposure to literate events, such as story reading with parents (e.g., Whitehurst et al., 1988). Because of its clearly delineated structure and semantically restricted context (Bruner, 1983), story reading presents an ideal language-learning situation for children with disabilities (Dale, Crain-Thoreson, Notari-Syverson, & Cole, 1996; Kirchner, 1991). Story reading also engages children in literate types of oral discourse, an experience often lacking in some children from ethnically diverse and lower socioeconomic groups (Heath, 1982; Snow, 1983). Story reading with parents and teachers, along with other media such as songs and videotapes, provides conversational topics to facilitate children's language development (Lemish & Rice, 1986). Children focus on different aspects of story reading with parents at different points of development, and adults vary the complexity of their language and task demands accordingly. Similarly, the activities in this book are designed to allow the participation of children with different ability levels and at different points of development within the same classroom. Suggestions are provided for teachers to adapt their questions and comments to each child's interests and developmental level.

- **Vocabulary**—At the earliest developmental levels (ages 1–2), children learn labels for objects through story reading (Ninio & Bruner, 1978). An interactive style of story reading, such as asking children many questions ["What's this a picture of?"], facilitates this development. As children become older (2–5 years and older for more complex language), they begin to listen to and remember syntactic constructions from stories. Snow and Goldfield (1983) found that children then would reuse these patterns in their speech. Appropriate teaching strategies include asking children to explain a part of the story ["What does that mean?"] and providing alternative ways of expressing complex ideas.
- **Narrative skills: Story structure and genre**—Children learn about story structure and narrative form through story reading with parents in the preschool years (Heath, Branscombe, & Thomas, 1986; Sulzby, 1985). They progress to more advanced levels of familiarity with genre (e.g., fiction and content books) and discipline (e.g., history and science books). Teaching strate-

gies include asking children to talk about these aspects of stories ["Is this a real story or a make-believe story?"] and calling children's attention to aspects of story structure, such as goals ["Why did the princess do that?"].

- **Literate discourse: Decontextualization**—The social nature of joint story reading allows the child to learn language as part of a dialogue. As the adult and the child reciprocally engage in discussions and comments about the story, the child learns essential pragmatic skills such as conversational turn taking, listening, and responding (Kirchner, 1991). Teaching strategies include following the child's lead, waiting for the child's turn, and expanding on the child's topic of interest. These basic conversational skills lay the foundation for later extended discourse characteristic of written language. Literate language is characterized by a removal from the here and now and by a separation of writer from reader or speaker from listener. This kind of decontextualized language is typical of the language in school settings. This section provides teachers and parents suggestions for how to engage with children in literate types of oral discourse (e.g., having children reconstruct past events, facilitating decontextualized language, asking open-ended questions, asking for explanations). The collection of activities in this section is intended to provide the linguistic vehicles for developing concepts about literacy and preparing for reading and writing instruction in ways that are developmentally appropriate and sensitive to the diversity among preschool children. By promoting oral abilities during the preschool years known to influence later reading development, the likelihood of a successful transition into kindergarten and first grade can be increased.

EARLY LITERACY GOALS AND OBJECTIVES

The following goals and objectives for each oral language skill are cross-referenced with the activities in this section. More specific definitions of skills and behaviors are provided in Appendix A.

Vocabulary

- **Words and sentences**—Child will use one-word utterances to label a variety of objects, people, and events. Child will use two-word utterances to express a variety of semantic intentions (e.g., agent–object, agent–action, action–object, existence, location, possession, negation, recurrence, attribution). Child will use a variety of adult-form sentences (e.g., declaratives, interrogatives, negatives).
  Activities: Show and Tell; Food Talk; Talking About Books; Enacting Storybooks; Portraits; What Did You Hear?; Feeling Objects; Treasure Boxes; Water Play: Floating Objects; My

Dream; Special Words; What Does This Mean?; Let's Say it Another Way!; Interviews; Brainstorming; From This to That; Let's Find Out!

Narrative Skills

- **Narrations of real events**—Child will relate events with beginning, middle, and end. Child will relate explicit causal and temporal sequences among events.
  Activities: Show and Tell; Food Talk; Portraits; What Did You Hear?; Water Play: Floating Objects; My Dream; Special Words; Let's Say it Another Way!; Interviews; Brainstorming; From This to That; Let's Find Out!
- **Book**—Child will attend to pictures in book and label pictures; child will make comments and ask questions about individual pictures. Child will tell story and link events based on pictures using conversational language. Child will form a written story based on pictures using reading intonation and wording.
  Activities: Talking About Books; Enacting Storybooks; Book Buddy
- **Narrations of fictional story**—Child will attend to story; child will add simple comments and ask questions. Child will relate and organize elements of story structure in a correct sequence (e.g., setting, theme, plot episodes, resolution).
  Activities: Talking about Books; Enacting Storybooks; Movie Reviews; Showtime

Literate Discourse

- **Conversations**—Child will maintain social interaction over two or more turns; child will initiate and maintain topic. Child will adapt information to level of listener.
  Activities: Show and Tell; Food Talk; Talking About Books; Enacting Storybooks; Book Buddy; Portraits; What Did You Hear?; Feeling Objects; I See, You See; Treasure Boxes; Interviews; Brainstorming; From This to That; Showtime
- **Categorical organization**—Child will use superordinate labels to indicate general categories.
  Activities: Show and Tell; Food Talk; What Did You Hear?; Feeling Objects; Treasure Boxes; Water Play: Floating Objects; Special Words
- **Decontextualization:** Child will generalize experiences to other settings. Child will provide explanations. Child will make predictions. Child will make interpretations and judgments. Child will distinguish fiction from real events.
  Activities: Show and Tell; Food Talk; Enacting Storybooks; What Did You Hear?; Treasure Boxes; Water Play: Floating Objects; My Dream; What Does This Mean?; Let's Say it Another

Way!; Interviews; Movie Reviews; Brainstorming; From This to That; Let's Find Out!

- **Interpretive/analytic discourse**—Child will use internal state words to express feelings (e.g., happy, sad) and motivations (e.g., want, like). Child will use cognitive words to refer to mental states (e.g., memory, idea, forget, think, know, understand). Child will use metalinguistic words to refer to the use of language (e.g., word, letter, sound, say, tell, call, read). Child will seek definitions of words.

  Activities: Talking About Books; Book Buddy; Portraits; What Did You Hear?; Feeling Objects; Treasure Boxes; My Dream; Special Words; What Does This Mean?; Let's Say it Another Way!; Interviews; Movie Reviews; Brainstorming; Showtime

SHOW AND TELL

Main Purpose To expand vocabulary, narrative skills, and literate discourse

Children learn they can communicate with others through speaking, writing, and reading. This activity develops pragmatic skills of sharing information among children. It also prepares children for literate discourse through learning to answer questions, describing objects and events, and providing explanations. The teacher facilitates appropriate communication among children and elicits language features that characterize literate discourse.

Materials Objects chosen by children, picture of object, written label of object

Description of the Activity This activity can be implemented during opening circle time or in smaller groups. Let children take turns showing and telling the other children about an object that they have brought from home. Ask each child to label and describe the object and to explain why he or she chose the object for the presentation. Encourage the other children to ask questions about the object that require literate discourse (e.g., explanations, predictions). When several show-and-tell items have been shared, ask children to make nonjudgmental comparisons ["Would you play with these objects differently?" "How are they the same?" "How do they differ?"]. Draw a picture, and write the name of each object to demonstrate the connection between language and print. Direct children's attention to the relationship among the name of each object, the picture, and the written label.

This activity develops the following behaviors and concepts that are related to early literacy:

Print/Book Awareness Symbolic representation—pictures; print—awareness of graphic symbols, writing; letter–sound correspondence—single sounds and letters

Metalinguistic Awareness Perception and memory for sounds—words

Oral Language Vocabulary—words and sentences; narrative skills—narrations of real events; literate discourse—conversations, categorical organization, decontextualization

ADULT–CHILD INTERACTIVE BEHAVIORS

High Demand/Low Support

Children will:

> describe explicit causal and temporal sequences among events, provide explanations, and adapt information to the level of the listener

Support Strategies

? **Open-ended questioning**

Invite children to ask questions about objects and to comment about personal experiences with similar objects.

> What else would you like to know about this?
> Is this like anything you have at home?

Ask questions that require children to provide explanations.

> Why is this your favorite stuffed toy?
> How does it work?

Encourage children to express temporal notions.

> When did this happen?

Providing feedback

Praise and encourage children's presentations.

> That's very interesting. I like that too.

Request children to clarify information, if necessary.

> Did you go before or after the puppet show?

Reinterpret information.

> Oh, you mean your cousin from Mexico gave you the doll.

Cognitive structuring

Point out contradictions in children's narrations.

> I'm not sure I understand. You said these poppies grew from seeds, but the birds ate all of the seeds and there were none left.

Help children sequence events.

> What happened after it rained?

Instructing

Provide models to encourage children to reword sentences.

Medium Demand/Medium Support

Children will:

> initiate and maintain the topic and relate events with a beginning, a middle, and an end

Support Strategies

? Open-ended questioning

Encourage children to initiate and describe the object.

> Tell us about this beautiful necklace.
> Where does it come from?

↻ Providing feedback

Praise and encourage children's presentations.

> That's very interesting. I like that, too.

Help continue the conversation by adding information related to the object or topic.

> It has very bright colors.

◈ Task regulation

Encourage children to respond to a set of structured questions as they prepare to show their objects.

> What is it called?
> What do you like to do with it?
> What do you like best about it?

î Instructing

Provide models to encourage children to repeat simple sentences.

Low Demand/High Support

Children show and label the object when it is their turn. They will:

> maintain social interaction over two or more turns

Support Strategies

↻ Providing feedback

Praise and demonstrate interest in the object.

> That's very cute.
> I'd like to know its name.

Help maintain the conversation by expanding on children's utterances.

> Ball. A red ball.

◈ Task regulation

Provide choices.

> Is it a cat or a lion?
> Do you play with it inside or outside?

î Instructing

Ask children to talk about their objects.

> Tell us what you brought to class.
> Tell us the name of your favorite toy.

Encourage peers to provide models.

> Claire, can you tell Kyle what that is?

Ask children to label features.

What's this?
What color is that?
Provide a model, and ask children to repeat.
Say "My dog is Snoopy."

Comments/Adaptations

Comments

This activity can also be done immediately after a classroom routine like play or snack time. Children can recall with what toy they most like to play or what their favorite food is.

Adaptations

Children with hearing impairments can communicate with sign language, which the adult translates for the rest of the group. Other basic signs can be taught to the other children.

Home Link

Encourage children to bring objects from home that represent their cultural backgrounds (e.g., clothing, jewelry, foods).

FOOD TALK

Main Purpose To develop expressive vocabulary, narrative skills, and literate discourse

Children develop descriptive vocabulary and repertoires of attributes to describe a range of objects. Children also refer to situations beyond the immediate context.

Materials Menu of snack items and foods children bring or are served by the school

Description of the Activity Refer to the foods on the snack menu; foods children bring for lunch, birthdays, or holiday treats; or pictures of food. Ask children to talk about the foods, using descriptive words. Prompt children with questions ["Yes, here's a carrot. What color is the carrot? Mmm. An orange carrot. What else could we say about it?"]. Encourage general discussion among children. When the topic seems exhausted, try going around the group asking each child to say one thing about the food being described. Accept and encourage all plausible responses, including repeating other children's descriptions. To expand the activity, ask children what they had for breakfast. Encourage children who had the same food (e.g., Cheerios, oatmeal) to describe what it was like (e.g., small, round, crunchy, rough, poured from a box, eaten with milk). Encourage children to describe a food across a range of attributes (e.g., size, shape, color, texture, smell). Children may want to associate the food with personal experiences, their feelings about the food, or other times they have eaten the food. Encourage all such verbal behavior, especially as it generates discussion among the children. Ask direct, simple questions of children reluctant to participate in group description. When possible, focus the discussion on description ["What does it taste like?" "What does it smell like?" "How does it make you feel?" "What does it make you think of?" "Where does it come from?" "How does it grow?" "What kind of package does it come in?" "What is your favorite way to eat it?"].

This activity develops the following behaviors and concepts that are related to early literacy:

Print/Book Awareness Symbolic representation—pictures, graphics; print—awareness of graphic symbols

Metalinguistic Awareness Perception and memory for sounds—words, phrases

| Oral Language | Vocabulary—words and sentences; narrative skills—narrations of real events; literate discourse—conversations, categorical organization, decontextualization |

ADULT–CHILD INTERACTIVE BEHAVIORS

High Demand/Low Support

Children engage in conversation about foods and expand these conversations to related topics. They will:

> describe explicit causal and temporal sequences among events, draw from their own experiences, and use superordinate labels to categorize foods

Support Strategies

| ? | Open-ended questioning | Encourage conversation by asking children questions about attributes, origins, and personal preferences of foods. |

| | Cognitive structuring | Encourage children to categorize and compare foods according to taste, origins, culinary use, and so forth. |

Medium Demand/Medium Support

Children engage in conversations about foods. They will:

> use a variety of adult-form sentences to describe attributes and make judgments about personal preferences

Support Strategies

| ? | Open-ended questioning | Encourage conversation by asking children questions about attributes and personal preferences of foods. |

| | Cognitive structuring | Provide categories for children to use when describing foods.
Tell us how it tastes, smells, and feels. |

| | Instructing | Participate in the conversation, and provide models by rewording and expanding on children's sentences. Ask direct questions about foods.
How does it taste?
Do you like it?
What's your favorite food? |

Low Demand/High Support

Children will:

> label foods and objects and engage in social interaction over two or more turns

Support Strategies

Task regulation

Comment on foods children are eating. Provide choices.

> Does the banana taste sweet or sour?

Instructing

Provide models by expanding on children's utterances. Ask direct questions.

> What are you drinking?
> What color is it?

Provide a model, and have children repeat.

> That's a muffin. What's that?

Comments/Adaptations

Adaptations

Children with hearing impairments can communicate using sign language that the adult translates for the rest of the group.

More Ideas

Have children talk about ethnic foods they eat at home.

Home Link

Parent Activity: Let's Use Words to Describe . . . !

TALKING ABOUT BOOKS

Main Purpose   To use print and language as tools of communication

Children learn to translate information gained through print into oral language to communicate to others. This activity develops the pragmatic skills for sharing information between children and the narrative skills of telling a story.

Materials   Books; magazines; newspaper

Description of the Activity   During group circle time, ask children to present a favorite book, magazine, or newspaper article from home or school to their peers. Ask the children to describe the story and to explain why they chose the story for the presentation. Help the children structure the story by asking questions about 1) the setting ["Where does the story take place?" "When?" "Who is in the story?"], 2) the theme ["What is it about?"], 3) the episodes ["What happens?"], and 4) the ending ["How does it end?"]. Invite children to ask questions about the story and to comment about personal experiences. Ask questions that require children to make predictions, and provide explanations and clarifications. Encourage the other children to ask questions about the story. In addition, help children become aware of writing conventions (e.g., title page, ending, reading of text from top to bottom and from left to right). Facilitate appropriate communication between children, and assist children in reconstructing the story (e.g., presence and correct sequencing of setting, theme, episodes, and ending).

This activity develops the following behaviors and concepts that are related to early literacy:

Print/Book Awareness   Print—book conventions, awareness of graphic symbols

Metalinguistic Awareness   Perception and memory for sounds—words, phrases

Oral Language   Vocabulary—words and sentences; narrative skills—narrations of fictional story; literate discourse—conversations, categorical organization, decontextualization, interpretive/analytic discourse

ADULT–CHILD INTERACTIVE BEHAVIORS

High Demand/Low Support

Children will:

> relate and organize elements of story structure in a coherent sequence, provide explanations, make predictions, distinguish

fiction from real events, and adapt the information to the level of the listener

Support Strategies

? **Open-ended questioning**

Ask children general questions.

What's the story about?
What happened?

Encourage children to make inferences and predictions.

How is she going to get to her mother's castle?
What if there were a big storm?

Ask children to provide explanations.

Why did the witch give him the magic plant?

Providing feedback

Request children to clarify information, if necessary.

Did the monkey climb up or jump down the coconut tree?
Who do you mean by he?

Reinterpret information.

Oh, you mean he was very frightened and couldn't remember the magic word?

Cognitive structuring

Review the separate elements of story structure and how they are connected to each other. Point out contradictions in children's narrations.

The monkey ran away? But you said he was a good tiger.

Help children organize and sequence their story.

Tell Zoe what happened after the bear ate all of the apples.

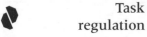 **Task regulation**

Provide visual cues (e.g., outlines on the chalkboard or paper sheets with blanks to fill in for separate elements of story structure).

 **Instructing**

Help children focus on specific elements of the story.

Where did it happen?
Who is the story about?
How does the story end?

Medium Demand/Medium Support

Children will:

relate events with a beginning, a middle, and an end and tell the story based on pictures

Support Strategies

?	**Open-ended questioning**	Ask children general questions.

> What's the story about?
> What happened?

Ask children to provide explanations.

> Why did the witch give him the magic plant?

Encourage children to relate objects and events to their own personal experiences.

> Have you ever seen a person dressed like that?
> Has this ever happened to you?

Cognitive structuring

Help children sequence events.

> What happened first?
> What did she do after she left?
> How did it end?

Remind children to use book illustrations as a guide to the story.

> The pictures show us what happens in the story.

Holding in memory

Remind children of the events told so far.

> The father told his son that he could make Abiyoyo disappear only if . . .

Instructing   Ask direct questions.
> What did the whale say to the shark?

Orient children to look at the pictures.
> What's in this picture?

Low Demand/High Support

Children will:
> attend to the story, add comments, and ask questions

Support Strategies

 Open-ended questioning   Encourage children to add comments and ask questions.
> Jamie, would you like to tell us something else about this picture?
> Is there anything more you want to know about Mr. Frog?

 Task regulation   Provide choices.
> Did she go to Grandma's or go home?

 Instructing   Help children formulate questions to ask a peer.
> Mary, ask Ruth what the three little pigs said to the wolf.

Ask direct questions about the story or the illustrations.
> What's the witch wearing?
> Where did the eagle fly?

Provide a model, and have children repeat.
> The owl sat on the big chestnut tree. Who sat on the tree?

Comments/Adaptations

Comment   Introduce a daily private reading time for children to look at books in the library area.

Adaptations   Translate sign language used by children with hearing impairments. Teach basic signs to all children.

Link with Print/ Book Awareness   Fill in a story grammar chart (see Figure 1 for examples of story elements) as children talk about books to demonstrate the structures commonly shared by all stories. Have children do book reviews.

Home Link   Parent Activities: Going Places—The Library (*Note:* Have parents help children complete a book review [see Figure 1 in this activity] for the child to bring back to class and share with peers.); Storybook Reading Routines; What Will Happen Next?

Book Review
Title:
Author:
Characters:
Setting:
Problem:
Events:

Figure 1.   An example of a book review form that can be sent home for children to complete with their parents.

Ladders to Literacy: A Preschool Activity Book
by Angela Notari-Syverson, Rollanda E. O'Connor, and Patricia F. Vadasy
©1998 Paul H. Brookes Publishing Co., Baltimore

ENACTING STORYBOOKS

Main Purpose

To develop literate discourse and awareness of the link between oral and written language

Through reading stories, children learn about objects, people, and events in the real world. By enacting the stories, children learn to relate print to their lives and to oral language. They also learn to play different roles and to communicate with others.

Materials

Books; costumes; puppets; toys; flannel board and figures

Description of the Activity

Read books and have children mime simple actions or implement activities related to the stories. For example, after reading *Brown Bear, Brown Bear, What Do You See?* (Martin, 1970) or *Polar Bear, Polar Bear, What Do You Hear?* (Martin & Carle, 1991), have the children pretend to be the animals. After reading *The Very Hungry Caterpillar* (Carle, 1969), go with the children to the grocery store and buy the foods the caterpillar ate or have the children paint or model them. Create paper bag prop stories. Put a familiar book into a paper bag with props (e.g., puppets, toy animals, dolls, objects, pictures) representing the characters and setting of the story. Have the children enact the stories. For example, present toy animals with *Brown Bear, Brown Bear, What Do You See?* Include stuffed animals, a troll, blue paper, and a toy bridge with *The Three Billy Goats Gruff* (Brown, 1957). Have children dramatize the stories with miniature toys, Velcro board figures, or puppets or by dressing themselves in costumes. Have children practice a favorite story and present it to the public (e.g., parents, other classrooms) as a play at the theater.

This activity develops the following behaviors and concepts that are related to early literacy:

Print/Book Awareness

Print—book conventions

Metalinguistic Awareness

Perception and memory for sounds—words, phrases

Oral Language

Vocabulary—words and sentences; narrative skills—narrations of fictional story; literate discourse—conversations, decontextualization, interpretive/analytic discourse

ADULT–CHILD INTERACTIVE BEHAVIORS

High Demand/Low Support

Children collaborate in planning actions and assigning roles. They will:

> relate and organize elements of story structure in a coherent sequence, make predictions and interpretations, distinguish fiction from real events, and use words that refer to mental states and use of language

Support Strategies

? Open-ended questioning

Ask questions to help children plan actions and assign roles.

> Who is in this story?
> What important things happened?
> What will Sara do?
> How can we make a stream?
> Can this happen for real?

Ask children about mental states and use of language.

> Did the goat know?
> What did the troll say?

Cognitive structuring

Help children sequence events.

> Who speaks first?

Define the notion of pretend, and explain differences between fictional and real events.

Holding in memory

Remind children of major characters and events of the story. Summarize what children have organized so far.

> We decided that Nick was going to pretend to be the caterpillar and Lara was going to be the butterfly.

Instructing

Help children focus on specific elements of the story.

> Tell Mike who this story is about.
> How does the story end?

Medium Demand/Medium Support

Children actively participate in enacting the story and playing imaginary roles. They will:

> provide explanations, draw from personal experiences, and use words to describe their feelings and desires (e.g., want, like, happy, sad)

Support Strategies

? **Open-ended questioning**

Encourage children to express feelings and draw from their own personal experiences.

> Who do you want to be?
> Who do you like the most?
> How does the princess feel?
> Have you ever seen a castle?

Ask questions that help children coordinate their actions and roles.

> Which role are you going to play?
> What do you do after he leaves?
> How will you know when to clap your hands?
> When do you jump across the stream?

Ask children for explanations.

> Why did she do that?
> Why was he sad?

Providing feedback

Request children to clarify information, if necessary.

> What do you mean?
> Did he forget?

Cognitive structuring

Help children sequence events.

> The wolf speaks first, then it's the pig's turn.

Holding in memory

Summarize events that children enacted.

> The caterpillar ate one apple, two pears, and three plums.

Provide reminders.

> It's the boa constrictor's turn now.

Task regulation

Provide visual cues (e.g., display pictures of major events to be enacted).

Low Demand/High Support

Children take on a simple role in the story. They will:

> maintain social interaction over two or more turns and use words and simple sentences

Support Strategies

Holding in memory

Provide reminders.

> The polar bear hears the lion roaring in his ear. Aaron, you're the lion.

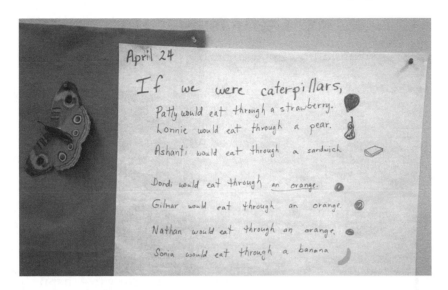

Task regulation	Provide visual cues (e.g., hold up a puppet or mask of a pig when it's the pig's turn to say something).
Instructing	Provide directions.

John, you speak now.
Talib, run around this circle.

Provide a model, and have children repeat.

The pigs say, "Not by the hair of my chinny chin chin." You say it.

Comments/Adaptations

Comments	Stories can also be created by the children. Have the children dictate a story, read it back to them, and have them enact it.
Adaptations	Use sign language, visual props, and body gestures to enhance the participation of children with hearing impairments.
Story	The Hungry Caterpillar

If we were caterpillars, Patty would eat through a strawberry. Lonnie would eat through a pear. Ashanti would eat through a sandwich. Dordi would eat through an orange. Gilmar would eat through an orange.

Home Link	Invite families to come to the performance, or videotape it and lend it to parents to view at home.

BOOK BUDDY

Main Purpose   To develop conversational and narrative skills

Children learn to engage in sustained social interaction with peers within the context of joint book reading routines. They learn to retell familiar, predictable stories and organize story elements in a coherent, logical sequence.

Materials   Familiar books

Description of the Activity   Propose predictable and repetitive storybooks with which children have become very familiar. Have children pair up with a buddy to look at the storybook together. Encourage children to pretend to read the book and to retell the story to each other ["Luis, can you read the duckling story to Ashanti?"]. Children who may need help should be paired with a more skilled peer, although children may also be paired with other children of equal skills. To the extent possible, allow children to choose partners.

This activity develops the following behaviors and concepts that are related to early literacy:

Print/Book Awareness   Print—book conventions, awareness of graphic symbols

Metalinguistic Awareness   Perception and memory for sounds—words, phrases

Oral Language   Vocabulary—words and sentences; narrative skills—book, narrations of fictional story; literate discourse—conversations, decontextualization, interpretive/analytic discourse

ADULT–CHILD INTERACTIVE BEHAVIORS

High Demand/Low Support

Children read and tell the story to their peers. They will:
> form a written story based on pictures using reading intonation and wording and adapt the information to the level of the listener

Support Strategies

? Open-ended questioning   Make children aware of their listener's perspective.
> Do you think David understood that?

222

	Providing feedback	Request children to clarify information, if necessary.
		Tell Tamiko who went up the mountain with him.

Providing feedback
: Request children to clarify information, if necessary.
: Tell Tamiko who went up the mountain with him.

Cognitive structuring
: Tell children to use pictures as a reference for them to organize and sequence their story.

Task regulation
: Have children look at books of familiar stories.

Instructing
: Directly elicit peer interactions.
: Ask Jessica if she knows what a ladder is.
: Help children focus on individual pictures.
: Say something about this picture to Annie.

Medium Demand/Medium Support

Children will:

tell the story to a peer using pictures and metalinguistic words to refer to the use of language

Support Strategies

Open-ended questioning
: Encourage use of metalinguistic words.
: What did the bear say?
: What does this word mean?

Cognitive structuring
: Encourage children to make connections among the pictures to form a story.
: Why is the lion roaring? The picture we saw before shows us why.
: Help children sequence events.
: What happens next?

Task regulation
: Give children familiar books. Encourage children to refer to the pictures.
: What happens in this picture?
: Let's see what's on the next page.

Instructing
: Have children practice repeated phrases in the book before they read it to a peer. Directly elicit peer interactions.
: Tell Louis what the bear did.
: Tell me what Hannah just said to you.
: Show Rafael this picture.

Low Demand/High Support

Children listen to a story told by a more advanced peer. They will:

attend to and comment on individual pictures and maintain social interaction for two or more turns

Support Strategies

? Open-ended questioning

Ask children questions about individual pictures.

What do you see?

Task regulation

Have children look at their favorite, often repeated books. Choose familiar books with repetitive rhyming verses.

Brown bear, brown bear, what do you see?

Give children choices.

Is this a big worm or a little worm?

Instructing

Provide models by expanding on children's utterances.

Yes, that's a cow. A brown cow.

Ask direct questions about the pictures.

What's this?

Direct children to initiate or respond to social interaction.

Tell Maya what this is.

Provide a model, and have children repeat.

That's a koala. What's that?

Comments/Adaptations

Comment

Introduce a daily 15-minute quiet reading time in the library area where children choose books to look at and read.

Home Link

Have children take home a favorite story to read to their siblings or parents.

PORTRAITS

Main Purpose	To develop expressive vocabulary and narrative skills
	Children expand their vocabulary and narrative skills by describing themselves (e.g., their bodies, feelings, ideas, and lives).
Materials	Paper; crayons; markers
Description of the Activity	Have children work in pairs to make portraits of each other. The portrait can be of the face only or of the entire body. Then have them label body parts and describe themselves and particular aspects of their lives (e.g., favorite activities and foods). Portraits can be made using a variety of methods including drawing, painting, playdough, making silhouettes by having children trace an outline of their body on large sheets of paper, and taking photographs. Children can also write or copy simple words or dictate ideas for adults to write.
	This activity develops the following behaviors and concepts that are related to early literacy:
Print/Book Awareness	Symbolic representation—pictures, graphics; print—awareness of graphic symbols, letter identification, writing
Metalinguistic Awareness	Perception and memory for sounds—words
Oral Language	Vocabulary—words and sentences; narrative skills—narration of real events; literate discourse—conversations, decontextualization, interpretive/analytic discourse

ADULT–CHILD INTERACTIVE BEHAVIORS

High Demand/Low Support

Children will:

> relate information about themselves describing explicit temporal and causal sequences among events, provide explanations, make interpretations and judgments, and use cognitive words to refer to mental states

Support Strategies

Open-ended questioning	Ask general questions.
	What would you like to tell me about yourself?

Encourage children to provide explanations, make interpretations and judgments, and use cognitive words to refer to mental states.

> Why do you like the library?
> Does this look right?
> What do you think this is?

Providing feedback

Manifest interest in the information children provide. Request clarifications.

> Does Snowy live with you in your house or on your grandfather's farm?

Task regulation

Ask specific questions about topics of interest.

> What's your favorite place for a field trip?
> What's your favorite pet?

Medium Demand/Medium Support

Children will:

> relate information using a variety of adult-like sentences, generalize experiences to other settings, and use internal state words to express feelings and motivations

Support Strategies

Open-ended questioning

Ask children questions about their daily lives and likes and dislikes.

> What do you do on the weekends?
> What do you like to have for dinner?

Providing feedback

Show interest in the information children provide.

> That was a great story about your birthday.

Task regulation

Ask specific questions about topics of interest.

> What's your favorite food?
> What's your favorite color?

Instructing

Directly elicit peer interactions.

> Ask Leigh what her favorite color is.

Low Demand/High Support

Children will:

> label objects and engage in social interaction over two or more turns

Support Strategies

Task regulation

Provide a set of questions for children to answer.

> Do you have sisters or brothers?
> Do you have a pet?
> Which color are your eyes?

Comment on present objects and actions.

> Eyes. You are painting the eyes.
> Green. That's green paint.

Provide choices.

> Do you want a crayon or a paintbrush?

Instructing

Have more skilled peers provide models. Provide models by expanding on children's utterances. Ask direct questions.

> What are you drawing?
> Which color is it?

Model and have children repeat.

> That's your nose. What is it?

Direct children to initiate or respond to social interaction.

> Tell Shona what this is.

Comments/Adaptations

Comments

Portraits can be used as a topic for Show and Tell. Children can present themselves to their peers, or a child can introduce another child to his or her peers at circle time.

Adaptations

Tape-record verbal portraits by children with visual or motor impairments.

Home Link

Send home a copy or a photograph of the portraits.

WHAT DID YOU HEAR?

Main Purpose   To develop vocabulary and literate discourse

Children use language to describe sounds they hear and make inferences and generalize experiences beyond the immediate context.

Materials   Objects that produce sounds; paper; crayons

Description of the Activity   Have children close their eyes and listen to the sounds around them. After approximately 1 minute, have them open their eyes and describe what they think happened while their eyes were closed. Children can also draw pictures, mime, or write words to describe their thoughts. While their eyes are closed, direct the children's attention to sounds that occur naturally in the classroom (e.g., water dripping, clock), sounds that occur outdoors (e.g., birds, cars), or sounds that you produce intentionally (e.g., feet stepping on the floor, musical instruments being played, paper being crumpled). You can also use records or audiotapes of common sounds (e.g., walking, running, clapping, laughing, sneezing) so that children do not need to close their eyes. After children have expressed their ideas, show them or have them identify the source of the sounds.

This activity develops the following behaviors and concepts that are related to early literacy:

Print/Book Awareness   Symbolic representation—graphics; print—writing

Metalinguistic Awareness   Perception and memory for sounds—environmental sounds, words

Oral Language   Vocabulary—words and sentences; literate discourse—categorical organization, decontextualization, interpretive/analytic discourse

ADULT–CHILD INTERACTIVE BEHAVIORS

High Demand/Low Support

Children will:

make personal interpretations about what the sounds may represent, use cognitive words to refer to mental states, and use superordinate labels to indicate categories

Support Strategies

? **Open-ended questioning** Ask questions to encourage children to make interpretations and use cognitive words.

> What do you suppose makes a sound like that?
> What do you think happened?
> What does this remind you of?

Providing feedback Make encouraging comments about children's guesses.

> That's a good answer, but remember that crows make loud noises.

Ask for clarifications.

> Why do you think it's a drum?

Cognitive structuring Help children categorize and make associations and distinctions between sounds and objects.

> This sound seemed like that of a vehicle.
> Did you notice that this bird made a louder sound than the one we heard before?

Point out contradictions.

> That's a good suggestion, but this sound is much louder. Snow doesn't make much noise.

Task regulation Provide verbal cues.

> I think it's the sound of someone who is happy.

Instructing Provide models for interpretive and cognitive use of words and general category labels.

Medium Demand/Medium Support

Children will:

> describe objects, sounds, and events using a variety of adult-like sentences; generalize experiences to other settings; and provide explanations

Support Strategies

? **Open-ended questioning** Encourage children to describe objects and events, relate them to their personal experiences, and provide explanations.

> Have you ever heard a sound like that before?
> Why does the wind make such a loud noise?

Providing feedback Make encouraging comments about children's guesses. Ask for clarifications.

> Why do you think it's a truck?

Cognitive structuring

Point out contradictions.

> Snow doesn't make much noise.

Task regulation

Provide children with clues that refer to concrete actions and personal experiences.

> This sound uses your hands.

Use sounds that are familiar to children or that are produced by objects that are present in the children's immediate environment.

Instructing

Provide models of relating personal experiences and providing explanations, and then ask children to do the same.

> I hear lots of crows by my house. Have you heard crows before?
>
> My book made a very loud noise when it fell because it's big and heavy. Why did your book make a loud noise?

Low Demand/High Support

Children will:

> label and describe a variety of objects, sounds, and actions

Support Strategies

Task regulation

Reproduce the sound when the children have their eyes open. Have children reproduce the sound themselves. Provide choices.

> Do you think that's rain or wind? Was that loud or soft?

Instructing

Ask direct questions.

> What did you hear?
> What was that?

Provide a model, and then elicit another response.

> That's thunder. What sound was that?

Comments/Adaptations

Comments

You can also try tape recording children's as well as staff's voices. Ask the children to guess whose voice they hear on the cassette tape. Ask them how they know whose voice is on the tape.

Home Link

Parent Activity: What Did You Hear?

FEELING OBJECTS

Main Purpose

To develop vocabulary and literate discourse

Children learn to express their ideas to communicate information to others as well as to use verbal information expressed by their peers. They also make inferences and judgments.

Materials

Familiar objects with interesting textures and shapes (e.g., shells, carrots, apples, cotton balls, mittens, Velcro strips); cardboard box or cloth bag; flipchart or chalkboard

Description of the Activity

Have children work together to guess the identity of an object that is hidden from their view and that they explore tactilely. The objects can be placed in a cloth bag or in a cardboard box. Children take turns exploring the object with their hands. They describe shape, texture, and size. Encourage children to compare their discoveries with those of their peers and to share information and ideas as to the identity of the object. Record children's descriptions of the object and guesses on a flipchart or a chalkboard. If multiple objects are used, encourage comparisons of the different qualities of each object.

This activity develops the following behaviors and concepts that are related to early literacy:

Print/Book Awareness

Symbolic representation—pictures, graphics; print—awareness of graphic symbols

Metalinguistic Awareness

Perception and memory for sounds—words

Oral Language

Vocabulary—words and sentences; literate discourse—conversations, categorical organization, decontextualization, interpretive/analytic discourse

ADULT–CHILD INTERACTIVE BEHAVIORS

High Demand/Low Support

Children describe and discuss the identity of the object. They will:

make judgments and inferences about the attributes and identity of the object, use cognitive words to refer to mental states, and use superordinate labels

231

Support Strategies

? Open-ended Encourage children to formulate hypotheses and to explain infer-
   questioning ences.

> What do you think it could be?
> What makes you think that?
> How do you know?

Providing Encourage children to talk aloud while they are feeling the object.
feedback
> Tell us how it feels now.

**Cognitive Help children use systematic strategies to explore objects and make
structuring** inferences about identity.

> You might want to start at the top and feel your way down.
> What's a fruit that's long and shaped like a half moon?

Holding in Summarize different characteristics.
memory
> You said it had two sharp points and a soft center.

Medium Demand/Medium Support

Children will:

> use a variety of adult-like sentences to describe the attributes
> and identity of the objects

Support Strategies

? Open-ended Encourage children to describe the object and what they think it
   questioning might be.

Providing Encourage children to talk aloud while they are feeling the object.
feedback
> Tell us what you feel.

Cognitive Provide verbal clues.
structuring
> It comes from a tree.

Point out contradictions.

> It can't be a leaf because it feels hard.

Holding in Summarize different characteristics.
memory
> You said it's cold and slippery.

Instructing Model and expand on children's utterances.

Low Demand/High Support

Children will:

> initiate and maintain a topic and label a variety of objects and actions and use two-word utterances to express a variety of semantic intentions

Support Strategies

Task regulation

Allow children to look at the object first, then conceal it and ask them to feel and describe it. Provide choices.

> Does it feel hard or soft?
>
> Is it a leaf or a nut?

Have similar objects or pictures visible to children. Have children explore and describe an object that is visible to them.

> Touch the leaf, and tell me how it feels.

Instructing

Ask direct questions.

> Which shape is it?

Model and expand on children's utterances.

> A nut. A big walnut.

Comments/Adaptations

Comment

Use objects that are representative of diverse cultural backgrounds (e.g., tropical fruits, clothing, musical instruments).

Adaptations

Use pictures and sign language with children who have hearing impairments. Translate signs for peers. Teach basic signs to other children. Use easily recognizable objects that require little exploration with children who have motor impairments.

Home Link

Parent Activity: Let's Use Words to Describe . . . !

I SEE, YOU SEE

Main Purpose

To facilitate the use of literate discourse

Children learn to remove themselves from their own point of view (decenter) and use language to describe another person's perspective.

Materials

Picture cards; crayons, markers; cardboard boxes; paint

Description of the Activity

Propose activities that require children to describe verbally another person's perspective. For example, prepare large cards that have different pictures on each side (e.g., two different animals or landscapes). After children have become familiar with both images, have one child stand on each side and describe what the other child sees. Large cardboard boxes can be decorated on the outside and inside using different colors, shapes, and themes (e.g., day and night). After children have explored both the outside and inside, one child crawls inside and describes the outside as the other child from the outside describes the inside.

This activity develops the following behaviors and concepts that are related to early literacy:

Print/Book Awareness

Symbolic representation—pictures, graphics; print—awareness of graphic symbols

Metalinguistic Awareness

Perception and memory for sounds—words

Oral Language

Vocabulary—words and sentences; literate discourse—conversations, categorical organization, decontextualization, interpretive/analytic discourse

ADULT–CHILD INTERACTIVE BEHAVIORS

High Demand/Low Support

Children will:

make interpretations and judgments about what they think another person sees, adapt information to the level of the listener, and use cognitive words to refer to mental states

Support Strategies

?

Open-ended questioning

Help children be aware that the other person's view differs from their own.

234

What does Kimara see inside the box?

Encourage children to use interpretive and cognitive words.

> What do you think Luis sees?
> How do you know that Dominique sees a sun?
> Do you remember what you saw on the other side?

| | **Providing feedback** | Reinterpret information. |

Reinterpret information.

> Oh, you mean it's a circle.

Cognitive structuring

Help children understand that people see things from different perspectives.

> When I stand on this side, I see the turtle upside down.
> Donna doesn't see the same thing as you.
> The bag looks different on the inside.

Have children view the same picture or object from different perspectives and compare similarities and differences.

> How is it the same?
> How is it different?

Holding in memory

Remind children about the differences in perspectives.

> Remember, this card had two sides, one with an apple and one with a duck.

Task regulation

Have children reexamine the pictures or objects from the other person's position. Use objects or pictures that will appear very different from different perspectives.

Medium Demand/Medium Support

Children will:

> use a variety of adult-like sentences to describe the pictures and objects to each other

Support Strategies

Open-ended questioning

Ask children to describe pictures and objects to each other from various perspectives.

> Amy, what do you see on the outside?
> Tamara, what do you see on the inside?

Task regulation

Use objects and pictures that are familiar to children (e.g., foods, favorite cartoon characters) and that have features that are easy to describe (e.g., bright colors).

Instructing   Provide models.

I see a girl on a swing in your picture.

Low Demand/High Support

Children will:

label objects, pictures, and their attributes and maintain social interactions over two or more turns

Support Strategies

  Task regulation   Have children choose pictures or objects to tell each other about. Use objects and pictures that are familiar to the children.

Instructing   Directly elicit social interaction.

Tell Scott what this is.

Ask direct questions.

What do you see?
What does Derek see?

Model, and have children imitate.

Comments/Adaptations

Adaptations   For children with visual impairments, use textured or scented objects and paste them on different sides of the cards or cardboard boxes.

Home Link   Parent Activity: Let's Use Words to Describe . . . !

TREASURE BOXES

Main Purpose	To develop narrative skills and the use of literate discourse
	Children learn to communicate personal feelings and facts to their peers and adults. They express likes, dislikes, judgments, and opinions.
Materials	Cardboard or metal boxes; crayons; paint materials
Description of the Activity	Have each child keep a personal treasure box for storing objects that have a special meaning. Children can create their own treasure box by decorating a cardboard shoebox. Throughout the year, encourage children to place special objects in their boxes. They may choose objects found during a field trip or on the school playground (e.g., rock, leaves, flowers) or objects from home (e.g., miniature toys, photographs). At regular times, have children take turns presenting their treasures to their peers, for example, during a show-and-tell activity. Encourage them to explain why they like the objects and what the objects mean to them.
	This activity develops the following behaviors and concepts that are related to early literacy:
Print/Book Awareness	Symbolic representation—pictures, graphics; print—awareness of graphic symbols, writing
Metalinguistic Awareness	Perception and memory for sounds—words
Oral Language	Narrative skills—narrations of real events; literate discourse—conversations, categorical organization, decontextualization, interpretive/analytic discourse

ADULT–CHILD INTERACTIVE BEHAVIORS

High Demand/Low Support

Children will:

use cognitive and metalinguistic words to explain personal meanings related to their objects

Support Strategies

Open-ended questioning	Ask questions that encourage use of cognitive and metalinguistic words.

237

What does this rock remind you of?
What do you know about this ring?
What does this mean to you?
Who told you that it belonged to your grandfather?

| | Providing feedback | Offer encouragement and praise. |

Providing
feedback

Offer encouragement and praise.

That's an interesting looking piece.

Instructing

Model use of cognitive and metalinguistic words.

I know that each nation has its own different stamps.
I read a story about a crab.

Medium Demand/Medium Support

Children will:

relate information about their objects and generalize experiences to other settings

Support Strategies

Open-ended
questioning

Ask questions to encourage children to generalize their experiences to other settings.

How do you use this at home?
Where did you find this?

Providing
feedback

Offer encouragement and praise.

That looks interesting.

Instructing

Ask direct questions.

This coin is from Mexico. Did you go to Mexico this summer?

Model associating objects with children's experiences.

We saw these shells yesterday when we went to the beach.

Low Demand/High Support

Children will:

use internal state words to express feelings and motivations regarding their objects

Support Strategies

Open-ended
questioning

Ask children questions to encourage expression of feelings.

Why do you like this?
Why is this your favorite?

	Providing feedback	Offer encouraging comments.

Providing feedback — Offer encouraging comments.
That's beautiful.

Instructing — Model use of internal state words.
I like this, too.
This makes me happy.

Comments/Adaptations

Home Link — Encourage children to bring from home objects that are part of their family's cultural background. Suggest to parents that they have their children create their own treasure boxes at home.

WATER PLAY: FLOATING OBJECTS

Main Purpose To develop literate discourse

Children use language to organize, explain, and interpret events and to develop the awareness of spoken language as a tool of thought.

Materials Water table; objects that float; objects that sink

Description of the Activity Provide children with objects of different shapes, sizes, and weights to play with in the water. Explain that some objects will float on the water whereas others will sink. Have children guess and then test whether an object will float or sink. Encourage children to verbalize their predictions, observations, and interpretations as well as to ask questions. Have children take notes on their observations and label and sort the objects into categories (e.g., sinks, floats). Encourage children to generate hypotheses about the reasons why some objects float and others sink. Explain notion of density (i.e., the little parts that make up the object all are close together or spread apart).

This activity develops the following behaviors and concepts that are related to early literacy:

Print/Book Awareness Print—awareness of graphic symbols, writing

Metalinguistic Awareness Perception and memory for sounds—words

Oral Language Vocabulary—words and sentences; literate discourse—categorical organization, decontextualization, interpretive/analytic discourse

ADULT–CHILD INTERACTIVE BEHAVIORS

High Demand/Low Support

Children will:

> use cognitive words, make predictions about whether an object will float or sink, compare the actual event with their expectations, and attempt to provide an explanation

Support Strategies

? **Open-ended questioning** Ask children to make predictions and provide explanations.

> What do you think it will do?
> What happens if we put in a wood spoon?
> Why did it sink?

| | Providing feedback | Encourage children to compare the actual event with their predictions. |

Encourage children to compare the actual event with their predictions.

> Tim said the cork would sink. What happened?

Cognitive structuring

Help children discover relationships between object characteristics and whether the object floats or sinks.

> Metal is packed really tightly, so it sinks. Wood is made of little parts that are more spread out, so it floats.
> This cork is bigger than the nail, but the cork floats and the nail sinks.

Task regulation

Have children make choices.

> Do you think it will sink or float?

Have familiar objects with clues about whether they will sink or float (e.g., a toy car and a wooden boat, a rock and a leaf).

Medium Demand/Medium Support

Children experiment with the objects. They will:

> use a variety of adult-like sentences to describe their observations and other related events

Support Strategies

Open-ended questioning

Encourage children to describe their observations.

> What do you see?
> What's happening?
> What's the pencil doing?

Providing feedback

Have children give verbal descriptions of events.

> Tell me what you're doing.

Describe events and objects for the children.

> Look, the twig is floating.

Task regulation

Have children make choices.

> Did it sink or float?

Have children choose their own objects with which to experiment.

> You pick two objects and see which one floats the best.

Low Demand/High Support

Children observe and play with objects and water. They will:

> label objects and events

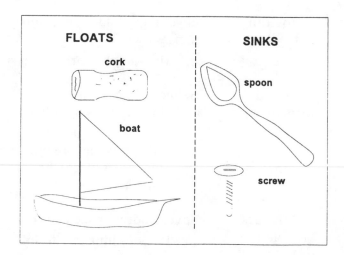

Support Strategies

?	Open-ended questioning	Ask children to describe events. What are you doing?

	Providing feedback	Describe events and objects for the children.
		   That's a leaf.
		   You're pouring the water into the cup.

	Task regulation	Have children choose and label objects to drop into the water.

	Instructing	Provide a model, and repeat the request.
		   This is a paper clip. What is this?
		Provide a model, and have children repeat.
		   The spoon went down. Can you say "down?"

Comments/Adaptations

Comments

This activity requires an introduction at circle time prior to the time children actually get to the water table. As a more structured alternative to a free play, water play table situation, a large transparent container can be set on a table for adults and children to take turns in experimenting with different objects. Children can also have their own containers.

**Link with Print/
Book Awareness**

Prepare a chart to list objects under categories (e.g., sinks, floats).

Home Link

Parent Activity: What Will Happen Next?

MY DREAM

Main Purpose	To develop the use of narrative skills and literate discourse
	Children learn to go beyond the immediate context and to think abstractly. They use language that refers to fictional events, objects, and situations that go beyond the here and now.
Materials	Paper; pictures; objects; props
Description of the Activity	Propose activities based on children's suggestions and interests that develop fictional scenarios and hypothetical thinking (e.g., "I have a dream . . ." "What if I were a grown-up?" "My dream school," "I live on the moon"). Emphasize the distinction between fiction and real events ["Could your dog really fly up to the moon, or are you just pretending?"]. Prepare materials and props related to the topics (e.g., costumes for pretend play, books with fictional stories, crayons and paper for children to draw on, paper to dictate words to the adult).
	This activity develops the following behaviors and concepts that are related to early literacy:
Print/Book Awareness	Print—book conventions, awareness of graphic symbols
Metalinguistic Awareness	Perception and memory for sounds—words, phrases
Oral Language	Vocabulary—words and sentences; narrative skills—narrations of real events; literate discourse—conversations, categorical organization, decontextualization, interpretive/analytic discourse

ADULT–CHILD INTERACTIVE BEHAVIORS

High Demand/Low Support

Children tell an oral story. They will:

> organize elements of story structure in a coherent sequence, make predictions, and explicitly distinguish fiction from real events

Support Strategies

? Open-ended questioning	Ask children general questions.
	What if you were an astronaut?

243

What do you do in your dream house?

Encourage children to make inferences and predictions.

Could dogs fly if they had wings?

Providing feedback

Request children to clarify information, if necessary.

Why would you want a pet dragon?

Reinterpret information.

Oh, you mean you like firefighters because your uncle is one.

Cognitive structuring

Help children sequence and connect events in a coherent manner.

What would you do after that?

Point out contradictions in children's narrations.

Coconut trees grow where it's warm. Would they grow in Alaska?

Task regulation

Have children begin by describing familiar experiences or immediate settings.

What's our classroom like? What would you like to have?

What does your dad do at work? Shall we pretend he does something else?

Instructing

Provide models.

My dream house would have a big swimming pool.

Ask direct questions about whether an event is real or fictional.

Could a dog really grow wings?

Is this for real?

Do elves really exist?

Medium Demand/Medium Support

Children will:

relate events with a beginning, a middle, and an end and draw on personal experiences and provide explanations

Support Strategies

Open-ended questioning

Ask children general questions.

What would you do in your dream school?

Ask children to provide explanations.

Why do you want to go to Mars?

Encourage children to relate objects and events to their own personal experiences.

Have you ever seen a spaceship?

Has this ever happened to you?

Cognitive structuring	Help children sequence events.
	What would you do first?

Task regulation	Have children describe familiar experiences or immediate settings.
	What's our classroom like?
	What's your house like?

Instructing	Ask direct questions.
	What would you like to be when you grow up?

Low Demand/High Support

Children will:

> use words and simple sentences and express feelings and motivations

Support Strategies

Open-ended questioning	Encourage children to express their likes, dislikes, feelings, and emotions.
	What do you like the best in our classroom?
	What's your favorite treat?
	What makes you feel good?
	What makes you angry?

Task regulation	Begin sentences, and have children fill in the blanks.
	I like to play with (blank).

Instructing	Provide a model, and elicit a response.
	I like our fish tank. What do you like?

Comments/Adaptations

Home Link	Send home a copy of the child's project. This activity is especially appropriate as a celebration of Martin Luther King, Jr.'s, Birthday.

SPECIAL WORDS

Main Purpose	To expand vocabulary and literate discourse
	Children learn to categorize words and to develop richer definitions for them. They learn about the attributes of objects and meanings and the use of language to organize and obtain knowledge.
Materials	Butcher paper; flipchart; chalkboard; colored felt pens or chalk; pictures; photographs; books; objects
Description of the Activity	In this activity, children identify words to describe and define "special words" consisting of basic level labels (e.g., dog, chair, apple) or of general categories (e.g., animals, furniture, food). Prepare relevant objects and pictures of interest to the children. Select or have children choose a picture or an object as the "special word" (e.g., clown). Ask the children to describe it, and record or draw their suggestions (e.g., a flowerpot hat, floppy shoes, polka-dot shirt, white make up, painted teardrop). Have some objects or pictures available to use as props. This activity can be done using a word wheel format whereby the teacher writes, draws, or pastes a picture of the "special word" in the middle of a circle and adds the words or pictures the children propose to describe the special word on the spokes of the wheel.
	The "special word" can also consist of a general category (e.g., animals, occupations, things/people in a circus), and children identify objects and people that belong to the category. Encourage children to provide different types of words (e.g., nouns, verbs, adjectives) ["What can this clown do?" What color is his nose?"], and organize the words according to their grammatical functions (e.g., names, actions, description). Have children practice using new words in sentences ["Who can say a sentence with the words 'shell' and 'likes lettuce'?"].
	This activity develops the following behaviors and concepts related to early literacy:
Print/Book Awareness	Print—book conventions, awareness of graphic symbols
Metalinguistic Awareness	Perception and memory for sounds—words, phrases
Oral Language	Vocabulary—words and sentences; narrative skills—narrations of real events; literate discourse—conversations, categorical organization, decontextualization, interpretive/analytic discourse

ADULT–CHILD INTERACTIVE BEHAVIORS

High Demand/Low Support

Children will:

> describe explicit causal and temporal sequences among events, use cognitive and metalinguistic words, and seek definitions of words

Support Strategies

? **Open-ended questioning**

Encourage use of cognitive and metalinguistic words.

> How do geese know when it's time to fly south?
> How do you say Happy Birthday in Spanish?
> What does gallop mean?
> What does the word beach make you think of?

Have children plan and choose categories.

> Here's a clown. Which kinds of things do we want to know about him?

Ask children to summarize.

> What did we find out about what police officers do?

Cognitive structuring

Explain definitions of categories and relationships among objects and events.

> Here we write all of the things we do with a computer and here all of the things we do with paper and pencil.
> I know lizards go with snakes because they are both reptiles.
> Pants and trousers are two words that mean the same thing.

Task regulation

Use novel words to encourage children to ask about their meanings. Ask children to define words or ask meanings of words suggested by peers.

Medium Demand/Medium Support

Children will:

> relate events with a beginning, a middle, and an end; use super-ordinate labels to indicate categories; and generalize experiences to other settings

Support Strategies

? **Open-ended questioning**

Ask general questions.

> Who else works in a circus?
> Which animals can swim?

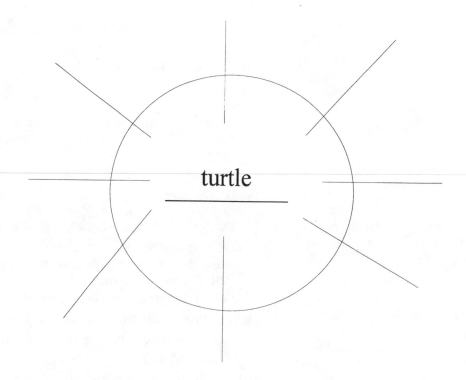

Encourage children to relate objects and events to their personal experiences.

> We saw a toad yesterday in the park. What did he look like? What did he do?

Holding in memory

Remind children of categories and words.

> Remember, here are the things we do in a park and here are the things we do at the library.

Task regulation

Ask children to choose among categories for a given object.

> A pumpkin. Is it a fruit or a vegetable?

Make discussions more concrete by providing objects or pictures of categories.

Instructing

Provide a model, and elicit a response.

> A bicycle is a vehicle. What's a bicycle?

Low Demand/High Support

Children will:

> use one-word utterances and simple sentences to describe objects and events

Support Strategies

?   Open-ended   Ask general questions.
        questioning   What can this clown do?
                              What does this clown wear?

        Task   Have children choose a topic or special word. Choose special words
        regulation   related to events recently experienced by the children. Have pic-
                          tures and props that serve as visual cues.

        Instructing   Provide practice in special words by reviewing lists or collections of
                          words or objects several times. Provide a model, and elicit a
                          response.
                              The turtle likes lettuce. What does he like?

Comments/Adaptations

Comments   The word wheel can be used to teach words in other languages. The
                English word can be written in the center, and children who speak
                other languages can give the translations for the teacher to write on
                the spokes.

Adaptations   Translate sign language used by children with hearing impair-
                ments. Teach basic signs to all children.

Home Link   Send home an activity sheet like the word wheel with instructions
                for children and parents to do together.

WHAT DOES THIS MEAN?

Main Purpose	To develop the use of literate discourse

Children learn that language can be used to organize and obtain knowledge. They seek out the meaning of words. They use verbs that refer to the uses of language (e.g., *I mean, You said*), words that reflect beliefs and attitudes (e.g., *I know, I think*), and words that provide explanations and make interpretations (e.g., *You know, It's because*).

Materials	Flipchart; crayon; chalkboard; chalk; objects; pictures; photographs; props; picture dictionary
Description of the Activity	Propose a word representing an object or event of interest to the children and for which children do not know the meaning. You might choose an unfamiliar word from a storybook read to the class, a word used by a colleague, or one proposed by the children themselves. For example, a child might ask what the word calf means. Provide a variety of verbal cues ["It's the same color and shape as a cow but smaller"] and visual cues (e.g., miniature toy animals, photographs) to help the children guess the meaning of the word. Encourage the children to ask for more information and to formulate their ideas. Explain and show children the use of picture dictionaries. Emphasize relationships and connections between related objects and events ["It looks like a snake, but it swims in water"].

This activity develops the following behaviors and concepts that are related to early literacy:

Print/Book Awareness	Symbolic representation—pictures, graphics; print—book conventions, awareness of graphic symbols
Metalinguistic Awareness	Perception and memory for sounds—words
Oral Language	Vocabulary—words and sentences; literate discourse—conversations, decontextualization, interpretive/analytic discourse

ADULT–CHILD INTERACTIVE BEHAVIORS

High Demand/Low Support

Children will:

> make interpretations and judgments, use cognitive and metalinguistic words, and define objects and events with superordinate labels

Support Strategies

?   Open-ended
questioning

Encourage children to ask questions, problem-solve, and formulate their hypotheses about the meanings of words.

> What do you think manatee could mean?
> What else do you want to know about this word?
> How could we find out what gourd means?

↻   Providing
feedback

Acknowledge children's hypotheses, and encourage them to continue to seek answers.

> Good guess.
> Keep thinking.

Ask children to make their reasoning explicit.

> Tell me why you think a gourd is an animal.

Propose interpretations of children's errors.

> Did you say a wombat was a bat because wombat ends with -bat?

⊞   Cognitive
structuring

Explain the notion of category.

> Some things are similar to each other. They go together.
> Papaya goes with pineapple and banana because they all are fruits.

Provide verbal descriptions based on similarities and differences.

> A tuba looks like a trumpet but makes a deeper sound.

ⓘ   Instructing

Provide models.

> A portrait means a painting or a drawing of a person.

Medium Demand/Medium Support

Children will:

> seek the meaning of words, provide explanations, and generalize experiences to other settings

Support Strategies

?   Open-ended
questioning

Encourage children to provide explanations and draw from their own experiences.

> What's the difference between a calf and a foal?
> Astonished means surprised. Have you ever been astonished?

↻   Providing
feedback

Give positive recognition to children's responses.

> Good guess.
> That's interesting.

Instructing   Encourage children to seek the meaning of words by drawing attention to unfamiliar words.

> Have you ever heard this word before?
> Is this a new word for you?

Model.

> I wonder what this word means.

Low Demand/High Support

Children will:

> label and comment on objects, pictures, and events

Support Strategies

Open-ended questioning   Ask general questions.

> What do you see on this picture?

Task regulation   Ask children to label or describe objects and pictures with which they are familiar.

Instructing   Ask direct questions.

> What's this?

Ask children to label or describe an object or picture following a peer model. Provide a model, and elicit a response.

> This is a calf. A calf is a baby cow. What's this?

Comments/Adaptations

Comment   Introduce objects from diverse cultural backgrounds or words in foreign languages (e.g., a Mardi Gras necklace, a Hawaiian lei, an audiotape of African dances, a hat from Korea).

Link with Print/ Book Awareness   Write some of the children's descriptions into short stories that can be read by the class and individual children at another time.

More Ideas   Have children select words to take home, and have parents look up the meanings in the dictionary.

Home Link   Parent Activity: Let's Use Words to Describe . . . !

LET'S SAY IT ANOTHER WAY!

Main Purpose

To develop vocabulary, narrative skills, and literate discourse

Children learn about the symbolic and arbitrary nature of language and print. They learn that objects, people, and events can be represented through the use of different symbolic systems. They learn about the conventions of language and print and their role in the communications of a specific group or culture.

Materials

Paper; crayons; objects presenting information about different cultures

Description of the Activity

During circle time, tell children different ways of saying and writing common words (e.g., hello, good-bye, thank you, yes, no) in foreign languages. If children in the class speak languages other than English, then choose their language and have them translate the words. Make labels in different languages for objects in the classroom, and draw children's attention to them during daily activities. Display boxes of products containing print in more than one language, such as Canadian products with English and French print. The purpose of this activity is not for children to learn specific words in foreign languages but to become aware that oral and written languages are specific to social groups and cultures. Encourage discussion about other countries, cultures, and traditions.

This activity develops the following behaviors and concepts that are related to early literacy:

Print/Book Awareness

Print—book conventions; awareness of graphic symbols

Metalinguistic Awareness

Perception and memory for sounds—words, phrases

Oral Language

Vocabulary—words and sentences; narrative skills—narrations of real events; literate discourse—decontextualization, interpretive/ analytic discourse

ADULT–CHILD INTERACTIVE BEHAVIORS

High Demand/Low Support

Children participate actively in discussions about other countries, cultures, and traditions and say words they know in foreign languages. They will:

> seek definitions of words, use cognitive and metalinguistic words, and make interpretations and judgments

Support Strategies

| | Open-ended questioning | Ask general questions. |

Ask general questions.

> What's it like in Mexico?
> What do people eat?
> What's the weather like?
> Which kinds of plants grow there?

Encourage children to make interpretations and use cognitive and metalinguistic words.

> What do you think "neko" means?
> What did you notice about the signs in Chinatown?

Cognitive structuring

Explain that different words and signs are used in different languages to represent the same object.

Task regulation

Provide visual and other contextual cues (e.g., pictures, objects, maps) to help children identify the meaning of foreign words.

Instructing

Ask direct questions.

> How do you say "hello" in Korean?
> How do we say "gato" in English?

Use peers as models. Provide models, and repeat request.

> The Koreans say "agno." How do you say "hello" in Korean?

Medium Demand/Medium Support

Children relate personal experiences and knowledge about countries and cultural traditions. They will:

> describe explicit causal and temporal sequences among events and generalize experiences to other settings

Support Strategies

Open-ended questioning

Encourage children to talk about their personal experiences with other countries and cultures.

> What did you see when you visited your grandma in Puerto Rico?
> How does your mother make tamales?
> How do you say "good night" in Mandarin?

Cognitive structuring

Help children sequence events.

> First, you light the candles. Then what?

Task regulation

Have children talk about a relevant book read in class or at home. Have children talk about objects they have brought to school from home.

Instructing

Model by talking about your own culture and personal experiences.

> Here's a story my grandfather told me about when he lived in China.

Ask children direct questions.

> How do you say "hello" in Hawaiian?
> What is Ramadan?

Low Demand/High Support

Children will:

> label and comment on objects, pictures, and events

Support Strategies

Open-ended questioning

Ask general questions.

> What's happening in this picture?
> What do you use this for?

Task regulation

Have children talk about objects that are familiar and present in the immediate environment.

Instructing

Ask direct questions.

> What's this?

Ask children to label or describe an object or picture following a peer model.

Provide a model, and elicit a response.

> This is a dog. "Ma" is the Thai word for dog. What's this?

Comments/Adaptations

Comments

This activity can be integrated within a reading of folktales or a Velcro board story. Children can create books themselves. Teach children songs in different languages. Make audiotapes of people speaking in different languages and accents. Visit ethnic stores that sell food, literature, and other objects from diverse cultures.

Link with Print/ Book Awareness

Use storybooks in other languages and that use different alphabetical systems (e.g., Greek, Russian, Chinese). Create books that describe and contain words from the cultures of the children in the class.

Home Link

Encourage children to bring from home books and songs in foreign languages and articles or souvenirs from other countries or cultures.

INTERVIEWS

Main Purpose	To use structured conversation as a tool to acquire knowledge
	Children learn that language can be used to obtain, give, and document information.
Materials	Tape recorder; pictures; labels
Description of the Activity	Have children identify topics of interest and related questions that can be answered by peers or other people in the class, school, home, or community. Children interview someone, record the interview on a tape recorder, and share it with the class. Encourage children to discuss the information presented. For the presentation of the interview, prepare simple visual materials (e.g., pictures, labels for objects) to accompany the conversation on the audiotape. Identify interesting simple questions that all children can answer ["What's your favorite food?"]. When listening to the tape, write each child's name and favorite food on a list.
	This activity develops the following behaviors and concepts that are related to early literacy:
Print/Book Awareness	Print—book conventions, awareness of graphic symbols
Metalinguistic Awareness	Perception and memory for sounds—words, phrases
Oral Language	Vocabulary—words and sentences; narrative skills—narrations of real events; literate discourse—conversations, decontextualization, interpretive/analytic discourse

ADULT–CHILD INTERACTIVE BEHAVIORS

High Demand/Low Support

Children participate in the discussion and provide personal interpretations of the information. They will:

> make interpretations and use cognitive and metalinguistic words

Support Strategies

? | Open-ended questioning

Encourage children to make interpretations and use cognitive and metalinguistic words.

> What do you think of that?

Do you remember what she said about traffic safety?
What did he mean when he said it depends on the weather?

| Providing feedback | Encourage children to evaluate the accuracy of their comprehension. |

Are there things you didn't understand?
Do you know what all those words mean?

| Holding in memory | Summarize parts of the interview for the children, and have them add comments. |

The doctor said that she went to school for 4 years before she started working in the hospital. Why do you think doctors need to study for so long?

Medium Demand/Medium Support

Children add comments to the discussion. They will:

generalize experiences to other settings

Support Strategies

| Open-ended questioning | Encourage children to talk about their own experiences. |

Have you ever tried that?
Did anything similar ever happen to you?
Do you know anybody else like that?

| Holding in memory | Summarize parts of the interview for the children, and have them add comments. |

| Task regulation | Provide visual props and pictures related to the content of the interview as reference for the children. |

| Instructing | Model adding comments about your own personal experiences related to the content of the interview. |

Low Demand/High Support

Children will:

use one- or two-word utterances to describe people and events and express a variety of semantics intentions

Support Strategies

| Open-ended questioning | Ask children general questions about the information presented. |

Where does a nurse work?
What does a pilot do?

Task regulation

Ask children to comment about objects and pictures related to the content of the interview.

>Who is in this photo?

Instructing

Provide a model.

>Ask Roberto, "What do you like to play?"

Model, and elicit a response.

>Monica's brother plays basketball. What does Monica's brother do?

Comments/Adaptations

Comments

Focus on issues of personal and cultural relevance. Interviews might include the school principal, the school janitor, or a child's parent who is a police officer or a doctor. Organize field trips and interview people on topics of interest (e.g., a farmer about his farm animals, passengers at a train station or airport about their destinations, a baker about making bread).

Link with Print/ Book Awareness

Develop fill-in-the-blank sheets to gather the information from each child, then discuss responses, write answers on paper, and encourage children to read each others' responses. Gather these responses into a class book that can be checked out and shared with families.

More Ideas

Have the children ask the same questions of a parent or an older sibling at home and then bring these responses back to class. Make a frequency chart to display how many family members answered with similar words.

Home Link

Ask parents to help their children interview people in their family or neighborhood (e.g., the store owner in the neighborhood who is from Mexico, the school nurse, a child's mother who is a dentist or a banker).

MOVIE REVIEWS

Main Purpose   To use narrative skills and literate types of oral discourse

Children learn to retell stories and events and to use forms of oral discourse that reflect opinions, beliefs, and critical judgments.

Materials   VCR/TV; videotape

Description of the Activity   Watch TV shows and short films appropriate for children. During the show, occasionally ask children to relate what they just saw, predict what might happen next, and express opinions and feelings about events and topics. Encourage children to ask questions during the viewing. When possible, relate topics to personal experiences. After the entire show or film has been viewed, have children relate the story or event.

This activity develops the following behaviors and concepts that are related to early literacy:

Print/Book Awareness   Symbolic representation—pictures, graphics

Metalinguistic Awareness   Perception and memory for sounds—words

Oral Language   Vocabulary—words and sentences; narrative skills—narrations of real events, narrations of fictional story; literate discourse—conversations, decontextualization, interpretive/analytic discourse

ADULT–CHILD INTERACTIVE BEHAVIORS

High Demand/Low Support

Children will:

> make predictions, interpretations, and judgments and will relate and organize elements of the story or structure in a coherent sequence

Support Strategies

? Open-ended questioning   Encourage children to make predictions.
> What do you think will happen next?

Encourage children to make interpretations and judgments.
> Now, what did she mean by that?
> Do you think that was a good thing to do?

Do you agree? Why?
Did you like what she did?

Providing feedback

Request children to clarify information, if necessary.

How did she ride home if she lost her horse?

Reinterpret information.

Oh, you mean he wasn't happy.

Cognitive structuring

Review the separate elements of story structure and how they are connected to each other. Point out contradictions in children's narrations.

You said he didn't have a boat, but he crossed the ocean.

Help sequence events.

What happened first?
What did he do after she left?
First, say what their names are.

Task regulation

Ask questions about specific elements of the story.

Where did it happen?
Who is the story about?
How does the story end?

Medium Demand/Medium Support

Children will:

relate events with a beginning, a middle, and an end; generalize experiences to other settings; and distinguish fiction from real events

Support Strategies

Open-ended questioning

Ask children general questions.

What's the movie about?
What happened?

Encourage children to relate events to their own personal experiences.

Have you ever seen an eagle?
Has this ever happened to you?
What's your house like?

Cognitive structuring

Help children sequence events.

What happened first?
How did it end?

Define the notion of pretend, and explain differences between fictional and real events.

Holding in memory

Summarize the story up to a point at which children can continue.

Instructing

Ask direct questions about the story.

What did the princess say to the king?

Ask direct questions about whether an event is real or fictional.

Could a raven really carry a boy across the ocean?
Is this for real?

Low Demand/High Support

Children attend to the videotape. They will:

ask questions, add simple comments, and use internal state words to express feelings

Support Strategies

Open-ended questioning

Encourage children to express their opinions and feelings.

What did you like about the story?
What made you scared?
What made the girl happy?
Why was she sad?

Task regulation

Stop the videotape occasionally, and ask children to comment.

What do you see here?

Provide children with corresponding books or pictures, and ask them to comment on the story.

Instructing

Model.

I liked it when they all danced together.

Ask direct questions to elicit opinions and feelings.

Did you like this?
Was it scary?
Was he sad?

Comments/Adaptations

Comments

Select videotapes that are culturally sensitive (e.g., documentaries about other countries, stories with characters that are from diverse cultures or who have disabilities). Show videotapes made of class activities or field trips. Use videotapes that address interpersonal themes, if appropriate.

Adaptations   Make sure the sound track enables children with visual impairments to follow the story line.

**Link with Print/
Book Awareness**   Write a few of the children's predictions on a large piece of paper. When the movie or story is over, review the predictions and ask the children whether any of these events occurred.

Home Link   Parent Activity: Movie Reviews

BRAINSTORMING

Main Purpose	To facilitate the use of literate discourse

Children learn to use literate forms of language as they formulate explanations and hypotheses about events and objects and propose solutions to specific problems.

Materials	Pictures; books; markers; crayons
Description of the Activity	Present children with specific situations that require them to explain an event or a process or to solve a problem. Problems can range from hypothetical situations with scenarios that address social and emotional issues ["Renee lost her mother at the zoo. What should she do?"] or explanations of events of personal interest to the children (e.g., thunderstorms, birth of animals) to descriptions of class science projects or immediate practical problems (e.g., how to make a sandwich). Situations can be presented in the form of a cartoon with characters and empty dialogue boxes. At the end of the brainstorming, ask children to dictate the content of the dialogue.

This activity develops the following behaviors and concepts that are related to early literacy:

Print/Book Awareness	Print—book conventions, awareness of graphic symbols
Metalinguistic Awareness	Perception and memory for sounds—words, phrases
Oral Language	Vocabulary—words and sentences; narrative skills—narrations of real events; literate discourse—conversations, decontextualization, interpretive/analytic discourse

ADULT–CHILD INTERACTIVE BEHAVIORS

High Demand/Low Support

Children will:
>   make predictions and judgments and use cognitive words

Support Strategies

Open-ended questioning	Encourage children to make hypotheses and predictions about events.

263

> What could Rebecca do to help Malcolm?
> What would happen if we turned off the light?
> What would you do if you got lost?

Encourage children to make judgments about proposed solutions.

> What do you think of Christina's idea?

Providing feedback

Acknowledge children's ideas in a positive manner, regardless of accuracy. Encourage children to evaluate and compare their predictions and hypotheses with actual events.

> Did it happen the way you expected?
> Which way did you think it would go? Which way did it really go?

Cognitive structuring

Emphasize relationships and similarities between events.

> The seed we planted in the sun grew faster.
> Chickens hatch from eggs, and so do snakes.

Holding in memory

Remind children of the purpose of brainstorming and the problem to be solved.

> José's mother speaks only Spanish, and his teacher speaks only English. How can they talk to each other?
> Remember, we planted the seeds in two different locations.
> We want to find out what to do if we get lost.

Medium Demand/Medium Support

Children will:

> describe explicit causal and temporal sequences among events and generalize experiences to other settings in proposing solutions

Support Strategies

Open-ended questioning

Ask general questions to encourage children to describe events.

> What did we see?
> What happened?
> What did Ruth do to make Donna feel better?

Encourage children to compare the proposed situation with their own experience.

> Has this ever happened to you?
> When someone pushes you, how do you feel?

Ask children to give explanations and make causal inferences between events.

> Why did it go faster?
> Why do you think the big one was louder?

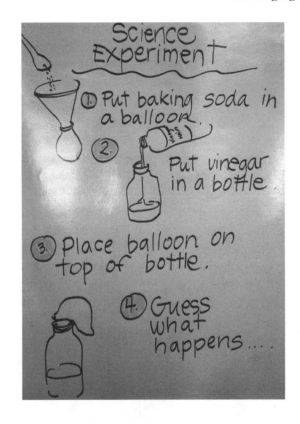

	Providing feedback	Ask children to provide clarifications.
		You said, "It blew up." What blew up?
		Provide interpretations.
		You mean your aunt speaks English and Spanish?
	Cognitive structuring	Help children sequence and organize events.
		What happened first?
		What happened after we poured the water?
	Holding in memory	Summarize events.
		Remember, Dan wanted his mother to see his Lego construction. She couldn't come to school, so Ann suggested we take a photo of it for Dan to take home.
	Task regulation	Provide visual cues such as props, charts, pictures, and drawings of events.
	Instructing	Ask specific questions.
		Who helped José's mother talk with the teacher?
		Would you be scared if you got lost?

Low Demand/High Support

Children will:

maintain social interaction over two or more turns and use words and a variety of adult-form sentences to describe objects and events

Support Strategies

? Open-ended questioning

Ask children to describe an object or an event.

What happened?
What do you see?

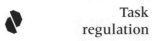 Task regulation

Provide visual cues that represent objects and events related to the situation. Provide children with choices.

Would you grab the toy or ask for a turn?
Is he happy or sad?

i Instructing

Model by describing objects and events. Expand on children's utterances.

Big. Yes, it grew much bigger when we blew into it.

Ask direct questions.

What's this?
What color is this?

Comments/Adaptations

Comments

This activity presents an excellent opportunity to address important social and emotional events that the children may experience (e.g., neighborhood violence, cultural discrimination).

Home Link

Parent Activity: What Will Happen Next?

FROM THIS TO THAT

Main Purpose

To facilitate vocabulary and the use of literate discourse

Children learn to use oral language to provide explanations, make predictions, and form judgments.

Materials

Related materials; paper; markers

Description of the Activity

Have children observe events during which a physical or visual change occurs. Encourage them to describe the different stages of the transformation process. For example, have them observe natural events related to weather changes (e.g., the wind that makes branches of trees bend, the sun that melts the snow). Prepare particular experiments (e.g., melt butter, freeze water). Discuss the change. The transformation of foods during cooking and baking is also an excellent activity in which to observe changes. During this activity, have children change positions to view the materials from different perspectives. For example, have the children look at the same object first when they are lying down and then when they are standing on top of a chair. Ask children to describe the difference.

This activity develops the following behaviors and concepts that are related to early literacy:

Print/Book Awareness

Symbolic representation—pictures; print—awareness of graphic symbols, letter identification, writing; letter–sound correspondence—single sounds and letters

Metalinguistic Awareness

Perception and memory for sounds—words

Oral Language

Vocabulary—words and sentences; narrative skills—narrations of real events; literate discourse—decontextualization, interpretive/analytic discourse

ADULT–CHILD INTERACTIVE BEHAVIORS

High Demand/Low Support

Children will:

provide explanations and make predictions

Support Strategies

? **Open-ended questioning**

Ask children to make predictions about events.

How did it change?
What do you think the vinegar will do to the egg?
What would happen if you added yellow paint to the blue paint?

Ask children to provide explanations.

Why did it melt?
What made the milk curdle?
Why does it look different under the magnifying glass?

Cognitive structuring

Emphasize relationships between events.

If you look at it closer, it looks bigger.
It was red before you added yellow.

Medium Demand/Medium Support

Children will:

describe explicit causal and temporal sequences among events
and generalize experiences to other settings

Support Strategies

Open-ended questioning

Ask general questions to encourage children to describe events.

What did we see?
What happened?
What's different?

Encourage children to relate events to their own experience.

Have you ever eaten ice cream in the sun?
Have you ever looked through a telescope?

Cognitive structuring

Help children sequence and organize events.

What happened first?
What happened after we boiled the eggs?

Holding in memory

Remind children of earlier events.

We poured water into the tray. We put it in the freezer, and it
turned into hard, frozen ice. Then we put the ice in the sun.
What happened?

Task regulation

Provide visual cues such as charts and drawings of the sequence of
events.

Instructing

Ask specific questions.

Which color was it before we started?
Which shape is it now?

When fall comes, our tree has red and gold leaves...

Outside our window, we can see our winter tree...

In spring, our tree has tiny pink flowers and new green leaves...

In summer, our tree has big green leaves to keep us cool when the weather is hot....

Low Demand/High Support

Children will:

use words and two-word utterances to describe objects and events

Support Strategies

?	Open-ended questioning	Ask children to describe an object or an event. What happened? What do you see?
❧	Task regulation	Provide visual cues. Here's some macaroni that hasn't been cooked. Provide choices. Are they hard or soft? Does it look bigger or smaller?
ⓘ	Instructing	Model by describing objects and events. Ask direct questions. What's this? Which color is this now?

Comments/Adaptations

Adaptations   Draw pictures, diagrams, and flowcharts for children with hearing impairments or language disabilities.

Link with Print/ Book Awareness   Write some of the children's descriptions into short stories that can be read by the class and individual children at another time.

Home Link   Encourage parents to discuss seasonal changes with their children. They can help children recognize signs of change by observing a familiar tree or garden during periods of rapid change, such as fall or spring.

LET'S FIND OUT!

Main Purpose

To use language and communication to gain knowledge about the world and to facilitate the use of literate discourse

Children learn to use language to understand and interpret events, to seek explanations and definitions, to categorize objects, to organize and summarize knowledge, to ask questions, to describe events, and to express feelings. Children learn to use different forms of communication and symbolic representation (e.g., oral language, drawings, print signs, photographs) to learn about events and to document new knowledge.

Materials

Project-related materials; paper; markers; pencils; books; notebooks; tape recorder; camera

Description of the Activity

This is a long-term activity that requires significant adult involvement and guidance. The idea is to develop two or three ongoing projects for children to participate in during the entire school year. It is important that each child get involved in a project in order to learn how to explore and develop a theme in depth. Children will learn about continuity in time and effort. They will learn how events are linked and sequenced. Children can propose the theme of the projects, adults can make suggestions based on questions or issues the children raise, or adults can observe children over several weeks and decide on two or three topics of interest. For example, children may ask questions about how things are made (e.g., food, paper, buildings, roads), how things work (e.g., cars, trucks, planes, trains), natural events (e.g., rain, snow, tornadoes), or events or people in the community (e.g., a new park, police, doctors, nurses). Pick the most appropriate topics that children suggest (e.g., those for which information is the easiest to obtain). Divide children into two or three groups, and help them plan how to develop the topic, define questions and problems, and identify strategies for gathering information (e.g., read books, interview experts, observe). Encourage the use of a variety of media to represent and document the information (e.g., photographs, drawings, audiotape). Help children to plan a way to summarize and disseminate the information (e.g., make a book, a poster, or a videotape). Involve children's families and experts from the community. For example, invite a police officer to come and talk about traffic safety or an architect to talk about how to build a house. Visit a bakery or a paper factory.

This activity develops the following behaviors and concepts that are related to early literacy:

Print/Book Awareness	Symbolic representation—pictures, graphics; print—book conventions, awareness of graphic symbols, letter identification, writing; letter–sound correspondence—single sounds and letters
Metalinguistic Awareness	Perception and memory for sounds—words
Oral Language	Vocabulary—words and sentences; narrative skills—narration of real events; literate discourse—decontextualization, interpretive/analytic discourse

ADULT–CHILD INTERACTIVE BEHAVIORS

High Demand/Low Support

Children participate in planning and organizing activities. They will:

> make predictions and judgments and describe explicit causal and temporal sequences among events

Support Strategies

?	**Open-ended questioning**	Assist children in planning and organizing events. How can we find out where honey comes from? Where could we find some books about tornadoes? Who could explain to us how the new park was planned?
↻	**Providing feedback**	Encourage children's ideas and incorporate them into the project as much as possible. Encourage children to evaluate the feasibility of their suggestions. I wonder if it's possible for us all to go and visit a hospital. Do we have enough money to buy a video on the national park? Ask for clarifications. Why do you think we need to take it apart?
⬛	**Cognitive structuring**	Help children find relationships between objects and events. The more letters we send, the more responses we might get. Help children sequence events. What should we do first? What do we need to do after we write the letter?
◐	**Holding in memory**	Summarize suggestions, decisions, and plans. Remind children of the purpose of the project.

	Task regulation	Assign different tasks to children according to their interests and backgrounds.
	Instructing	Assign specific tasks.

> Sondra, will you draw us a picture of our school?
> Ask your parents to help you look for pictures of bees in magazines.

Medium Demand/Medium Support

Children will:

> relate events with a beginning, a middle, and an end; provide explanations; and generalize experiences to other settings

Support Strategies

? Open-ended questioning

Ask children general questions.

> What would you like to know about spiders?

Ask children to provide explanations.

> Why do we need to write a letter?

Encourage children to relate objects and events to their own personal experiences.

> Is there a bakery near your house?
> Did you see any spider webs this morning?

	Cognitive structuring	Help children sequence events.
		First, we should take a photo.
	Holding in memory	Summarize suggestions, decisions, and plans. Remind children of the purpose of the project.
	Task regulation	Have children describe what they have done in the project so far.
	Instructing	Assign specific tasks.

Assign specific tasks.

How about if Yayoi puts together all of the signs in this box?

Ask specific questions.

What is bread made of?
What are spider webs for?

Low Demand/High Support

Children will:

use two-word utterances to express a variety of semantic intentions

Support Strategies

Open-ended questioning

Ask children to describe an object or an event.

What are you drawing?
What do you see?

Providing feedback

Describe what children see or are doing.

That's a photo of a queen bee.
You're painting the box.

Task regulation

Make the recording of observations or collecting information concrete.

Let's look at our chart and see how many shells we had last week. Count with me.
(After counting) How many shells did you bring today? How shall we record that on the chart?

Instructing

Model by describing objects and events. Expand on children's utterances.

Honey. Yes, honey tastes sweet.

Ask direct questions.

What's this?

Comments/Adaptations

More Ideas   Involve parents by telling them the topic that their child is researching. Send parents regular updates on the progress of the project. Encourage parent contributions in terms of ideas and direct participation.

Home Link   Parent Activity: Going Places—The Museum

SHOWTIME

Main Purpose	To develop vocabulary and literate discourse
	Children learn to work together to coordinate dialogues. They use language to communicate and understand ideas and to plan and guide actions.
Materials	Related materials
Description of the Activity	Prepare a short, simple drama or musical event for the children to perform at a special occasion (e.g., a festivity such as Christmas or Hanukkah) or at the end of the school year. Have children suggest themes, dialogues, and songs. This activity presents a good opportunity to teach children about folktales, songs, and other characteristics of a variety of cultures. For example, children can learn to sing songs from their own culture or that of their peers.
	This activity develops the following behaviors and concepts that are related to early literacy:
Print/Book Awareness	Symbolic representation—pictures, graphics; print—awareness of graphic symbols, writing
Metalinguistic Awareness	Perception and memory for sounds—words
Oral Language	Vocabulary—words and sentences; literate discourse—decontextualization, interpretive/analytic discourse

ADULT–CHILD INTERACTIVE BEHAVIORS

High Demand/Low Support

Children participate in planning and organizing activities. They will:

> make predictions, interpretations, and judgments and use cognitive and metalinguistic words

Support Strategies

? Open-ended questioning	Assist children in planning and organizing events.
	Which songs go best with the story?
	Which costumes should we wear?
	When should we send out invitations?
	Encourage children to make judgments.

Do you think it's a good idea to have three different colors?

Ask children about mental states and use of language.

What does this word mean?
Do you understand what to sing?

| | Providing feedback | Encourage children's ideas and incorporate them into the project as much as possible. Request children to clarify information, if necessary. |

What do you mean?
Did you forget?
Who is he?

| | Cognitive structuring | Help children sequence events. |

What should we sing first?
What do we say before Pat and Pedro do their dance?

| | Holding in memory | Summarize suggestions, decisions, and plans. |

So we decided to have the songs first and then the dances.

| | Instructing | Assign specific tasks. |

I think Rosa should play the drum.
Ramona and MaryLou can design the invitations.
The Swan Team is in charge of making the tree.

Medium Demand/Medium Support

Children will:

provide explanations and use adult-form sentences to describe events

Support Strategies

| | Open-ended questioning | Ask children general questions. |

What do the dancers do while Pamela sings?
What's this song about?

Ask children to provide explanations.

Why do we need four people to be dragons?

| | Task regulation | Have children describe their roles and responsibilities. |

| | Instructing | Ask specific questions. |

From which country is this dance?
Who is on our list of invitations?

Low Demand/High Support

Children will:

use two-word utterances to express a variety of semantic intentions

Support Strategies

? Open-ended questioning

Ask children to describe an object or an event.

What are you coloring?
What's Sara doing?

Providing feedback

Describe what children see or are doing.

That's Alberto's bird costume.
You're painting the box.

Instructing

Provide extra practice and cues for children's roles.

Right, Alberto. You be the bird who sings before the dance.

Model by describing objects and events. Expand on children's utterances.

Leaf. Yes, a green leaf.

Provide directions.

Your turn, Heather, to play the drum.

Ask direct questions.

What's this?

Comments/Adaptations

Comments

Themes should be familiar (e.g., a favorite story or fairy tale), and dialogues should be kept simple (e.g., one sentence monologues). Actions and visual props should be relied on heavily to guide the story of the drama. Videotape rehearsals and performances.

Home Link

Invite parents to come to the performance. Have children prepare the invitations.

EARLY LITERACY OBSERVATION FORM

Child's name: _____

Oral Language

1. Words I know   2. Things I say about what I do, what I feel, and what I think   3. Stories I can tell

Date	What I did or said

Ladders to Literacy: A Preschool Activity Book
by Angela Notari-Syverson, Rollanda E. O'Connor, and Patricia F. Vadasy
©1998 Paul H. Brookes Publishing Co., Baltimore

ORAL LANGUAGE CHECKLIST
Behaviors observed

Name: _____

Scoring: Dates: _____ _____ _____

2 = Consistently/independently   1 = Sometimes/partly   0 = Not yet   Activity: _____ _____ _____

Notes:

A = Assumed   NO = No opportunity   R = Report   H = Help   M = Modifications

I. VOCABULARY
Words and Sentences

A. Uses one-word utterances to label a variety of objects, people, and events _____( )_____( )_____( )

B. Uses two-word utterances to express a variety of semantic intentions (agent-object, agent-action, action-object, existence, location, possession, negation, recurrence, attribution) _____( )_____( )_____( )

C. Uses a variety of adult-form sentences (e.g., declarative, interrogative, negative) _____( )_____( )_____( )

II. NARRATIVE SKILLS
Narrations of Real Events

A. Relates events with beginning, middle, and end _____( )_____( )_____( )

B. Describes explicit causal and temporal sequences among events (uses: because, before, after) _____( )_____( )_____( )

Book

C. Attends to and labels pictures in book _____( )_____( )_____( )

D. Makes comments and asks questions about individual pictures _____( )_____( )_____( )

E. Tells story and links events based on pictures using conversational language _____( )_____( )_____( )

F. Forms written story based on pictures using reading intonation and wording _____( )_____( )_____( )

Narrations of Fictional Story

G. Attends to story _____( )_____( )_____( )

H. Adds simple comments and asks questions _____( )_____( )_____( )

_____
continued

Ladders to Literacy: A Preschool Activity Book
by Angela Notari-Syverson, Rollanda E. O'Connor, and Patricia F. Vadasy
©1998 Paul H. Brookes Publishing Co., Baltimore

ORAL LANGUAGE CHECKLIST
(continued)

Name: _____

I. Relates and organizes elements of story structure in a
   coherent sequence (setting, theme, episodes, resolution)   _____( )_____( )_____( )

III. LITERATE DISCOURSE

Conversations

A. Maintains social interaction over two or more turns   _____( )_____( )_____( )

B. Initiates and maintains topic   _____( )_____( )_____( )

C. Adapts information to level of listener   _____( )_____( )_____( )

Categorical Organization

D. Uses superordinate labels to indicate general categories   _____( )_____( )_____( )

Decontextualization

E. Generalizes experiences to other settings   _____( )_____( )_____( )

F. Provides explanations   _____( )_____( )_____( )

G. Makes predictions   _____( )_____( )_____( )

H. Makes interpretations and judgments   _____( )_____( )_____( )

I. Distinguishes fiction from real events   _____( )_____( )_____( )

Interpretive/Analytic Discourse

J. Uses internal state words to express feelings and motivations
   (e.g., happy, sad, want, like)   _____( )_____( )_____( )

K. Uses cognitive words to refer to mental states (e.g., memory,
   idea, forget, think, know, understand)   _____( )_____( )_____( )

L. Uses metalinguistic words to refer to the use of language
   (e.g., word, letter, sound, say, tell, mean, call, read)   _____( )_____( )_____( )

M. Seeks definitions of words   _____( )_____( )_____( )

Ladders to Literacy: A Preschool Activity Book
by Angela Notari-Syverson, Rollanda E. O'Connor, and Patricia F. Vadasy
©1998 Paul H. Brookes Publishing Co., Baltimore

SCAFFOLDING STRATEGIES CHECKLIST

Child's name: _____

Date: _____ _____ _____

Activity: _____ _____ _____

Circle strategies used during activity:	Used	Did it help?	Used	Did it help?	Used	Did it help?
Open-ended questioning descriptions predictions and planning explanations relating to the child's experience	□Y □N	□Y □N	□Y □N	□Y □N	□Y □N	□Y □N
Providing feedback encouragements evaluations thinking aloud clarification requests interpretation of meaning acknowledgments and information talk	□Y □N	□Y □N	□Y □N	□Y □N	□Y □N	□Y □N
Cognitive structuring rules and logical relationships sequencing contradictions	□Y □N	□Y □N	□Y □N	□Y □N	□Y □N	□Y □N
Holding in memory restating goals summaries and reminders	□Y □N	□Y □N	□Y □N	□Y □N	□Y □N	□Y □N
Task regulation matching interests and experience rearranging elements reducing alternatives making more concrete	□Y □N	□Y □N	□Y □N	□Y □N	□Y □N	□Y □N
Instructing modeling orienting direct questioning elicitations coparticipation	□Y □N	□Y □N	□Y □N	□Y □N	□Y □N	□Y □N

Ladders to Literacy: A Preschool Activity Book
by Angela Notari-Syverson, Rollanda E. O'Connor, and Patricia F. Vadasy
©1998 Paul H. Brookes Publishing Co., Baltimore

References

Adams, M.J. (1990). *Beginning to read: Thinking and learning about print.* Cambridge, MA: MIT Press.

Arno, E. (1970). *The gingerbread man.* New York: Scholastic.

Arter, J., & Spandel, V. (1991). *Using portfolios of student work in instruction and assessment.* Portland, OR: Northwest Regional Educational Laboratory.

Ball, E.W. (1993). Assessing phoneme awareness. *Language, Speech, and Hearing Services in Schools, 24,* 130–139.

Ball, E.W., & Blachman, B.A. (1991). Does phoneme awareness training in kindergarten make a difference in early word recognition and developmental spelling? *Reading Research Quarterly, 26,* 49–65.

Barker, R.G. (1968). *Ecological psychology.* Palo Alto, CA: Stanford University Press.

Ben-Dror, I., Bentin, S., & Frost, R. (1995). Semantic, phonologic, and morphologic skills in reading disabled and normal children: Evidence from perception and production of spoken Hebrew. *Reading Research Quarterly, 30,* 876–893.

Bentin, S., & Leshem, H. (1993). On the interaction between phonological awareness and reading acquisition: It's a two-way street. *Annals of Dyslexia, 43,* 2–29.

Berk, L.E., & Winsler, A. (1995). *Scaffolding children's learning: Vygotsky and early childhood education.* Washington, DC: National Association for the Education of Young Children.

Blachman, B. (1994). What we have learned from longitudinal studies of phonological processing and reading, and some unanswered questions. *Journal of Learning Disabilities, 27*(5), 287–291.

Bodrova, E., & Leong, D.J. (1996). *Tools of the mind: The Vygotskian approach to early childhood education.* Englewood Cliffs, NJ: Prentice-Hall.

Brady, S., Gipstein, M., & Fowler, A. (1992, April). *The development of phonological awareness in preschoolers.* Paper presented at the annual conference of the American Educational Research Association, San Francisco.

Brett, J. (1990). *Goldilocks and the three bears.* New York: G.P. Putnam's Sons.

Bricker, D., & Cripe, J.J. (1992). *An activity-based approach to early intervention.* Baltimore: Paul H. Brookes Publishing Co.

Bridge, C., Winograd, P., & Haley, D. (1983). Using predictable materials versus preprimers to teach beginning sight words. *The Reading Teacher, 36*(9), 884–891.

Bronfenbrenner, U. (1979). *The ecology of human development: Experiments by nature and design.* Cambridge, MA: Harvard University Press.

Brown, M. (1957). *The three billy goats gruff.* San Diego: Harcourt Brace Jovanovich.

Bruner, J. (1983). *Child's talk: Learning to use languages.* New York: Norton.

Bus, A.G., van Ijzendoorn, M., & Pellegrini, A.D. (1995). Joint book reading makes for success in learning to read: A meta-analysis on intergenerational transmission of literacy. *Review of Educational Research, 65,* 1–21.

Byrne, B. (1992). Studies in the acquisition procedure for reading: Rationale, hypotheses, and data. In P. Gough, L. Ehri, & R. Treiman (Eds.), *Reading acquisition* (pp. 1–34). Hillsdale, NJ: Lawrence Erlbaum Associates.

Byrne, B., & Fielding-Barnsley, R. (1993). Evaluation of a program to teach phonemic awareness to children: A 1–year follow-up. *Journal of Educational Psychology, 85,* 104–111.

Byrne, B., Freebody, P., and Gates, A. (1992). Longitudinal data on relations between word reading strategy, comprehension, and reading time. *Reading Research Quarterly, 27,* 141–151.

Carle, E. (1969). *The very hungry caterpillar.* New York: Philomel Books.

Catts, H.W. (1993). The relationship between speech-language impairments and reading disabilities. *Journal of Speech and Hearing Research, 36,* 948–958.

Chomsky, C. (1972). Stages in language development and reading exposure. *Harvard Educational Review, 42,* 1–33.

Clay, M.M. (1979). *The early detection of reading difficulties* (3rd ed.). Auckland, New Zealand: Heinemann.

Clay, M.M. (1993). *Reading recovery: A guidebook for teachers in training.* Auckland, New Zealand: Heinemann.

Cohen, L.G., & Spenciner, L.J. (1994). *Assessment of young children.* White Plains, NY: Longman.

Cook-Gumperz, J., & Gumperz, J.J. (1981). From oral to written culture: The transition to literacy. In M.F. Whiteman (Ed.), *Writing: The nature, development, and teaching of written communication: Vol. 1. Variation in writing: Functional and linguistic cultural difference* (pp. 89–110). Hillsdale, NJ: Lawrence Erlbaum Associates.

Crain-Thoreson, C., & Dale, P.S. (1992). Do early talkers become early readers? Linguistic precocity, preschool language and emergent literacy. *Developmental Psychology, 28,* 421–429.

Cross, T.G. (1978). Mother's speech and its association with rate of linguistic development in young children. In N. Waterson & C. Snow (Eds.), *The development of communication* (pp. 199–216). New York: John Wiley & Sons.

Cunningham, A.E. (1990). Explicit vs. implicit instruction in phonemic awareness. *Journal of Experimental Child Psychology, 50,* 429–444.

Dale, P., Crain-Thoreson, C., Notari-Syverson, A., & Cole, K. (1996). Parent–child storybook reading as an intervention technique for young children with language delays. *Topics in Early Childhood Special Education, 16,* 213–235.

Diaz, R.M., Neal, C.J., & Vachio, A. (1991). Maternal teaching in the zone of proximal development: A comparison of low- and high-risk dyads. *Merrill-Palmer Quarterly, 37,* 83–108.

Dickinson, D., & Smith, M. (1996, April). *Grade two reading comprehension: Contributions of preschool, kindergarten and grade one experiences.* Paper presented at the annual conference of the Society for the Scientific Study of Reading, New York.

Dickinson, D., & Snow, C. (1987). Interrelationships among prereading and oral language skills in kindergartners from two social classes. *Early Childhood Research Quarterly, 2,* 1–25.

Dickinson, D.K., Du Temple, J., Hirschler, J., & Smith, M. (1992). Book reading with preschoolers: Co-construction of text at home and at school. *Early Childhood Research Quarterly, 7,* 323–346.

Dyson, A.H. (1984). Emerging alphabetic literacy in school contexts. *Written Communication, 1,* 5–55.

Edge, N. (1988a). *I can read colors.* Salem, OR: Nellie Edge Resources.

Edge, N. (1988b). *The opposite song.* Salem, OR: Nellie Edge Resources.

Felton, R.H. (1992). Early identification of children at risk for reading disabilities. *Topics in Early Childhood Special Education, 12,* 212–229.

Ferreiro, E., & Teberosky, A. (1982). *Literacy before schooling.* Exeter, NH: Heinemann.

Fey, M. (1986). *Language intervention with young children.* San Diego: College Hill Press.

Forman, G. (1993). Multiple symbolization in the Long Jump Project. In C. Edwards, L. Gandini, & G. Forman (Eds.), *The hundred languages of children: The Reggio Emilia approach to early childhood education* (pp. 171–188). Norwood, NJ: Ablex.

Fowler, A.E. (1991). How early phonological development might set the stage for phoneme awareness. In S.A. Brady & D.A. Shankweiler (Eds.), *Phonological processes in literacy* (pp. 97–117). Hillsdale, NJ: Lawrence Erlbaum Associates.

Fox, B., & Routh, D. (1975). Analyzing spoken language into words, syllables and phonemes: A developmental study. *Journal of Psycholinguistic Research, 4,* 331–342.

Fry, P.S. (1992). *Fostering children's cognitive competence through mediated learning experiences: Frontiers and future.* Springfield, IL: Charles C Thomas.

Galda, L., Pellegrini, A.E., & Cox, S. (1989). A short-term longitudinal study of preschoolers' emergent literacy. *Research in the Teaching of English, 23,* 292–309.

Galdone, P. (1970). *The three little pigs.* New York: Houghton Mifflin.

Goswami, U., & Bryant, P. (1992). Rhyme, analogy, and children's reading. In P. Gough, L. Ehri, & R. Treiman (Eds.), *Reading acquisition* (pp. 49–64). Hillsdale, NJ: Lawrence Erlbaum Associates.

Grammer, R. (1983). Can you sound just like me? Finger Play, and Ready Set. On *Can you sound just like me?* [cassette/album]. Brewerton, NY: Red Note Records.

Greenman, J. (1988). *Caring spaces, learning places: Children's environments that work.* Redmond, WA: The Exchange Press.

Gutierrez-Clellen, V., & Quinn, R. (1993). Assessing narratives of children from diverse cultural/linguistic groups. *Language, Speech, and Hearing Services in Schools, 24,* 2–9.

Haddock, M. (1976). Effects of an auditory and an auditory visual method of blending instruction on the ability of prereaders to decode synthetic work. *Journal of Educational Psychology, 68,* 825–831.

Hanline, M.F., & Fox, L. (1994). The use of assessment portfolios with young children with disabilities. *Assessment in Rehabilitation and Exceptionality, 1,* 40–57.

Heath, S.B. (1982). What no bedtime story means: Narrative skills at home and at school. *Language in Society, 11,* 49–78.

Heath, S.B. (1983). *Ways with words: Language, life and work in communities and classrooms.* New York: Cambridge University Press.

Heath, S.B., Branscombe, A., & Thomas, C. (1986). The book as a narrative prop in language acquisition. In B. Schieffelin & P. Gilmore (Eds.), *The acquisition of literacy: Ethnographic perspectives* (pp. 16–34). Norwood, NJ: Ablex.

Heller, R. (1989). *Many luscious lollipops.* New York: Grosset & Dunlap.

Hill, E. (1981). *Spot's first walk.* New York: G.P. Putnam's Sons.

Hoff-Ginsberg, E. (1991). Mother–child conversation in different social classes and communicative settings. *Child Development, 61,* 782–796.

Juel, C. (1988). Learning to read and write: A longitudinal study of 54 children from first through fourth grades. *Journal of Educational Psychology, 80,* 437–447.

Juel, C. (1996). What makes literacy tutoring effective? *Reading Research Quarterly, 31,* 268–289.

Katims, D. (1991). Emergent literacy in early childhood special education: Curriculum and instruction. *Topics in Early Childhood Special Education, 11,* 69–84.

Katzen, M., & Henderson, A. (1994). *Pretend soup and other real recipes: A cookbook for preschoolers and up.* Berkeley, CA: Tricycle Press.

Kirchner, D.M. (1991). Reciprocal book reading: A discourse based intervention strategy for the child with atypical language development. In T.M. Gallagher (Ed.), *Pragmatics of language: Clinical practice issues* (pp. 307–332). San Diego: Singular.

Lemish, D., & Rice, M.L. (1986). Television as a talking picture book: A prop for language acquisition. *Journal of Child Language, 13,* 251–274.

Lewkowicz, N. (1980). Phonemic awareness training: What to teach and how to teach it. *Journal of Educational Psychology, 72,* 686–700.

Lundberg, I., Frost, J., & Peterson, O. (1988). Effects of an extensive program for stimulating phonological awareness in preschool children. *Reading Research Quarterly, 23,* 263–284.

Maclean, M., Bryant, P., & Bradley, L. (1987). Rhymes, nursery rhymes, and reading in early childhood. *Merrill-Palmer Quarterly, 33,* 255–281.

Mahoney, G., & Powell, A. (1988). Modifying parent–child interaction: Enhancing the development of handicapped children. *Journal of Special Education, 22,* 82–96.

Markman, E. (1987). How children constrain the possible meaning of words. In U. Neisser (Ed.), *Concepts and conceptual development: Ecological factors in categorization* (pp. 255–287). Cambridge, England: Cambridge University Press.

Martin, B. (1970). *Brown bear, brown bear, what do you see?* New York: Holt, Rinehart & Winston.

Martin, B., & Carle, E. (1990). *Polar bear, polar bear, what do you hear?* New York: Holt, Rinehart & Winston.

Maxim, G. (1997). Developmentally appropriate maps skills instruction. *Childhood Education, 73,* 206–211.

McCormick, C.E., Kerr, B.M., Mason, J.M., & Gruendel, E. (1992). Early Start: A literacy-rich prekindergarten program for children academically at risk. *Journal of Early Intervention, 16,* 79–86.

McCormick, C.E., & Mason, J.M. (1986). Intervention procedures for increasing preschool children's interest in and knowledge about reading. In W.H. Teale & E. Sulzby (Eds.), *Emergent literacy: Writing and reading* (pp. 90–115). Norwood, NJ: Ablex.

McLane, J.B., & McNamee, G.D. (1990). *Early literacy.* Cambridge, MA: Harvard University Press.

Meisels, S.J. (1993). Remaking classroom assessment with the work sampling system. *Young Children, 48*(5), 34–40.

Morrow, L.M. (1989). *Literacy development in the early years: Helping children read and write.* Englewood Cliffs, NJ: Prentice-Hall.

Neuman, S.G., & Roskos, S. (1993). *Language and literacy learning in the early years: An integrated approach.* San Diego: Harcourt Brace Jovanovich.

Ninio, A., & Bruner, J. (1978). The achievement and antecedents of labelling. *Journal of Child Language, 7,* 565–573.

Norris, J.A., & Hoffman, P.R. (1990). Language intervention within naturalistic environments. *Language, Speech and Hearing Services in Schools, 21,* 72–84.

Notari-Syverson, A., & Losardo, A. (1996). Assessing children's language in meaningful contexts. In K.N. Cole, P.S. Dale, & D.J. Thal (Eds.), *Communication and language intervention series: Vol. 6. Assessment of communication and language* (pp. 257–279). Baltimore: Paul H. Brookes Publishing Co.

Notari-Syverson, A., O'Connor, R., Jenkins, J., & Drinkwater, S. (1997, March). *Phonological awareness in young children with disabilities: Metacognitive abilities and effects of instruction.* Paper presented at the American Educational Research Association Meeting, Chicago.

Notari-Syverson, A., O'Connor, R., & Vadasy, P. (1996, April). *Facilitating language and literacy development in preschool children: To each according to their needs.* Paper presented at the American Educational Research Association Meeting, New York. (ERIC Document ED 395 692)

O'Connor, R.E., Jenkins, J.R., Slocum, T.A., & Leicester, N. (1993). Teaching phonemic awareness skills to at-risk kindergarten children: The link to reading. *Exceptional Children, 59,* 532–546.

O'Connor, R.E., Notari-Syverson, A., & Vadasy, P. (1996). Ladders to literacy: The effects of teacher-led phonological activities for kindergarten children with and without disabilities. *Exceptional Children, 63,* 117–130.

O'Connor, R.E., Notari-Syverson, A., & Vadasy, P.F. (1998). First grade effects of teacher-led phonological activities in kindergarten for children with mild disabilities: A follow-up study. *Learning Disabilities Research and Practice, 13,* 43–52.

Olswang, L.B., Bain, B.A., & Johnson, G.A. (1992). Using dynamic assessment with children with language disorders. In S. Warren & J. Reichle (Eds.), *Communication and language intervention series: Vol 1. Causes and effects in communication and language intervention* (pp. 187–215). Baltimore: Paul H. Brookes Publishing Co.

Palmer, H. (n.d.). Letter sounds. On *Ideas, thoughts and feelings: Experiences in discovery and independent thinking* [cassette]. Freeport, NY: Educational Activities.

Pellegrini, A.D., Perlmutter, J.C., Galda, L., & Brody, G. (1990). Joint reading between black Head Start children and their mothers. *Child Development, 61,* 443–453.

Peña, E.D. (1996). Dynamic assessment: The model and its language applications. In K.N. Cole, P.S. Dale, & D.J. Thal (Eds.), *Communication and language intervention series: Vol. 6. Assessment of communication and language* (pp. 281–307). Baltimore: Paul H. Brookes Publishing Co.

Piaget, J. (1971). *Science of education and the psychology of the child.* New York: Viking Press.

Pressley, M., Hogan, K., Wharton-McDonald, R., & Mistretta, J. (1996). The challenges of instructional scaffolding: The challenges of instruction that supports student thinking. *Learning Disabilities Research and Practice, 11*(3), 138–146.

Puckett, M.B., & Black, J.K. (1994). *Authentic assessment of the young child.* New York: Macmillan.

Raffi. (1985). Apples and bananas. On *One light, one sun* [cassette]. Camridge, MA: Rounder Records.

Rogoff, B. (1986). Adult assistance of children's learning. In T.E. Raphael (Ed.), *The contexts of school-based literacy* (pp. 27–40). New York: Random House.

Scarborough, H.S., Dobrich, W., & Hager, M. (1991). Preschool literacy experience and later reading achievement. *Journal of Learning Disabilities, 24,* 508–511.

Schickedanz, J.A. (1989). The place of specific skills in preschool and kindergarten. In D.S. Strickland & L.M. Morrow (Eds.), *Emerging literacy: Young children learn to read and write* (pp. 96–106). Newark, DE: International Reading Association.

Share, D.L., Jorm, A.F., Maclean, R., & Matthews, R. (1984). Sources of individual differences in reading acquisition. *Journal of Education Psychology, 76,* 1309–1324.

Slocum, T.A., O'Connor, R.E., & Jenkins, J.R. (1993). Transfer among phonological manipulation skills. *Journal of Educational Psychology, 85,* 618–630.

Smith, B. (1994). *Through writing to read: Classroom strategies for supporting literacy.* New York: Routledge.

Snow, C.E. (1983). Literacy and language: Relationships during the preschool years. *Harvard Educational Review, 53,* 165–189.

Snow, C.E., & Goldfield, B.A. (1983). Turn the page please: Situation-specific language acquisition. *Journal of Child Language, 10,* 551–569.

Snow, C.E., & Ninio, A. (1986). The contracts of literacy: What children learn from learning to read books. In W.H. Teale & E. Sulzby (Eds.), *Emergent literacy: Writing and reading* (pp. 116–138). Norwood, NJ: Ablex.

Snow, C.E., & Weisman, Z. (1996, April). *Grade two reading comprehension: Contributions of home language experiences.* Paper presented at the annual conference of the Society for the Scientific Study of Reading, New York.

Sulzby, E. (1985). Children's emergent reading of favorite storybooks: A developmental study. *Reading Research Quarterly, 20,* 458–481.

Sulzby, E., & Teale, W. (1991). Emergent literacy. In R. Barr, M. Kamil, P. Mosenthal, & D. Pearson (Eds.), *Handbook of reading research* (Vol. 2, pp. 727–757). New York: Longman.

Swinson, J., & Ellis, C. (1988). Telling stories to encourage language. *British Journal of Special Education, 15,* 169–171.

Tannen, D. (1982). The oral/literate continuum in discourse. In D. Tannen (Ed.), *Spoken and written language: Exploring orality and literacy* (pp. 1–16). Norwood, NJ: Ablex.

Teale, W.H. (1984). Reading to young children: Its significance for literacy development. In H. Goelman, A.A. Oberg, & F. Smith (Eds.), *Awakening to literacy* (pp. 110–121). Exeter, NH: Heinemann.

Teale, W.H. (1988). Developmentally appropriate assessment of reading and writing in the early childhood classroom. *The Elementary School Journal, 89*(2), 173–183.

Tharp, R.G., & Gallimore, R. (1988). *Rousing minds to life: Teaching, learning, and schooling in social context.* Cambridge, England: Cambridge University Press.

Torgeson, J., Morgan, S., & Davis C. (1992). Effects of two types of phonological awareness training on word learning in kindergarten children. *Journal of Educational Psychology, 84,* 364–370.

Torgeson, J.K., Wagner, R.K., & Rashotte, C.A. (1994). Longitudinal studies of phonological processing and reading. *Journal of Learning Disabilities, 27,* 276–286.

Treiman, R., & Zukowski, A. (1996). Children's sensitivity to syllables, onsets, rimes, and phonemes. *Journal of Experimental Child Psychology, 61,* 193–215.

Tunmer, W.E., Herriman, M.L., & Nesdale, A.R. (1988). Metalinguistic abilities and beginning reading. *Reading Research Quarterly, 23,* 134–158.

Vandervelden, M.C., & Siegel, L.S. (1995). Phonological recoding and phoneme awareness in early literacy: A developmental approach. *Reading Research Quarterly, 30,* 854–875.

Vellutino, F., & Scanlon, D. (1987). Phonological coding, phonological awareness, and reading ability: Evidence from a longitudinal and experimental study. *Merrill-Palmer Quarterly, 33,* 321–363.

Vygotsky, L. (1978). *Mind in society: The development of higher psychological processes.* Cambridge, MA: Harvard University Press.

Watson, R. (1989). Literate discourse and cognitive organization: Some relations between parents' talk and 3-year-olds' thought. *Applied Psycholinguistics, 10,* 221–236.

Weinstein, C.S. (1987). Designing preschool classrooms to support development: Research and reflection. In C.S. Weinstein & T.G. David (Eds.), *Spaces for children: The build environment and child development* (pp. 159–185). New York: Plenum.

Wells, G. (1985). Preschool literacy-related activities and success in school. In D.R. Olson, N. Torrance, & A. Hildyard (Eds.), *Literacy, language and learning* (pp. 229–255). Cambridge, England: Cambridge University Press.

Wells, G. (1990). Talk about text: Where literacy is learned and taught. *Curriculum Inquiry, 20,* 369–405.

Wertsch, J.V. (1985). Adult–child interaction as a source of self-regulation in children. In S.R. Yussen (Ed.), *The growth of reflecting in children* (pp. 69–97). New York: Academic Press.

Whitehurst, G., Epstein, J.N., Angell, A.L., Payne, A.C., Crone, D.A., & Fischel, J.E. (1994). Outcomes of an emergent literacy intervention in Head Start. *Journal of Educational Psychology, 86*(4), 542–555.

Whitehurst, G.H., Falco, F.L., Lonigan, C.J., Fischel, J.E., Debaryshe, B.D., Valdez-Menchaca, M.C., & Caulfield, M. (1988). Accelerating language development through picture book reading. *Developmental Psychology, 24,* 552–559.

Wood, D., Bruner, J.S., & Ross, G. (1976). The role of tutoring in problem-solving. *Journal of Child Psychology and Psychiatry, 17,* 89–100.

Yopp, H. (1988). The validity and reliability of phonemic awareness tests. *Reading Research Quarterly, 23,* 159–177.

Yopp, H. (1992). Developing phonemic awareness in young children. *The Reading Teacher, 45*(9), 696–703.

Appendix A

Ladders to Literacy
Preschool Checklist

The *Ladders to Literacy* Preschool Checklist is a curriculum-based assessment tool designed to assess the early literacy development of young children during daily classroom activities. It provides teachers with a systematic and easy-to-use format to observe and compare children's progress over multiple points in time. Because the items in the checklist correspond to the goals suggested in the curriculum activities, the assessment provides a basis for formulating developmentally appropriate educational goals for young children with disabilities. The skills and behaviors included in the checklist cover a broad range of abilities typical for children 3–6 years of age. In order to provide useful information about preschool children with significant delays, items that refer to skills typical of younger children have also been included. The selection of skills and behaviors was based on an extensive review of the current literature on early literacy and language development. The checklist was reviewed by experts and was pilot-tested by early childhood and early childhood special education teachers.

The purpose of the checklist is to monitor the individual child's learning on an ongoing basis, not to determine the child's status with respect to developmental norms. Data collected during pilot-testing, however, suggest that many children have mastered the skills and the behaviors covered in the checklist by the time they enter kindergarten.

The main characteristics of the checklist are the following:

1. Play based—Skills are elicited during play activities with miniature toys, looking at storybooks, and drawing pictures.
2. Flexible—The assessment process can be adapted to the characteristics of the individual child; activities and materials can be adapted to different situations and needs.

3. Educationally relevant—Skills are developmentally sequenced within content areas and constitute meaningful and functional behaviors that can be incorporated in educational goals.
4. Comprehensive—The content covers early literacy development across three major areas: print/book awareness, metalinguistic awareness, and oral language.

ADMINISTRATION PROCEDURES AND PROTOCOL

The *Ladders to Literacy* Preschool Checklist should be administered in the context of play and daily routine activities with the child in a familiar environment. Whenever possible, allow the child to show behaviors spontaneously or within interactive play and conversation. Behaviors should be elicited, only if necessary, through direct questioning or visual cues. Throughout the testing, vary materials, order of presentation, and types of elicitation strategies in response to the child's behaviors. If the child shows no evidence of being able to perform a task consistently and independently, then the tester can provide cues and prompts (e.g., modeling) to gain information about the child's responsiveness to instruction and the kinds of adult support or scaffolding strategies that are the most helpful in assisting the child to master a skill. You can collect information by observing and testing children during general classroom activities. At times, however, it may be more economical to plan activities that will specifically elicit the behaviors that need to be observed. A description of three activities that together offer opportunities to elicit all of the items in the checklist is provided.

Suggested Protocol

Assemble a variety of toys and materials to stimulate literacy and language behaviors, such as small animal and human figures, vehicles, blocks, books, paper, and crayons. Keep these materials in a box or a bag near the play area where you can set out one or two or a few in a small grouping, as needed, while conducting the assessment. Familiarize yourself with the three areas to be assessed by reading through the definitions and indicators. Although the ordering of play events will follow the child's direction (spending more or less time with particular props that stimulate and maintain the child's interest), it is important to provide settings and scenarios in which the child can demonstrate the behaviors and knowledge of concern. You may wish to videotape assessments initially in order to focus on eliciting behaviors rather than on scoring them. With videotaped sessions, you will be able to score behaviors more critically, recognize at which points you might improve the presentation to engage children more actively, or identify instances in which you might scaffold tasks dynamically to find the most useful instructional strategies to share with other teachers and parents.

You may refer to videotaped sessions from early and later in a school year when discussing a child's literacy and language development with his or her parents.

We have found the following three scenarios particularly helpful:

1. Play with figures and blocks.

    Materials: Animal and human figures; car; blocks

    Begin by pulling the figures out of a box or a bag, one at a time. Ask the child to name the animal. If there is no response, then encourage identification and naming ["Where's the bear? Would you like to hold him? Say 'bear'"]. Encourage conversation and make-believe play by gradually introducing more animals and figures. Possible conversation starters include the following: ["My name is (blank). What's your name?" "This bear's name is Bob Bear. Who is this? He has soft fur" (stroke fur). Do you want to touch his fur? How does that feel? Which color is Bob Bear?"]. If the child does not readily engage in make-believe play, then begin the play yourself ["This bear needs a place to live. Shall we build him a house?"]. *Try to elicit* symbolic representation (play), vocabulary, narrations of events, and literate discourse skills.

    You can talk about the child's toys or clothing or ask the child to name things and teachers in the room. You can also ask the child to talk about events that happened at home or in other settings ["Did you have breakfast this morning? What did you eat?"]. *Try to elicit* vocabulary, narrations of events, and literate discourse skills.

    Figures and blocks can also be used to elicit metalinguistic knowledge, such as repetition of words and sounds ["This bear likes to say everything I say. You be the bear. GRRRR" (Child repeats "GRRRR")]. Try words, phrases, short sentences, and longer ones if the child succeeds at easier levels. Encourage the child to repeat individual sounds (/m/) and series of two, then three individual sounds (/m/-/a/) with short pauses between them. We have used the Magic Password activity with animal figures to elicit rhyming and phonological awareness:

    ["Let's build a house with these blocks." (Build a low rectangular wall with the child, and place an animal figure inside.) "The house has a special door that will open only if you say the magic password. The dog wants to go out and play. Let's help him find the magic word"].

    - Rhyming: ["The magic password rhymes with mat"] (or house, sand, kitten, tree)
    - Blending: ["The magic password is base-ball"] (or o-pen; m-an; d-o-g)

- Segmenting: ["The magic password is the first sound in fff-fat"] (or ssssnake, pickle)

   Try to elicit perception and memory for sounds, word awareness, and phonological skills

2. Play with books.

   Materials: Storybook

   Show the child any simple storybook with a variety of pictures, or use the child's book. Encourage the child to identify pictures, to name objects, to tell about the pictures, or to retell the story. Hand the book to the child to explore orientation, page turning, and awareness of words on the page.
   Try to elicit symbolic representation (pictures), book conventions, awareness of graphic symbols, word awareness, phonological skills, narrative skills, and literate discourse.
   Refer to repeating words or letters in the text to encourage the child to identify a specific word ["Can you find tiger on this page?"] and letter knowledge ["Here's tiger. It starts with t. Can you find another t? What sound does t make?"]. *Try to elicit* awareness of graphic symbols, letter identification, and letter–sound correspondence; and perception and memory for sounds and word awareness
   After reading the story, ask the child to relate elements of story structure and encourage decontextualization ["Who is this about? How did he get into trouble? Can you think of another way to solve the problem? Did this really happen?"]. *Try to elicit* narrative skills and literate discourse.

3. Play with paper and crayons.

   Materials: Paper; crayons

   Ask the child to draw a picture and tell you about it. Print the child's name while the child watches ["What does this say? Yes, that's your name. Which letter is this?"]. (Point to letters in name.) Use the child's name to elicit more knowledge about individual letters and their function ["What are the letters in your name? Which sound does this one make? I know a song about letters: a b c d e f g . . ."]. (Encourage the child to sing it with you.) Explore writing with the child. (Give a pencil to the child.) ["Can you write your name? Here's O"]. (Draw an "O.") ["Can you draw an O? Do you know other letters?"]. (If child tries to copy, then write t, s, m, and other common letters, and encourage scribbles or letters.) *Try to elicit* symbolic representation: graphics; writing; letter–sound correspondence; phonological skills; narrative skills; literate discourse.

Drawing can also elicit information about rhymes. (Draw a star.) ["Here's a star. I know a rhyme about a star"]. Encourage the child to recite "Twinkle, Twinkle, Little Star" and other rhymes, and provide motivation for invented spelling ["Let's label your picture. What shall we write?"]. *Try to elicit* knowledge of rhymes; perception and memory for sounds and words; and writing.

Scoring—Points

2: Child consistently and independently performs the entire task.
1: Child performs part of task or performs task inconsistently.
0: No evidence that child can perform the task.

The following notes (to be indicated in parentheses next to score) allow teachers to record additional information about the testing and the child's performance:

A: Most tasks are organized according to a developmental sequence or in order of increasing difficulty. If a child performs a higher level task, then it is not necessary to directly test less complex tasks. In this case, give the child a score of 2 for the task and indicate an A for Assumed.

NO: Use NO for No Opportunity if it is not possible to present a specific task to the child.

R: If necessary, ask parents or teachers for information about tasks that were not tested and indicate R for Reported.

H: Indicate H if the child performed the task with adult assistance (with help). (See notes under comments and most helpful supports.)

M: Modification for specific disabilities. In some cases it will be necessary to modify the administration of an item (e.g., use of sign language with a child with a hearing impairment; of large, brightly colored objects for a child with a visual impairment). Indicate M next to appropriate score. If useful, note the specific type of modification.

Comments and Most Helpful Supports

A space is provided for the tester to note useful observations that may help better understand the child's performance as well as provide suggestions for appropriate educational approaches. If the child shows no evidence of being able to perform a task consistently and independently, then the tester can provide supports and prompts (e.g., questioning, modeling) to gain information about the child's responsiveness to instruction. Supports will vary for an individual child and the nature of the tasks. Possibilities include repeating words at a slower pace; modeling; and providing verbal, visual, and physical cues. For some items, specific strategies are indicated under the heading "Supports." A comprehensive list of instructional strategies is provided in Chapter 2 (scaffolding strategies).

I. SYMBOLIC REPRESENTATION

Play

A. Child uses symbols in play.
Task definition/examples: Engage in play with miniature toys, and observe whether the child uses objects to represent other objects or mimes pretend actions and objects.

Scoring:

2: Child consistently uses a variety of symbols and sequences of multiple symbolic acts with objects in play.
1: Child uses simple symbolic acts with objects.
0: No evidence of symbolic play.

Pictures

B. Child identifies objects, people, and actions represented in pictures.
Task definition/examples: Look at books, pictures, and photographs; and observe whether the child names or points to objects, people, and actions illustrated in the pictures.

Scoring:

2: Child consistently identifies a variety of objects, people, and actions.
1: Child identifies two to three objects, people, and actions.
0: No evidence the child can perform the task.

Graphics

C. Child scribbles.
Task definition/examples: Give the child crayons and paper and encourage the child to draw.

Scoring:

2: Child draws lines and circles and fills most of the page.
1: Child makes two to three marks on paper.
0: No evidence the child can perform the task.

D. Child names figures after execution.
Task definition/examples: Ask the child to draw a figure, and observe whether the child says what the drawing represents. If not, then ask the child directly.

Scoring:

2: Child spontaneously says what the drawing represents.
1: Child names figure following adult's request.
0: No evidence the child can perform the task.

E. Child draws recognizable figures.
Task definition/examples: Ask the child to draw a figure, and evaluate whether the drawing is recognizable. If not, then ask the child directly.

Scoring:

2: Child's drawing is recognizable without need for explanations.
1: Child's drawing is recognizable after the child gives some explanation.
0: No evidence the child can perform the task.

II. PRINT

Book Conventions

A. Child turns pages.
Task definition/examples: Look at a picture book with the child, and observe how the child handles the book. If necessary, ask the child to open the book and turn the pages.

Scoring:

2: Child turns most pages.
1: Child turns two to three pages.
0: No evidence the child can perform the task.

B. Child orients book correctly and knows where book begins and ends.
Task definition/examples: Look at a picture book with the child, and observe whether the child places the book upright, starts with the front page, and finishes with the last page. If necessary, ask the child to show the front and last pages.

Scoring:

2: Child orients the book correctly and shows front and last pages.
1: Child orients the book correctly *or* shows front and/or last page.
0: No evidence the child can perform the task.

C. Child knows that print, not pictures, tells the story.

Task definition/examples: Look at a picture book with the child, and observe whether the child demonstrates interest in the print (e.g., asks what the words say, points to words while telling the story). If necessary, ask the child what in the book tells the story.

Scoring:

2:   Child asks about meaning of print *or* points to words.
1:   Child focuses on print as well as pictures but does not demonstrate understanding that print has meaning.
0:   No evidence the child can perform the task.

D.   Child knows that text begins at top left corner of page and reads from left to right.
Task definition/examples: Look at a picture book with the child, and ask the child to show where the text begins and the direction in which to read.

Scoring:

2:   Child points to top left corner of page when asked ["Show me where to start reading"] and indicates correct direction in response to ["Which way do I go?"].
1:   Child points to top left corner of page when asked ["Show me where to start reading"] or indicates correct direction in response to ["Which way do I go?"].
0:   No evidence the child can perform the task.

Awareness of Graphic Symbols

E.   Child reads environmental print (e.g., logos, road signs, cereal boxes).
Task definition/examples: Have available pictures with common signs or boxes (e.g., cereal, toothpaste, McDonald's products) with logos, and observe whether the child recognizes the logos. If necessary, ask the child directly.

Scoring:

2:   Child recognizes a variety of signs.
1:   Child recognizes one or two signs.
0:   No evidence the child can perform the task.

F.   Child recognizes a few memorized words in print (e.g., name).
Task definition/examples: Print familiar words or show the child simple print in a picture book, and observe whether the child recognizes a few words (e.g., mom, love, dog, names of siblings or classmates).

Scoring:

2: Child recognizes more than one word in addition to name.
1: Child recognizes name.
0: No evidence the child can perform the task.

G. Child identifies a printed word.
Task definition/examples: Show the child a written text, and ask the child to point to or circle a word. For example, tell the child ["I'd like to read you a word. Show a word for me to read to you"]. The purpose of this task is not for the child to read words but for you to assess the child's understanding of the concept of a word.

Scoring:

2: Child points to a word by beginning with the first letter and indicating the entire length of the word in a left-to-right direction.
1: Child places finger on part of a word.
0: No evidence the child can perform the task.

H. Child reads simple words.
Task definition/examples: While looking at books or writing, observe whether the child can read novel words by sounding out letters.

Scoring:

2: Child reads more than one unfamiliar word.
1: Child reads one unfamiliar word or parts of unfamiliar words.
0: No evidence the child can perform the task.

Letter Identification

I. Child recites part of alphabet.
Task definition/examples: While looking at books or writing, ask whether the child can say the alphabet or the names of some letters.

Scoring:

2: Child recites at least 10 letters.
1: Child recites one or two letters.
0: No evidence the child can perform the task.

Supports:

Sing the alphabet song. Can the child sing the song with you? Can the child sing it independently?

J. Child names single letters.

Task definition/examples: While looking at books or writing, point to common letters and ask the child to name the letters. Begin with most common letters (e.g., s, t, m, a) and the first letter in the child's name.

Scoring:

2: Child names at least 10 letters.
1: Child names one or two letters.
0: No evidence the child can perform the task.

Writing

K. Child copies shapes.
Task definition/examples: Draw a vertical and horizontal line, a cross, a circle, and a square; and ask the child to copy them. Draw the shapes one at a time, and have the child copy before drawing the next shape.

Scoring:

2: Child reproduces all shapes in a manner that makes them recognizable (e.g., straight-sided figures [squares] are clearly distinguished from curves [circles]).
1: Child reproduces drawings that distinguish between open and closed figures (e.g., a line and a cross are differentiated from a circle, but a square and a circle may be similar).
0: No evidence the child can perform the task.

L. Child copies letters.
Task definition/examples: Print letters, and ask the child to copy them. Print the letters one at a time, and have the child copy before printing the next letter.

Scoring:

2: Child's reproduction is recognizable.
1: Child's reproduction approximates model.
0: No evidence the child can perform the task.

M. Child copies a few words (e.g., name).
Task definition/examples: Print or show words in a book, and ask the child to copy them.

Scoring:

2: Child copies all letters in correct sequence.
1: Child copies some letters.
0: No evidence the child can perform the task.

N: Child pretends to write.
Task definition/examples: Give the child paper and crayons, and ask the child to write a message or a letter.

Observe whether the child intends the scribbles as writing.

Scoring:

2: Child scribbles lines or letter-like forms and verbalizes a message.
1: Child scribbles lines or letter-like forms but does not verbalize a message.
0: No evidence the child can perform the task.

O. Child writes name independently.
Task definition/examples: Ask the child to write his or her name (e.g., on his or her drawing of a figure).

Scoring:

2: Child writes name correctly.
1: Child writes name partially or with incorrect spelling.
0: No evidence the child can perform the task.

P. Child writes a few familiar letters and words.
Task definition/examples: Ask the child to write some letters and words (e.g., about his or her drawing of a figure).

Scoring:

2: Child writes at least 10 letters and at least three familiar words correctly in addition to his or her name or uses invented spelling with letters that relate to sound.
1: Child writes two or three letters and one familiar word in addition to his or her name.
0: No evidence the child can perform the task.

Q. Child uses invented spelling (related letters) to write messages.
Task definition/examples: Ask the child to write a message or a story (e.g., about his or her drawing of a figure). Observe whether the child creates his or her own spelling for new words. In invented spelling, words may not be properly spaced, and one letter may represent an entire syllable (e.g., krs for cross).

Scoring:

2: Child writes a sequence of related words independently using invented spelling with letters that relate to sound.
1: Child writes familiar letters independently in long strings or in random order.
0: No evidence the child can perform the task.

III. LETTER–SOUND CORRESPONDENCE

Single Sounds and Letters

A. Child says most common sound for all letters.
Task definition/examples: While looking at books or writing, ask the child to say the sound for individual letters.

Scoring:

2: Child says sounds for at least 10 letters in addition to s, t, m, b, and a.
1: Child says sound for high-frequency letters: s, t, m, b, and a.
0: No evidence the child can perform the task.

B. Child selects a letter to represent a sound.
Task definition/examples: While looking at books or writing, say individual sounds and ask the child to point to or write the corresponding letter.

Scoring:

2: Child selects letters for at least six sounds.
1: Child selects letters for one or two sounds.
0: No evidence the child can perform the task.

Words

C. Child uses letter sounds to write words.
Task definition/examples: Ask the child to write a word (e.g., about his or her drawing of a figure), and observe whether the child says the sound before writing the corresponding letter.

Scoring:

2: Child writes at least one word independently using letter sounds to write words (e.g., word is phonetically correct, kat for cat).
1: Child writes two letters to form a word using letter sounds.
0: No evidence the child can perform the task.

METALINGUISTIC AWARENESS

I. PERCEPTION AND MEMORY FOR SOUNDS

Environmental Sounds

A. Child uses sounds to represent objects and animals.
Task definition/examples: Play with miniature toys or look at picture books, and encourage the child to say animal sounds (e.g., grrr, meow) or make sounds of objects (e.g., brrrr for a car).

Scoring:

2: Child uses sounds to represent several animals and objects.
1: Child uses one sound to represent an animal or an object.
0: No evidence the child can perform the skill.

B. Child identifies the source of sounds.
Task definition/examples: Play with toy animals, objects that make noise, or musical instruments. Make sounds, and ask the child to identify which object produced the sound.

Scoring:

2: Child identifies source of at least three different sounds.
1: Child identifies source of one sound.
0: No evidence child can perform the skill.

Words

C. Child repeats short words.
Task definition/examples: While participating in activities with the child (e.g., pretend play, drawing, looking at books), say a short (one-syllable) word and ask the child to repeat it (e.g., bear).

Scoring:

2: Child consistently repeats words that closely resemble those modeled.
1: Child repeats at least one word modeled or attempts many words with low or inconsistent accuracy.
0: No evidence child can perform the skill.

D. Child repeats multisyllabic words.
Task definition/examples: While participating in activities with the child (e.g., pretend play, drawing, looking at books), say a word with two, three, or four syllables

(e.g., tiger, elephant, artichoke, rhinoceros), and ask the child to repeat it.

Scoring:

2: Child consistently repeats words that closely resemble those modeled.
1: Child repeats at least one word modeled, or child attempts many words with low or inconsistent accuracy.
0: No evidence child can perform the skill.

Phrases

E. Child repeats phrases (e.g., repetitive lines in familiar songs, nursery rhymes, stories).
    Task definition/examples: While participating in activities (e.g., pretend play, drawing, looking at books, singing songs, reciting rhymes) with the child, ask the child to repeat phrases (at least two-word utterances) and repetitive lines from songs and texts (e.g., *The Three Little Pigs* [Galdone, 1970], *The Gingerbread Man* [Arno, 1970]).

Scoring:

2: Child consistently repeats phrases understandably.
1: Child repeats phrases in at least one instance, but not consistently, or child attempts two words with low or inconsistent accuracy.
0: No evidence child can perform the skill.

Phonemes

F. Child repeats single phonemes after a short delay (1–2 seconds).
    Task definition/examples: While participating in activities with the child (e.g., pretend play, drawing, looking at books), say an isolated phoneme (the sound made by a single letter or letters pronounced as single units, such as /t/, /k/, /m/, and /a/). Ask the child to repeat the sound after a 1-second pause. You may have to use a physical prompt throughout this series of tasks to help the child wait 1 second before responding (e.g., holding a hand up in a stop position, pointing to yourself and the child as a *my turn, your turn* signal) ["Let's play copycat. First, I'll say a sound, then you say the same sound after me." (Point to yourself.) "/M/." (Point to child.) "Now it's your turn"].

Scoring:

2: Child consistently repeats sounds that closely resemble those modeled.

1: Child repeats at least one sound modeled, or child attempts many sounds with low or inconsistent accuracy.

0: No evidence child can perform the skill.

G. Child repeats two to three phonemes after a short delay (1–2 seconds).

Task definition/examples: While participating in activities with the child (e.g., pretend play, drawing, looking at books), say a series of two or three isolated phonemes (e.g., /m/ /a/, /s/ /p/ /i/). Ask the child to repeat the sounds after a 1-second pause. Make the task into a game ["Let's play copycat. First I'll say some sounds, then you say the same sounds after me." (Point to self.) "/M/ /a/." (Point to the child.)].

Scoring:

2: Child consistently repeats sounds that closely resemble those modeled by the teacher.

1: Child repeats at least one set of sounds modeled by the teacher, or child attempts many sets with low or inconsistent accuracy.

0: No evidence child can perform the task.

H. Child discriminates between two phonemes (same/different).

Task definition/examples: While participating in activities with the child (e.g., pretend play, drawing, looking at books), say two phonemes in isolation (/m/ /m/; /m/ /p/), and ask the child to tell whether the sounds were the same or different. If the child has difficulty with the concept of different, then ask ["Are these the same?"]. The child can respond by saying "yes" or "no" or by nodding and head shaking.

Scoring:

2: The child consistently responds correctly by using the words (same/different) or by consistently indicating when pairs of sounds are the same.

1: The child responds correctly more than 50% of the time.

0: No evidence child can perform the task. Watch out for children who always respond yes or always respond no (score all yes/all no responses to varied pairs as 0).

II. WORD AWARENESS

Words

A. Child identifies a word from a spoken sentence.
Task definition/examples: While participating in activities (e.g., pretend play, drawing, looking at books) with the child, say a sentence (e.g., "The rabbit eats carrots"), and ask the child to tell you a word from the sentence.

Scoring:

2: The child identifies several words (e.g., rabbit, bites, eats).
1: The child identifies one word.
0: No evidence child can perform the task.

B. Child identifies the longer word of two spoken words.
Task definition/examples: While participating in activities with the child (e.g., pretend play, drawing, looking at books), say words of different length (e.g., baseball and cat), and ask the child to tell you which is the longer word.

Scoring:

2: Child consistently identifies the longer word.
1: Child identifies the longer word once.
0: No evidence child can perform the task.

C. Child plays with the pronunciation of a word.
Task definition/examples: Sing songs or play name games, and have the child modify words. For example, have the child say "apple" with an /o/ or say child's first name beginning with a different letter (e.g., Betty: Netty, Jetty, Detty).

Scoring:

2: The child consistently modifies new words according to request.
1: The child repeats a few familiar modified words (e.g., lyrics in songs created in class).
0: No evidence the child can perform the task.

III. PHONOLOGICAL SKILLS

Rhyming

A. Child says common rhymes along with teacher or peers.
Task definition/examples: Say common nursery rhymes, and observe whether the child repeats the words along with you. These rhymes may include hand motions,

tunes ("Baa, Baa, Black Sheep"), or both ("The Itsy Bitsy Spider," "I'm a Little Teapot").

Scoring:

2: Child says all words and attempts hand motions, if used.
1: Child attempts part of the rhyme; says some phrases along with the teacher.
0: No evidence child can perform the task; child does only the motions but does not say the words of the rhyme.

B. Child fills in last word in rhyme.
Task definition/examples: Recite rhymes the child is familiar with, and have the child fill in the last word of the rhyme lines ["Humpty Dumpty sat on a (blank)" (wall)].

Scoring:

2: Child fills in several lines of rhyme.
1: Child fills in one line of rhyme.
0: No evidence child can perform the task.

C. Child says common rhymes independently.
Task definition/examples: Same as IIIB, but have the child say a rhyme alone, without assistance.

Scoring:

2: Child says the whole rhyme understandably without assistance (also give 2 points if specific word errors are minimal and do not affect the rhyme or flow of the tale).
1: Child says some words or phrases in a rhyme independently but requires prompting to start or continue.
0: No evidence child can perform the task.

D. Child recognizes that pairs of words do or do not rhyme.
Task definition/examples: Say two words in isolation ["Listen to these words. Do they rhyme? Heart, smart" "Do these words rhyme? Cat, meow"], and ask the child to tell whether they rhyme.

Scoring:

2: The child consistently judges rhymes correctly.
1: The child judges more than half of the items correctly.
0: No evidence child can perform the task. Watch out for children who always respond yes or always re-

spond no (score all yes/all no responses to varied pairs as 0).

E. Child says a rhyming word for a target word.
    Task definition/examples: While participating in activities with the child (e.g., pretend play, drawing, looking at books), say a word, and ask the child to say a word (or rhyming nonword) that rhymes with it ["Rhyme with dime"].

Scoring:

2: The child consistently produces a rhyming word or nonword.
1: The child produces a rhyme to one target word.
0: No evidence child can perform the task; child repeats the target word, but does not produce a rhyming word.

Alliteration

F. Child recognizes words that start with the same sound.
    Task definition/examples: While participating in activities (e.g., looking at an alphabet book), say words that share a common initial sound and words that do not, and ask the child to say whether they start with the same sound ["Apple and ant. Do they start with the same sound?"].

Scoring:

2: Child recognizes words consistently.
1: Child recognizes one or two pairs of words correctly.
0: No evidence the child can perform the task. Watch out for children who always respond yes or always respond no (score all yes/all no responses to varied pairs as 0).

G. Child says word that starts with the same sound.
    Task definition/examples: While participating in activities (e.g., looking at an alphabet book), ask the child to say a word that shares a common initial sound with the target word ["Man. Tell me a word that starts with the same sound as man"].

Scoring:

2: Child consistently gives words with common initial sounds to several target words.
1: Child gives word with common initial sound to one target word.
0: No evidence the child can perform the task.

Blending

H. Child blends syllables into words.
Task definition/examples: While participating in activities with the child (e.g., pretend play, drawing, looking at books), say real words in separated syllables (e.g., el-e-phant; tur-tle; tel-e-phone), and ask the child to guess the word.

Scoring:

2: Child consistently blends the syllables into the correct word.
1: Child responds correctly to at least one item or blends some of the syllables in a longer word but does not say the entire word (e.g., child says either tele or vision, after the teacher says tel-e-vi-sion).
0: No evidence child can perform the task. Score as 0 if the child repeats the word in segmented syllables as pronounced by the examiner.

I. Child blends words with sounds pronounced in onset-rime format (e.g., m-ake).
Task definition/examples: While participating in activities with the child, say a word in onset-rime fashion, and have the child pronounce the word normally ["Guess this word: M-ike"].

Scoring:

2: The child consistently blends words correctly and pronounces them without distortion. If the child repeats a word in an onset-rime fashion but then says it correctly with the prompt ["What word?"], award the full 2 points ["Guess this word. M-ike." (Child replies "M-ike.") "What word?" (Child replies "Mike.")].
1: The child blends words pronounced in a stretched fashion (e.g., Mmmike, Sssam).
0: No evidence child can perform the task; child repeats the word in an onset-rime format without pronouncing it normally.

Supports:

Ask the child to repeat a word, then add ["Say it fast!"]. If the child does not respond, then ask the child to say it again, and ask ["What word is that?"]. Say words that begin with a continuous sound (e.g., vowels, f, l, m, n, r, s, v, z) in a stretched fashion.

J. Child blends three to four phonemes into words (e.g., s-a-t; m-a-n).

Task definition/examples: While participating in activities (e.g., pretend play, drawing, looking at books) with the child, say a word in isolated phonemes ["S-a-t"; "m-a-n"], and have the child pronounce the word normally ["Guess this word. F-o-g"].

Scoring:

2: The child consistently blends words correctly and pronounces them without distortion. If the child at first mimics the examiner but then says it correctly with the prompt ["What word?"], award the full 2 points.
1: The child blends a few words correctly.
0: No evidence child can perform the task; child repeats the segmented word without pronouncing it normally.

Segmentation

K. Child segments words into syllables (e.g., clapping or saying words in syllables).
Task definition/examples: While participating in activities with the child (e.g., pretend play, drawing, looking at books), say words with two to five syllables (e.g., lion, albatross, television), and encourage the child to say the word divided into syllables.

Scoring:

2: After a few examples, the child consistently says words independently in rhythm with the correct number of syllables. The child can but need not accompany the responses with physical motions. The child's response is correct if it contains the correct number of syllables as the word is commonly spoken, even if the child divides the word slightly differently from the syllable divisions used in spelling (e.g., instead of na-tion, the child says /nash-un/).
1: The child consistently and correctly says words in syllables *along with* the teacher but does not do it independently, or child segments a few familiar words (e.g., name).
0: No evidence child can perform the task; child does task only with direct assistance, such as the examiner's holding the child's hands and physically assisting the clapping prompt.

Supports:

Many children find this task easier if they are also taught to clap, tap, or stomp the word in syllables ["Let's clap turtle." (Lead the children for several examples.) "Tur" (clap) "tle" (clap)]. Assist the child physically (as in 0 above), then ask the child to segment the same words without assistance.

L. Child identifies first sound in words.
    Task definition/examples: While participating in activities with the child (e.g., pretend play, drawing, looking at books), say isolated words in a normal tone of voice, and ask the child to say the first sound in each word ["What's the first sound in tip?"].

    Scoring:

    2: The child consistently says the correct first sound of words. Two points are awarded whether the child stretches (e.g., /mmm/) or iterates (e.g., t-t-t) the first sound or says the sound conventionally, provided the sound is isolated from the rest of the word.
    1: The child says the correct response when the examiner repeats the word and stretches the first sound (e.g., sssnake, fffat, Mmmike).
    0: No evidence child can perform the task; the child repeats the word as pronounced by the teacher.

M. Child separates words into onset-rime.
    Task definition/examples: Onset (composed of initial consonant or consonant cluster) and rime (referring to the vowel and remaining consonants), for example b-at, is an instructional compromise between the whole word and the phoneme, which may be too difficult for some children. While participating in activities (e.g., pretend play, drawing, looking at books) with the child, say an isolated word, and ask the child to segment the word in an onset-rime fashion (e.g., B-ob; c-at).

    Scoring:

    2: The child segments all items correctly into onset-rime. Award 2 points also if the child correctly segments the words into all constituent phonemes (correct responses: b-at or b-a-t), as saying all phonemes represents a higher level of phoneme knowledge than the onset-rime task requires.
    1: The child segments at least one example independently.
    0: No evidence child can perform the task.

    Supports:

    This task is best taught through modeling with examples. Children may benefit initially from a physical prompt, such as moving the head from side to side as the word is divided, or using visual and physical cues (e.g., two paper squares [one representing onset and the other representing rime] that can be separated or joined as the word is segmented or blended).

N. Child segments one-syllable words into three to four phonemes.
    Task definition/examples: While participating in activities with the child, say words with three to four phonemes (e.g., cat, lake, tops, best, stop), and ask the child to segment the word into separate phonemes (e.g., c-a-t; l-a-ke; t-o-p-s; b-e-s-t; s-t-o-p).

Scoring:

2: The child segments all items correctly into all constituent phonemes.
1: The child segments at least one example independently.
0: No evidence child can perform the task; child repeats segmented words.

Supports:

See supports for onset-rime in Segmentation: M, but use three to four squares joined to represent the word.

ORAL LANGUAGE

I. VOCABULARY

Words and Sentences

A. Child uses one-word utterances to label a variety of objects, people, and events.
Task definition/examples: While participating in activities (e.g., games, drawing, looking at books) with the child, observe whether the child labels objects, people, and events.

Scoring:

2: Child uses more than 50 different words.
1: Child uses at least three different words.
0: No evidence the child can perform the task.

B. Child uses two-word utterances to express a variety of semantic intentions (meanings) (e.g., agent-object, agent-action, action-object, existence, location, possession, negation, recurrence, attribution).
Task definition/examples: While participating in activities with the child, observe whether the child uses two-word utterances to express a variety of semantic intentions or meanings.

Scoring:

2: Child uses two-word utterances to express at least five different semantic intentions.
1: Child uses two-word utterances to express at least two different semantic intentions.
0: No evidence the child can perform the task.

C. Child uses a variety of adult-form sentences (e.g., declaratives, interrogatives, negatives).
Task definition/examples: While participating in activities (e.g., games, drawing, looking at books) with the child, observe whether the child uses a variety of adult-form sentences.

Scoring:

2: Child uses at least three different types of adult-form sentences correctly.
1: Child uses at least two different types of sentences that approximate adult-form.
0: No evidence the child can perform the task.

II. NARRATIVE SKILLS

Narrations of real events

A. Child relates events with a beginning, a middle, and an end.

Task definition/examples: Ask the child to tell you about a former event ["What did you do this morning?"], and observe whether the child relates a sequence of events organized as a beginning, a middle, and an end.

Scoring:

2: Child relates all three points of an action (beginning, middle, and end).
1: Child relates one or two parts of an action.
0: No evidence the child can perform the task.

B. Child describes explicit causal and temporal sequences among events (uses: because, before, after).

Task definition/examples: Ask the child to tell you about a former event ["What did you do last weekend?"], and observe whether the child relates a sequence of events and makes explicit causal (e.g., because) and temporal (e.g., yesterday, first, then, later, before, after) relations between actions.

Scoring:

2: Child relates at least three actions in a sequence, using appropriate causal and temporal clauses.
1: Child relates at least three actions in a sequence, using simple, repetitive causal and temporal clauses (because . . . , because . . . ; and then . . . , and then . . .).
0: No evidence the child can perform the task.

Book

C. Child attends to and labels pictures in book.

Task definition/examples: Look at picture storybooks with the child, and observe whether the child looks at the pictures and points to and labels objects represented in the pictures.

Scoring:

2: Child points to or labels pictures.
1: Child looks at pictures.
0: No evidence the child can perform the task.

D. Child makes comments and asks questions about individual pictures.

Task definition/examples: Look at picture storybooks with the child, and observe whether the child comments about objects, people, or actions represented in the pictures.

Scoring:

2: Child says at least a short sentence about objects, people, or actions in pictures.
1: Child verbalizes information other than labels about objects, people, or actions in pictures.
0: No evidence the child can perform the task.

E. Child tells story and links events based on pictures, using conversational language.
Task definition/examples: Look at picture storybooks with the child and observe whether the child relates a story based on the pictures and identifies main characters and events.

Scoring:

2: Child identifies characters and relates a sequence of events that link the actions represented in the pictures and convey the gist of the story.
1: Child identifies one character and relates a sequence of events that link at least two actions represented in the pictures.
0: No evidence the child can perform the task.

F. Child forms written story based on pictures using reading intonation and wording.
Task definition/examples: Look at picture storybooks with the child, and observe whether the child uses reading intonation and wording when relating a story based on the pictures.

Scoring:

2: Child uses reading intonation and wording when relating a sequence of events that link the actions represented in the pictures and convey the gist of the story.
1: Child uses reading intonation and wording when relating a sequence of events that link at least two actions presented in the pictures.
0: No evidence the child can perform the task.

Narrations of Fictional Story

G. Child attends to story.
Task definition/examples: Read or tell the child a short story (e.g., about his or her drawing or toy animals) with a setting, a theme, episodes, and a resolution.

Scoring:

2: Child attends to the entire story.
1: Child attends to part of the story.
0: No evidence the child can perform the task.

H. Child adds simple comments and asks questions.
Task definition/examples: Read or tell the child a short story (e.g., about his or her drawing or toy animals) with a setting, a theme, episodes, and a resolution.

Scoring:

2: Child adds comments or asks questions independently during and at the end of the story.
1: Child adds comments or asks questions when prompted by the adult.
0: No evidence the child can perform the task.

I. Child relates and organizes all elements of story structure in a coherent sequence (e.g., setting, theme, episodes, resolution).
Task definition/examples: Read or tell the child a short story (e.g., about his or her drawing or toy animals) with a setting, a theme, episodes, and a resolution; and ask the child to retell you the story.

Scoring:

2: Child retells the story and organizes the setting, theme, episodes, and resolution in the correct sequence.
1: Child retells part of the story.
0: No evidence the child can perform the task.

III. LITERATE DISCOURSE

Conversations

A. Child maintains social interaction over two or more turns.
Task definition/examples: Play games or look at a book with the child, and observe whether the child uses non-verbal and/or verbal means of communication (e.g., eye contact, smile, gestures) to maintain social interaction.

Scoring:

2: Child maintains social interaction over at least two consecutive turns.
1: Child responds to a single social interaction.
0: No evidence the child can perform the task.

B. Child initiates and maintains topic.
Task definition/examples: While participating in activities (e.g., games, drawing, looking at books) with the

child, observe whether the child proposes a topic to talk about and maintains the topic.

Scoring:

2: Child initiates and maintains topic over at least two consecutive turns.
1: Child responds verbally and in an appropriate manner to adult's verbal communication.
0: No evidence the child can perform the task.

C. Child adapts information to level of listener.
Task definition/examples: While engaged in a conversation, observe whether the child takes into account the level of knowledge of the listener (e.g., explains context of events, gives names and definitions of characters).

Scoring:

2: Child relates information so that it is understandable to listener.
1: Child gives additional information if requested by listener.
0: No evidence the child can perform the task.

Categorical Organization

D. Child uses superordinate labels to indicate general categories.
Task definition/examples: While participating in activities with the child, observe whether the child uses a variety of superordinate category terms (e.g., animals, food, clothes) as opposed to basic level labels (e.g., dog, cookie, pants).

Scoring:

2: Child uses a variety of different superordinate labels.
1: Child uses a few common superordinate labels.
0: No evidence the child can perform the task.

Decontextualization

E. Child generalizes experiences to other settings.
Task definition/examples: While participating in activities with the child, observe whether the child relates present events to other personal experiences. Ask questions ["Has this ever happened to you?"].

Scoring:

2: Child draws from experiences in other settings to understand or interpret present event. For example, child says "I know how it works! My mother showed me how to push the button."

1: Child associates present event to own experience. For example, child says "I have a dog at home, too."

0: No evidence the child can perform the task.

F. Child provides explanations.

Task definition/examples: While participating in activities with the child, ask the child to explain actions and ideas.

Scoring:

2: Child explains a variety of actions and ideas.

1: Child explains immediate and personal actions.

0: No evidence the child can perform the task.

G. Child makes predictions.

Task definition/examples: While participating in activities with the child, ask the child to make predictions ["What do you think will happen?"].

Scoring:

2: Child consistently predicts a variety of plausible or fanciful events.

1: Child makes predictions based on regular and familiar routines.

0: No evidence the child can perform the task.

H. Child makes interpretations and judgments.

Task definition/examples: While participating in activities with the child, observe whether the child expresses opinions or judgments or makes inferences. Ask questions ["What do you think of this?" "Why do you think she did that?"].

Scoring:

2: Child makes inferences and expresses critical judgments.

1: Child expresses likes and dislikes and/or makes simple associations between events.

0: No evidence that the child can perform the task.

I. Child distinguishes fiction from real events.

Task definition/examples: While participating in activities involving imaginary events (e.g., symbolic play, drawing pictures, reading stories) with the child, observe whether the child explicitly verbalizes that events are fictional. Ask questions ["Is this for real?"].

Scoring:

2: Child uses words such as "pretend" or "not for real" to distinguish fiction from real events.

1: Child responds with "yes" or "no" to questions about whether events are pretend or real.

0: No evidence the child can perform the task.

Interpretive/Analytic Discourse

J. Child uses internal state words to express feelings and motivations (e.g., happy, sad, want, like).

Task definition/examples: While conducting activities with the child, observe whether the child uses internal state words (e.g., "I like ice cream," "The puppy looks sad").

Scoring:

2: Child uses a variety of internal state words.

1: Child uses at least one internal state word.

0: No evidence the child can perform the task.

K. Child uses cognitive words to refer to mental states (e.g., memory, idea, forget, think, know, understand).

Task definition/examples: While conducting activities with the child, observe whether the child uses cognitive words (e.g., "I know how to do this," "My dad forgot his lunch").

Scoring:

2: Child uses a variety of cognitive words.

1: Child uses at least one cognitive word.

0: No evidence the child can perform the task.

L. Child uses metalinguistic words to refer to the use of language (e.g., word, letter, sound, say, tell, mean, call, read).

Task definition/examples: While conducting activities with the child, observe whether the child uses metalinguistic words (e.g., "She said, 'Hi,'" "My mom told me").

Scoring:

2: Child uses a variety of metalinguistic words.

1: Child uses at least one metalinguistic word.

0: No evidence the child can perform the task.

M. Child seeks definitions of words.

Task definition/examples: While conducting activities with the child, observe whether the child asks for the definition and meaning of words. For example, the child asks, "What does this word mean?"

Scoring:

2: Child explicitly asks for the definition of unfamiliar words. For example, child asks "What does that mean?"
1: Child reacts to an unfamiliar word by asking simple questions. For example, child asks "What's that?"
0: No evidence the child can perform the task.

LADDERS TO LITERACY
Preschool Checklist

Name: _____   Date of Birth: _____

Dates of Assessments: __/__/__   __/__/__   __/__/__

Total Score: _____   _____   _____

Tester: _____

Print/Book Awareness   Metalinguistic Awareness   Oral Language

Score: ___ ___ ___   Score: ___ ___ ___   Score: ___ ___ ___

Scoring: 2 = Consistently/independently   1 = Sometimes/partly   0 = Not yet

Notes: A = Assumed   NO = No opportunity   R = Report   H = Help   M = Modifications

                                            __/__/__   __/__/__   __/__/__
                                                   (dates of assessments)

PRINT/BOOK AWARENESS

I.   SYMBOLIC REPRESENTATION

Play

   A.   Uses symbols in play   ___( ) ___( ) ___( )

Pictures

   B.   Identifies objects, people, and actions represented in pictures   ___( ) ___( ) ___( )

Graphics

   C.   Scribbles   ___( ) ___( ) ___( )

   D.   Names figures after execution   ___( ) ___( ) ___( )

   E.   Draws recognizable figures   ___( ) ___( ) ___( )

II.   PRINT

Book Conventions

   A.   Turns pages   ___( ) ___( ) ___( )

   B.   Orients book correctly, knows where book begins and ends   ___( ) ___( ) ___( )

   C.   Knows that print, not pictures, tells the story   ___( ) ___( ) ___( )

   D.   Knows that text begins at top left corner of page, is read from left to right   ___( ) ___( ) ___( )

(continued)

Ladders to Literacy: A Preschool Activity Book
by Angela Notari-Syverson, Rollanda E. O'Connor, and Patricia F. Vadasy
©1998 Paul H. Brookes Publishing Co., Baltimore

LADDERS TO LITERACY Preschool Checklist *(continued)*

Name: _____

Scoring: 2 = Consistently/independently   1 = Sometimes/partly   0 = Not yet

Notes: A = Assumed   NO = No opportunity   R = Report   H = Help   M = Modifications

_/_/_   _/_/_   _/_/_
(dates of assessments)

Awareness of Graphic Symbols

E.   Reads environmental print (e.g., logos, road signs, cereal boxes)   ____( ) ____( ) ____( )

F.   Recognizes a few memorized words in print (e.g., name)   ____( ) ____( ) ____( )

G.   Identifies a printed word   ____( ) ____( ) ____( )

H.   Reads simple words   ____( ) ____( ) ____( )

Letter Identification

I.   Recites part of alphabet   ____( ) ____( ) ____( )

J.   Names single letters   ____( ) ____( ) ____( )

Writing

K.   Copies shapes   ____( ) ____( ) ____( )

L.   Copies letters   ____( ) ____( ) ____( )

M.   Copies a few words (e.g., name)   ____( ) ____( ) ____( )

N.   Pretends to write   ____( ) ____( ) ____( )

O.   Writes name independently   ____( ) ____( ) ____( )

P.   Writes a few familiar letters and words   ____( ) ____( ) ____( )

Q.   Uses invented spelling (related letters) to write messages   ____( ) ____( ) ____( )

III.   LETTER–SOUND CORRESPONDENCE

Single Sounds and Letters

A.   Says most common sound for each letter   ____( ) ____( ) ____( )

B.   Selects a letter to represent a sound   ____( ) ____( ) ____( )

Words

C.   Uses letter sounds to write words   ____( ) ____( ) ____( )

Print/Book Awareness score: ____   ____   ____

Comments and most helpful prompts:

_____

(continued)

Ladders to Literacy: A Preschool Activity Book
by Angela Notari-Syverson, Rollanda E. O'Connor, and Patricia F. Vadasy
©1998 Paul H. Brookes Publishing Co., Baltimore

LADDERS TO LITERACY Preschool Checklist *(continued)*

Name: _____

Scoring: 2 = Consistently/independently   1 = Sometimes/partly   0 = Not yet
Notes: A = Assumed   NO = No opportunity   R = Report   H = Help   M = Modifications

___/___/___   ___/___/___   ___/___/___
(dates of assessments)

METALINGUISTIC AWARENESS

I.   PERCEPTION AND MEMORY FOR SOUNDS

Environmental Sounds

A.   Uses sounds to represent objects and animals   ____( ) ____( ) ____( )

B.   Identifies the source of sounds   ____( ) ____( ) ____( )

Words

C.   Repeats short words   ____( ) ____( ) ____( )

D.   Repeats multisyllabic words   ____( ) ____( ) ____( )

Phrases

E.   Repeats phrases (e.g., repetitive lines in familiar songs, nursery rhymes, and stories)   ____( ) ____( ) ____( )

Phonemes

F.   Repeats single phonemes after a short delay (1–2 seconds)   ____( ) ____( ) ____( )

G.   Repeats two to three phonemes after a short delay (1–2 seconds)   ____( ) ____( ) ____( )

H.   Discriminates between two phonemes (same/different)   ____( ) ____( ) ____( )

II.   WORD AWARENESS

Words

A.   Identifies a word from a spoken sentence   ____( ) ____( ) ____( )

B.   Identifies the longer word of two spoken words   ____( ) ____( ) ____( )

C.   Plays with the pronunciation of a word   ____( ) ____( ) ____( )

III.   PHONOLOGICAL SKILLS

Rhyming

A.   Says common rhymes along with teacher or peers   ____( ) ____( ) ____( )

B.   Fills in last word in rhyme   ____( ) ____( ) ____( )

C.   Says common rhymes independently   ____( ) ____( ) ____( )

D.   Recognizes that pairs of words do or do not rhyme   ____( ) ____( ) ____( )

E.   Says a rhyming word for a target word   ____( ) ____( ) ____( )

(continued)

Ladders to Literacy: A Preschool Activity Book
by Angela Notari-Syverson, Rollanda E. O'Connor, and Patricia F. Vadasy
©1998 Paul H. Brookes Publishing Co., Baltimore

LADDERS TO LITERACY Preschool Checklist *(continued)*

Name: _____

Scoring: 2 = Consistently/independently   1 = Sometimes/partly   0 = Not yet

Notes: A = Assumed   NO = No opportunity   R = Report   H = Help   M = Modifications

___/___/___   ___/___/___   ___/___/___

(dates of assessments)

Alliteration

F. Recognizes words that start with the same sound ____( ) ____( ) ____( )

G. Says a word that starts with the same sound ____( ) ____( ) ____( )

Blending

H. Blends syllables into words ____( ) ____( ) ____( )

I. Blends words with sounds pronounced in onset-rime format (e.g., m-ake) ____( ) ____( ) ____( )

J. Blends three to four phonemes into words (e.g., s-a-t, m-a-n) ____( ) ____( ) ____( )

Segmentation

K. Segments words into syllables (e.g., clapping, saying words in syallables) ____( ) ____( ) ____( )

L. Identifies first sound in words ____( ) ____( ) ____( )

M. Separates words into onset-rime ____( ) ____( ) ____( )

N. Segments one-syllable words into three to four phonemes ____( ) ____( ) ____( )

Metalinguistic Awareness score: _____ _____ _____

Comments and most helpful prompts:

(continued)

Ladders to Literacy: A Preschool Activity Book
by Angela Notari-Syverson, Rollanda E. O'Connor, and Patricia F. Vadasy
©1998 Paul H. Brookes Publishing Co., Baltimore

Name: _____

Scoring: 2 = Consistently/independently   1 = Sometimes/partly   0 = Not yet
Notes: A = Assumed   NO = No opportunity   R = Report   H = Help   M = Modifications

__/__/__   __/__/__   __/__/__
(dates of assessments)

ORAL LANGUAGE

I.   VOCABULARY

Words and Sentences

A.   Uses one-word utterances to label a variety of objects, people, and events   ____( ) ____( ) ____( )

B.   Uses two-word utterances to express a variety of semantic intentions (meaning) (e.g., agent-object, agent-action, action-object, existence, location, posses-sion, negation, recurrence, attribution)   ____( ) ____( ) ____( )

C.   Uses a variety of adult-form sentences (e.g., declarative, interrogative, negative)   ____( ) ____( ) ____( )

II.   NARRATIVE SKILLS

Narrations of Real Events

A.   Relates events with beginning, middle, and end   ____( ) ____( ) ____( )

B.   Describes explicit causal and temporal sequences among events (uses: because, before, after)   ____( ) ____( ) ____( )

Book

C.   Attends to and labels pictures in book   ____( ) ____( ) ____( )

D.   Makes comments and asks questions about individual pictures   ____( ) ____( ) ____( )

E.   Tells story and links events based on pictures using conversational language   ____( ) ____( ) ____( )

F.   Forms written story based on pictures using reading intonation and wording   ____( ) ____( ) ____( )

Narrations of Fictional Story

G.   Attends to story   ____( ) ____( ) ____( )

H.   Adds simple comments and asks questions   ____( ) ____( ) ____( )

I.   Relates and organizes elements of story structure in a coherent sequence (setting, theme, episodes, resolution)   ____( ) ____( ) ____( )

(continued)

Ladders to Literacy: A Preschool Activity Book
by Angela Notari-Syverson, Rollanda E. O'Connor, and Patricia F. Vadasy
©1998 Paul H. Brookes Publishing Co., Baltimore

LADDERS TO LITERACY Preschool Checklist *(continued)*

Name: _____

Scoring: 2 = Consistently/independently   1 = Sometimes/partly   0 = Not yet

Notes: A = Assumed   NO = No opportunity   R = Report   H = Help   M = Modifications

___/___/___   ___/___/___   ___/___/___
(dates of assessments)

III. LITERATE DISCOURSE

Conversations

A. Maintains social interaction over two or more turns   ___( ) ___( ) ___( )

B. Initiates and maintains topic   ___( ) ___( ) ___( )

C. Adapts information to level of listener   ___( ) ___( ) ___( )

Categorical Organization

D. Uses superordinate labels to indicate general categories   ___( ) ___( ) ___( )

Decontextualization

E. Generalizes experiences to other settings   ___( ) ___( ) ___( )

F. Provides explanations   ___( ) ___( ) ___( )

G. Makes predictions   ___( ) ___( ) ___( )

H. Makes interpretations and judgments   ___( ) ___( ) ___( )

I. Distinguishes fiction from real events   ___( ) ___( ) ___( )

Interpretive/Analytic Discourse

J. Uses internal state words to express feelings and motivations (e.g., happy, sad, want, like)   ___( ) ___( ) ___( )

K. Uses cognitive words to refer to mental states (e.g., memory, idea, forget, think, know, understand)   ___( ) ___( ) ___( )

L. Uses metalinguistic words to refer to the use of language (e.g., word, letter, sound, say, tell, mean, call, read)   ___( ) ___( ) ___( )

M. Seeks definitions of words   ___( ) ___( ) ___( )

Oral Language score: ____   ____   ____

Comments and most helpful prompts:

Ladders to Literacy: A Preschool Activity Book
by Angela Notari-Syverson, Rollanda E. O'Connor, and Patricia F. Vadasy
©1998 Paul H. Brookes Publishing Co., Baltimore

Appendix B

Early Literacy Activities for Children and Parents

A Parent's Guide to Easy Times to Do These Activities

Activities that may help your child's early reading skills—what a great idea! And activities that use play as a means of learning about books and print really sound fun. You care and want your child to grow up to be the best reader he or she can be. But when can you find the time to use these activities? You know how little time you have to set aside just for activities like these—even if they are fun and develop early reading skills. Well, if these are your thoughts, then these activities are made for you! They are perfect for you and your child:

- They are written *especially for busy parents* who work, cook, drive to and from errands, and have busy, active lives.
- They are designed so that *you can do them while you are doing other things,* such as washing the dishes and driving the car.
- They are *short and easy to do.*
- They are *fun* for both children and parents.
- They *help your child learn skills* that contribute to reading.

To make them easy to use, the activities have been arranged by routines that will be familiar to every parent. So, you can pick the activities that you can do when you are busy with your hands (when you are driving the car or folding laundry) or those that are good at bedtime. Most of the activities take only a few minutes to do—so you can fit one into a trip to the grocery store, when you are waiting in the check-out line, or waiting for the microwave to heat dinner. We know that parents think that reading is very important. These short, easy activities are a parent's dream for how to fit successful learning activities into the family's active daily schedule.

WHEN YOU HAVE NO HANDS FREE

(Driving the car, fixing dinner, doing laundry, bathtime, and so forth) First Sound; Let's Use Words to Describe . . . !; Movie Reviews; Nursery Rhymes; Print in the World; Say it Fast; Sing a Song; Tell Me a Word that Rhymes with . . . !; That's My Name!; What Did You Hear?; What Will Happen Next?

WHEN YOU'RE SITTING DOWN TOGETHER

(Eating a meal, waiting in the laundromat, riding the bus, and so forth) Diaries; Let's Use Words to Describe . . . !; Writing Messages

WHEN GRANDPARENTS OR RELATIVES ARE VISITING

Draw a Picture; Getting to Know Books; Let's Dance!; Let's Draw the Building You Made!; Magic Password; Magnetic Letters; Making Signs; Measuring; My Very Own Book; Nursery Rhymes; Recipes; Scribbling; That's My Name!; Writing Messages

WHEN YOUR CHILD AND FRIENDS ARE TOGETHER

Let's Draw the Building You Made!; Magnetic Letters; Making Signs; Measuring; Recipes; Scribbling; Writing Messages

WHEN YOU HAVE SOME TIME ON A RAINY DAY

Art Portfolios; Draw a Picture; Getting to Know Books; Let's Dance!; Let's Draw the Building You Made!; Magic Password; Making Signs; Mapping the Territory; Measuring; My Very Own Book; Print in the Home; Print in the World; Recipes; Scribbling; Storybook Reading Routines; That's My Name

WHEN YOU HAVE JUST A FEW MINUTES BETWEEN ACTIVITIES

(Waiting in the grocery line, taking a walk, and so forth) First Sound; Let's Use Words to Describe . . . !; Movie Reviews; Nursery Rhymes; Print in the Home; Print in the World; Tell Me a Word that Rhymes with . . . !; That's My Name!; What Did You Hear?; What Will Happen Next?; Writing Messages

AT BEDTIME

Diaries; Getting to Know Books; Nursery Rhymes; Sing a Song; Storybook Reading Routines

ON A WALK OR AT THE PARK

Say it Fast; Tell Me a Word that Rhymes with . . . ; What Did You Hear?; What Will Happen Next?

SPECIAL TRIPS

Going Places—The Library; Going Places—The Museum; Going Places—The Zoo

ART PORTFOLIOS

Children often put a lot of effort into their drawings. Sometimes they express important things about their feelings and experiences. Why not keep these creative works and collect them in a special art portfolio file? It will be fun to look back at them later with your child and remember special events and experiences together. You can buy a cardboard art portfolio in an art supply store or use a large department store box to store the drawings, collages, and other artworks.

Ladders to Literacy: A Preschool Activity Book
by Angela Notari-Syverson, Rollanda E. O'Connor, and Patricia F. Vadasy
©1998 Paul H. Brookes Publishing Co., Baltimore

DIARIES

Give your child a spiral notebook to use as a diary. On a regular basis, encourage your child to draw pictures or dictate some comments about an event that happened during the day. Remember to note the dates. It will be fun to look back at these pages later together.

Ladders to Literacy: A Preschool Activity Book
by Angela Notari-Syverson, Rollanda E. O'Connor, and Patricia F. Vadasy
©1998 Paul H. Brookes Publishing Co., Baltimore

DRAW A PICTURE

Children use drawing to stand for writing. When children scribble and draw, they learn that the marks made on paper can mean something. These activities prepare children to understand that writing is a means of communicating a message. Encourage your child to draw or paint a picture and to tell you about the picture. Let your child choose the subject. If your child does not have any ideas that day, then suggest that he or she draw a person, favorite animal, toy or object, or recent event (for example, going to the zoo or park). Your child may tell you spontaneously things about the picture before, during, or after he or she has drawn or painted the picture. If your child does not say anything, then ask him or her some questions ["What shall we call this?" "What's happening?" "Tell me about your picture"]. Write down exactly what your child says, and read back his or her dictation.

Ladders to Literacy: A Preschool Activity Book
by Angela Notari-Syverson, Rollanda E. O'Connor, and Patricia F. Vadasy
©1998 Paul H. Brookes Publishing Co., Baltimore

FIRST SOUND

Have your child choose a word (for example, bear). Ask him or her to identify the first sound of that word (for example, the sound for b is /b/). If your child is unable to find the first sound, then help him or her ["B-b-b-bear"]. Then together try to think of other words that begin with the same sound and that are related to the chosen word (for example, brown, big). Have your child compose sentences with words that begin with the same sound (for example, Big brown bear . . .).

Ladders to Literacy: A Preschool Activity Book
by Angela Notari-Syverson, Rollanda E. O'Connor, and Patricia F. Vadasy
©1998 Paul H. Brookes Publishing Co., Baltimore

GETTING TO KNOW BOOKS

In English, we begin to read books at the front, not at the back, and words go from top to bottom and from left to right. Teach your child how to hold a book correctly and to turn pages in the correct direction. When your child begins to show interest in the print and not only the story, run your fingers under the words that you read. Highlight the left-to-right, top-to-bottom orientation of the written text. As your child begins to know some letters, ask him or her to point to a word that starts with the same letter as his or her name.

Ladders to Literacy: A Preschool Activity Book
by Angela Notari-Syverson, Rollanda E. O'Connor, and Patricia F. Vadasy
©1998 Paul H. Brookes Publishing Co., Baltimore

GOING PLACES—THE LIBRARY

Your local library is a great place to visit with your child. There you can find books, magazines, videotapes, music, and newspapers for adults and children of all ages. You can check out books for your child and you to take home, or you can spend time browsing through materials and searching for information on computers. You can get all kinds of information at the library not only on books but also on events and activities taking place in town as well as educational programs. Libraries also distribute other useful information such as bus schedules and tax forms. Some libraries even have play areas to keep younger children busy. And, of course, the librarians are always available to assist you. All this and at no charge! Many libraries will issue library cards to children of any age as long as they are accompanied by their parents, and many times children are not charged overdue fines if they forget to return their books on time.

Ladders to Literacy: A Preschool Activity Book
by Angela Notari-Syverson, Rollanda E. O'Connor, and Patricia F. Vadasy
©1998 Paul H. Brookes Publishing Co., Baltimore

GOING PLACES—THE MUSEUM

There are many types of museums that children will enjoy. Science museums have exhibits that help children understand how all sorts of things work. At natural history museums, children can learn all about animals, bugs, oceans, and volcanoes. Art museums introduce children to paintings and sculptures. Find out what is available in your area. Most museums have at least one day a month when entry is free of charge. Visit the museum with your child. Talk together about what you see. Read aloud the descriptive labels of the art pieces that your child has picked as his or her favorites. In some exhibitions, you can also watch movies or get information from a computer. Take home the brochures and use them later to show other people and to tell them what you saw.

Ladders to Literacy: A Preschool Activity Book
by Angela Notari-Syverson, Rollanda E. O'Connor, and Patricia F. Vadasy
©1998 Paul H. Brookes Publishing Co., Baltimore

GOING PLACES—THE ZOO

Going to the zoo is always a special treat for both children and adults. Animals are always a great topic for conversations with children. Use this opportunity to encourage language by asking questions and responding to your child's comments. Also point out animal names and other familiar words and letters on the written descriptive labels. Take photographs, and create a scrapbook with pictures of animals you saw. Have your child dictate labels and descriptions for the photographs. Your child can also draw and write about the zoo trip after you return home.

Ladders to Literacy: A Preschool Activity Book
by Angela Notari-Syverson, Rollanda E. O'Connor, and Patricia F. Vadasy
©1998 Paul H. Brookes Publishing Co., Baltimore

LET'S DANCE!

Children learn about rhythm by moving their bodies to music. Exploring rhythm helps children become sensitive to the temporal quality or the duration of sounds. Sing a song or listen to music that has different rhythms. With your child, dance to the different beats, clap hands, or use a drum. Begin with slow, regular, even beats, and later introduce uneven beats with variations in intensity and tempo. Relate movements to personal experiences ["Let's move slowly and pretend we are heavy elephants!" "Let's move fast and pretend we are flying on a plane!"]. Listen to some classical, Latin, or folk music. Talk about how the music makes you feel. What does it make you think of? Ask your child to draw a picture that goes with the music.

Ladders to Literacy: A Preschool Activity Book
by Angela Notari-Syverson, Rollanda E. O'Connor, and Patricia F. Vadasy
©1998 Paul H. Brookes Publishing Co., Baltimore

LET'S DRAW THE BUILDING YOU MADE!

Children often build things that need to be torn apart during cleanup time. Encourage your child to make a record of his or her accomplishments before the construction is torn apart. Compliment your child on the construction, then say something to encourage him or her to record it ["I can see you put lots of effort into making your castle so high. Let's draw a picture of it before you put the blocks away. That way we'll always remember what it looks like"]. You might start out by showing your child how to sketch and talk about what you are doing. Encourage your child to join in ["First, I'm drawing the blocks that make up the bottom layer. Now I'm making it higher. See how the color changes to yellow for the top row? Where's a yellow pen?"]. After your child has drawn the picture, ask your child to label the picture ["What shall we call it?"]. Help your child label the picture with meaningful letters or a few words to help him or her remember the construction.

Ladders to Literacy: A Preschool Activity Book
by Angela Notari-Syverson, Rollanda E. O'Connor, and Patricia F. Vadasy
©1998 Paul H. Brookes Publishing Co., Baltimore

LET'S USE WORDS TO DESCRIBE . . . !

Although children learn some descriptive words (for example, big) when they are very young, adults need to encourage other kinds of description. Children have strong opinions about food, so a wonderful way to start is to have your child talk about its color, texture, shape, smell, and taste. You can help your child develop a descriptive vocabulary by using these words around mealtime and in everyday conversation. On a walk outdoors, call your child's attention to the rough, spiky leaves of a tree or the striped, velvety petals of a flower. You can encourage your child to describe and classify things in the world around you (for example, help your child find things that are purple, things that taste sweet, or things that are shiny). The possibilities are endless. As you describe and classify with your child, you also develop the essential vocabulary that will help him or her successfully start in school.

MAGIC PASSWORD

Children learn to rhyme and to understand that words are made up of parts (for example, b-a-t, mom-my, un-der). Have your child enact pretend play activities with toy animals, blocks, and other materials. Tell your child that the animals have to guess a magic password to gain access to or to leave a location (for example, barn, zoo, trap, magic cave). Pretend you are the guardian and the child is the animal. Tell your child that the magic password can be a word that rhymes ["You have to say the magic password. Tell me a word that rhymes with dog"]. Then try asking your child to give you a password that is fragmented into syllables or sounds (for example, Pop-si-cle). When you are reading together or see a sign, point out to your child a written word ["Can you read this word?" (cat) "What word rhymes with cat?" "Can you read this word?" (hamburger) "Can you break it into parts?"].

Ladders to Literacy: A Preschool Activity Book
by Angela Notari-Syverson, Rollanda E. O'Connor, and Patricia F. Vadasy
©1998 Paul H. Brookes Publishing Co., Baltimore

MAGNETIC LETTERS

Arrange magnetic letters on the refrigerator, and encourage your child to play with them in a variety of ways when you are in the kitchen together. By taking them off of the refrigerator and putting them back on, your child can learn about colors, shapes, letter names, and sounds. Spell your child's name often, and leave it on the refrigerator so that your child will learn to recognize it. Do the same for other names of people and objects that are important to your child. Older children can read and write simple words with the letters. You can also use the letters to write simple messages. If, for example, you are going to the zoo, then you can write "zoo" and talk about the outing during breakfast. Use the letters to attach to pictures or photographs of the words you write (for example, Dad and a photograph of Dad, cat and a picture of a cat). Use a letter to attach to a picture of an object with a name that begins with that letter of the alphabet (for example, the letter O and a picture of an orange). You can also play matching games (for example, choosing a letter and having your child find the same letter) and word guessing games (for example, choosing a letter and thinking of words that begin with that letter).

Ladders to Literacy: A Preschool Activity Book
by Angela Notari-Syverson, Rollanda E. O'Connor, and Patricia F. Vadasy
©1998 Paul H. Brookes Publishing Co., Baltimore

MAKING SIGNS

Children learn about words and how sounds and symbols go together as they make signs to use in their play. Help your child make signs he or she can use as part of construction activities (for example, Stop!, Go around, Open, Closed, Exit). As your child finds a need for new signs, help him or her create meaningful signs that can be placed around the house (for example, a picture of a crayon to label the drawer or box in which your child keeps coloring materials).

Ladders to Literacy: A Preschool Activity Book
by Angela Notari-Syverson, Rollanda E. O'Connor, and Patricia F. Vadasy
©1998 Paul H. Brookes Publishing Co., Baltimore

MAPPING THE TERRITORY

Children can learn that maps represent real places by developing models and drawings of areas familiar to them. For example, landscapes can be created by playing with sand in a sandbox. Help your child to model familiar home or neighborhood features and to talk about how these features are arranged. Encourage your child to enact pretend play scenes using these landscapes as contexts ["How will the bear walk to the store?" "Shall we go down this street?"]. Talk about events that occurred in these contexts ["Remember when we went bike riding? Where did we go?"]. Encourage your child to recall events related to the outing. Use paper and crayons to draw with your child a model of the park or your child's favorite room. Talk about where objects would be located, and add details to the drawing ["Where shall we put the swings? Are they close to the trees or far away?"]. Use print to label objects (for example, stove, table) and activities (for example, cooking, eating).

Ladders to Literacy: A Preschool Activity Book
by Angela Notari-Syverson, Rollanda E. O'Connor, and Patricia F. Vadasy
©1998 Paul H. Brookes Publishing Co., Baltimore

MEASURING

Science requires the use of reading and writing skills. For example, writing records of observations and taking measurements are important scientific activities. Practice literacy skills as you and your child do simple science projects. 1) Keep track of your child's height. Make your own growth chart (for example, tape a long strip of paper against a wall) or use an already-made growth chart. Mark your child's height, and then have your child measure with a measuring tape and record the numbers and observation dates. 2) Plant beans or seeds. Help your child measure the growth of the plants and record the heights and dates as well as other observations in a notebook or on a graph. 3) Have a long-jump competition. Mark the starting point of the jump with tape or another object. Use a measuring tape with easy-to-read numbers to measure the jumps. Help your child read the numbers on the tape and record the length of the jumps along with the names of the competitors. 4) Use blocks to measure different objects. Have your child stack blocks next to different objects until the tower reaches the same height as the objects. Help your child count the blocks, record numbers, or draw lines that correspond to the different heights. Compare the differences.

Ladders to Literacy: A Preschool Activity Book
by Angela Notari-Syverson, Rollanda E. O'Connor, and Patricia F. Vadasy
©1998 Paul H. Brookes Publishing Co., Baltimore

MOVIE REVIEWS

After watching a television show or a movie with your child, set aside a few minutes to talk about what you watched. Ask your child to tell you about the story or topic and what he or she liked and disliked about the show. This will help your child develop communication and narrative language skills and learn how to express opinions and make judgments. Ask questions that will help your child learn about the sequence and causes of events ["When did that happen?" "What happened next?" "Why did he do that?"].

Ladders to Literacy: A Preschool Activity Book
by Angela Notari-Syverson, Rollanda E. O'Connor, and Patricia F. Vadasy
©1998 Paul H. Brookes Publishing Co., Baltimore

MY VERY OWN BOOK

With your child, paste photographs or pictures from magazines in a notebook or on sheets of paper that can be stapled together. Write a short sentence to go with the pictures. You can make books about special events (for example, a vacation or a trip) or about topics of interest to your child (for example, dinosaurs, astronauts, fish).

Ladders to Literacy: A Preschool Activity Book
by Angela Notari-Syverson, Rollanda E. O'Connor, and Patricia F. Vadasy
©1998 Paul H. Brookes Publishing Co., Baltimore

NURSERY RHYMES

We all know that children take great delight in nursery rhymes. Rhyming during the preschool years helps children to learn to read more easily in first grade. Read traditional Mother Goose nursery rhymes and other rhyming books and songs with your child. Have some pictures of familiar nursery rhymes for your child to color and place in prominent places (for example, the bathroom mirror, the car dashboard, the refrigerator). Encourage your child to say the rhymes along with you.

Ladders to Literacy: A Preschool Activity Book
by Angela Notari-Syverson, Rollanda E. O'Connor, and Patricia F. Vadasy
©1998 Paul H. Brookes Publishing Co., Baltimore

PRINT IN THE HOME

The best way for a child to learn about literacy is to see how reading and writing are integral parts of daily home routines. Have books, newspapers, and magazines in your house; and show your child their value by reading them yourself. Whenever you have a chance, show your child that print is a source of information (for example, cook from a written recipe, use a manual to fix a piece of equipment, look in the telephone book to find a telephone number). Place pictures and bookshelves in your house, especially in your child's room. Use a message board, chalkboard, or the refrigerator to display simple messages, drawings, songs, or nursery rhymes. Create a special place with a small table, chair, and crayons for your child to draw or write. Visit bookstores and libraries so your child has books of his or her own to read and look at.

Ladders to Literacy: A Preschool Activity Book
by Angela Notari-Syverson, Rollanda E. O'Connor, and Patricia F. Vadasy
©1998 Paul H. Brookes Publishing Co., Baltimore

PRINT IN THE WORLD

Learning to read and to write is a process that begins at a very early age. Children are continually exposed to many forms of print (for example, signs, labels, logos, symbols). On outings and at home with your younger child(ren), draw their attention to road signs; grocery store, gas station, and restaurant logos; signs in restaurants (for example, men's and women's bathrooms); and letters on cereal boxes. There are so many different kinds of signs in our homes and communities. It will be fun to see which ones your child likes and learns to identify. Suggest that your child might want to make some signs for the house. Give your child some cardboard to draw signs for his or her room, the kitchen, the front door, or your pet's corner.

Ladders to Literacy: A Preschool Activity Book
by Angela Notari-Syverson, Rollanda E. O'Connor, and Patricia F. Vadasy
©1998 Paul H. Brookes Publishing Co., Baltimore

RECIPES

Preparing food can help a child understand the relationship between printed directions and the organized actions of one or more person(s), and the results are delicious. Children learn that print can be used to label and identify ingredients as well as to record and to remember steps in sequence. Let your child help you decide on a favorite recipe to cook together on a rainy day. The recipe could be as simple as a peanut butter and jelly sandwich. Examine labels with your child, and ask sequencing and quantity questions as your recipe progresses ["I have the bread ready. What is our next step?" "How much jelly do you think we should use?" "What happens when there is too much jam?"]. Look for children's recipe books in bookstores or at your local library.

Ladders to Literacy: A Preschool Activity Book
by Angela Notari-Syverson, Rollanda E. O'Connor, and Patricia F. Vadasy
©1998 Paul H. Brookes Publishing Co., Baltimore

SAY IT FAST

Breaking down words into syllables and sounds helps the child become aware that words not only have meaning but also are characterized by sounds. It also helps your child understand the sound–letter association involved in reading and writing. During daily activities (for example, driving in your car, walking to the grocery store), play word games with your child. Say a word by breaking it down into syllables ["Look! There's a spi-der!"]. Have your child guess the word ["Can you say that word fast?"].

Ladders to Literacy: A Preschool Activity Book
by Angela Notari-Syverson, Rollanda E. O'Connor, and Patricia F. Vadasy
©1998 Paul H. Brookes Publishing Co., Baltimore

SCRIBBLING

Scribbling is the very first step to writing. Even though your child's early attempts to write may not resemble conventional letters and words, do not worry because they will eventually. Encourage your child to write pretend words and messages and to tell you what they may mean. Create a writing scrapbook. Paste photographs or draw pictures, and have your child pretend to write something about the picture. What will your child write? Your child may write a short message consisting of a shape or a straight line or a longer message with full lines of scribbling, perhaps some letter-like forms, and, later, even recognizable words and letters.

Ladders to Literacy: A Preschool Activity Book
by Angela Notari-Syverson, Rollanda E. O'Connor, and Patricia F. Vadasy
©1998 Paul H. Brookes Publishing Co., Baltimore

SING A SONG

Singing a song is a fun and natural way to help children become sensitive to the different qualities and sounds of words. During daily activities (for example, driving in your car, bathtime), sing favorite songs with your child, especially songs with words that rhyme. Once your child becomes familiar with the words, you can take turns at singing verses. Eventually, you can invent your own songs together and even play with nonsense words and verses!

Ladders to Literacy: A Preschool Activity Book
by Angela Notari-Syverson, Rollanda E. O'Connor, and Patricia F. Vadasy
©1998 Paul H. Brookes Publishing Co., Baltimore

STORYBOOK READING ROUTINES

The first important thing that children need to experience about literacy is the pleasure involved in reading stories together with an adult. You can begin sharing picture storybooks with your child from a very early age. Find a quiet place and time (bedtime is usually a good time) to look at books on a regular basis. You can encourage exploration of the books and print by talking with your child about the pictures, pointing to words as you read, and asking your child to tell or read the story to you (if your child is so inclined). Listen and respond to your child's comments and questions. Associate characters and events in the book with the child's own experience. Story time with your child is a wonderful way to stimulate a love for books and pleasant anticipation for learning to read in school.

Ladders to Literacy: A Preschool Activity Book
by Angela Notari-Syverson, Rollanda E. O'Connor, and Patricia F. Vadasy
©1998 Paul H. Brookes Publishing Co., Baltimore

TELL ME A WORD THAT RHYMES WITH . . . !

We use language to communicate ideas and feelings; but we also use language when we tell jokes, invent poems, and use slang. Rhyming is one way of playing with the sounds of words that you can practice with your child. Take turns guessing words that rhyme with each other or that sound the same. Let your child be creative by inventing nonsense words, too, as long as they rhyme. Rhyming helps children learn to read. It helps children understand that not only do words have meaning, but they also are composed of collections of sounds.

Ladders to Literacy: A Preschool Activity Book
by Angela Notari-Syverson, Rollanda E. O'Connor, and Patricia F. Vadasy
©1998 Paul H. Brookes Publishing Co., Baltimore

THAT'S MY NAME!

One of the first printed words children learn to recognize is their own name. Find ways for your child to see his or her name in print. Make a name tag for his or her bedroom door and for objects that belong to him or her. Write your child's name on his or her drawings and on letters and cards to family members. Once your child has learned to recognize his or her name, teach your child letter names, beginning with the first letter. Point out other words in the environment that start with the same first letter.

Ladders to Literacy: A Preschool Activity Book
by Angela Notari-Syverson, Rollanda E. O'Connor, and Patricia F. Vadasy
©1998 Paul H. Brookes Publishing Co., Baltimore

WHAT DID YOU HEAR?

At home or on a walk to a park, listen for sounds that may occur and for which the source is not directly in sight (for example, water dripping in another room, a bird or an animal up in a tree, a car around the bend). Draw your child's attention to the sound. Ask your child to describe the sound, guess from where it came, and what he or she thinks happened. This guessing game can be really fun. It will help your child improve listening skills, problem-solve, and develop the ability to use language to describe objects and events.

Ladders to Literacy: A Preschool Activity Book
by Angela Notari-Syverson, Rollanda E. O'Connor, and Patricia F. Vadasy
©1998 Paul H. Brookes Publishing Co., Baltimore

WHAT WILL HAPPEN NEXT?

Reading and writing help us describe and document events in the past and future and in far-away settings. This is an activity to do when reading familiar stories and during familiar routines (for example, mealtime, bedtime, bathtime). Invite your child to tell you what will happen next in the story or what will happen next on your drive to the grocery store. Predicting events helps your child go beyond the immediate here-and-now. It will help your child when he or she begins to read.

Ladders to Literacy: A Preschool Activity Book
by Angela Notari-Syverson, Rollanda E. O'Connor, and Patricia F. Vadasy
©1998 Paul H. Brookes Publishing Co., Baltimore

WRITING MESSAGES

In school, your child is learning that print is a tool for communication. Your child is learning how spoken words can be captured on paper and preserved for others to read. Each day, your child's teacher will write a message with the children, telling about important events that take place in the classroom. At the end of the day, the teacher might ask the children to tell about a significant event that happened to them and record it to be reread the following day. You can encourage your child to use written messages at home. Ask your child to dictate a short message to give to an older sibling or other adults in the home, send to friends or teachers at school, or mail to relatives. Encourage your child to write or copy a few words and draw or paste pictures to communicate a message. You can also leave written messages for your child. For example, you can write a short note or draw a picture of an upcoming event or a weekend outing (for example, the zoo, the grocery store, a mountain hike). Writing and reading messages are fun ways to stimulate literacy.

Ladders to Literacy: A Preschool Activity Book
by Angela Notari-Syverson, Rollanda E. O'Connor, and Patricia F. Vadasy
©1998 Paul H. Brookes Publishing Co., Baltimore

Appendix C

Glossary

Alliteration Recognition or production of words with common initial sounds.

Blending Combining sounds (e.g., syllables, phonemes) together to form words (d-o-g becomes dog).

Book conventions Book handling behaviors such as turning pages; orienting the book correctly; knowing where the book begins and ends; knowing that print, not the pictures, tells the story; and knowing that text begins at the top left corner of the page and is read from left to right.

Categorical organization The grouping of objects into categories (e.g., animals, food, people).

Compound word Word consisting of two or more elements that have meaning.

Continuous sounds Sounds that can be prolonged without interruption (e.g., short vowels, f, l, m, n, r, s, v, z).

Decentration The ability to take into account different points of view or to view an object from a different perspective (e.g., to view a word in terms of its sound as well as its meaning).

Decontextualized language Type of language that refers to objects and events that are detached from the immediate context; deals with the remote and the abstract, such as stories beginning "Once upon a time . . ."

Emergent literacy Perspective that considers literacy a complex sociological, psychological, and linguistic activity that begins in the very early years.

Environmental print Signs, labels, and logos present in the daily environment and community (e.g., road signs, food packages, store fronts).

Interpretive/analytic discourse Type of oral language organized around interpretation and meaning (providing definitions and explanations) rather than experience.

Invented spelling Writing typical of young children, based on an idiosyncratic letter–sound correspondence strategy that differs from the conventional system (e.g., FLR for flower).

Literacy Activities and skills associated directly with the use of print; includes reading, writing, interpreting text, and playing alphabet games.

Literate discourse Type of oral language that contains characteristics of written forms of language (e.g., detachment from the here and now, explicitness of reference and meaning, complex syntactic structures, high degree of cohesion).

Metacognition Ability to reflect on and control one's cognitive processes.

Metalinguistic awareness Ability to reflect on, manipulate, and talk about linguistic forms (e.g., to isolate the first sound in spoken words, to produce a rhyming word).

Onset Initial consonant or consonant cluster of a word (e.g., bat: onset is /b/).

Phoneme Smallest linguistic unit of sound in a word (the sound produced by a letter or letter group).

Phonology Aspect of language concerned with the rules governing the structure, distribution, and sequencing of speech sound patterns.

Pragmatic skills Skills that relate to the use of language to communicate in social contexts.

Referent Person, action, or event to which a word refers and for which a word serves as a symbol.

Rime Part of a word (vowel and consonants) following the onset (e.g., bat's rime is -at).

Scaffolding Dynamic process during adult–child interactions in which the adult varies levels of task demands and support in response to the child's changing competence.

Segmentation Separation of words into smaller sounds such as syllables (e.g., banana can be segmented into three syllables: ba-na-na) or phonemes (e.g., bat can be segmented into b-at or b-a-t).

Semantic intentions Meanings characteristic of children's early two-word utterances. These include agent-action (Daddy run), action-object (throw ball), agent-object (Mommy book), locative (sit chair), possession (Mommy hat), existence (that doggie), negation (no birdie), recurrence (more crackers), and attribution (yellow flower).

Semantics Aspect of language concerned with the rules that govern the meaning or content of words and sentences.

Stop sounds Sound articulated with a complete obstruction of the passage of breath (e.g., b, d, g, h, k, p, t).

Story structure Narrative framework that specifies the underlying relationship of the story components (e.g., setting, theme, episodes, resolution).

Superordinate level labels Labels that categorize objects and events at an abstract, general level (e.g., animals, people, food) as opposed to basic level labels that describe particulars (e.g., dog, Mama, apple).

Symbol Something that represents or stands for something else.

Symbolic representation Use of a variety of symbolic media (e.g., language, drawing, imaginative actions) to evoke nonpresent realities.

Syntax Organizational rules specifying word order, sentence organization, and word relationships.

Appendix D

Additional Resources

RHYMING

Brown, M.W. (1957). *Goodnight moon.* New York: Harper & Row.

Brown, R. (1994). *What rhymes with snake?* New York: Tambourine Books.

Cauley, L.B. (1992). *Clap your hands.* New York: G.P. Putnam's Sons.

Cole, J., & Calmenson, S. (1991). *The eentsy, weentsy spider: Fingerplays and action rhymes.* New York: Mulberry Books.

Degen, B. (1983). *Jamberry.* New York: HarperCollins.

Edge, N. (1988a). *I can read colors.* Salem, OR: Nellie Edge Resources.

Edge, N. (1988b). *The opposite song.* Salem, OR: Nellie Edge Resources.

Edge, N. (1992). *Make friends with Mother Goose.* Salem, OR: Nellie Edge Resources.

Fleming, D. (1991). *In the tall, tall grass.* New York: Holt, Rinehart & Winston.

Gregorich, B. (1984a). *Beep, beep.* Grand Haven, MI: School Zone Publishing.

Gregorich, B. (1984b). *Gum on the drum.* Grand Haven, MI: School Zone Publishing.

Guarino, D. (1989). *Is your mama a llama?* New York: Scholastic.

Hennessy, B.G. (1989). *The missing tarts.* Middlesex, England: Puffin Books.

Kalish, M., & Kalish, L. (1993). *Bears on the stairs.* New York: Scholastic.

Langstaff, J. (1991). *Oh, a hunting we will go.* New York: Aladdin Books.

Loomans, D., Kolberg, K., & Loomans, J. (1991). *Positively Mother Goose.* Tiburon, CA: H.J. Kramer.

Martin, B., & Carle, E. (1991). *Polar bear, polar bear, what do you hear?* New York: Holt, Rinehart & Winston.

McMillan, B. (1990). *One sun: A book of terse verse.* New York: Holiday House.

Milios, R. (1988). *Bears, bears, everywhere.* Chicago, IL: Children's Press.

Pelham, D. (1990). *Sam's sandwich.* New York: Dutton Children's Books.

Seuss, Dr. (1957). *The cat in the hat.* New York: Random House.

Shaw, N. (1986). *Sheep on a jeep.* Boston: Houghton Mifflin.

Shaw, N. (1989). *Sheep on a ship.* Boston: Houghton Mifflin.

Silverstein, S. (1964). *A giraffe and a half.* New York: HarperCollins.

Wadsworth, O. (1971). *Over in the meadow.* New York: Scholastic.

Williams, S. (1989). *We went walking.* San Diego: Harcourt Brace Jovanovich.

Witty, B. (1992). *The racoon on the moon.* Grand Haven, MI: School Zone Publishing.

SYLLABLE SEGMENTATION

Heller, R. (1989). *Many luscious lollipops.* New York: Grosset & Dunlap.

ALPHABET/ALLITERATION

Barrett, J. (1980). *Animals should definitely not act like people.* New York: Aladdin Books.

Dragonwagon, C. (1992). *Alligator arrived with apples: A potluck alphabet feast.* New York: Aladdin Books.

Gregorich, B. (1985). *Elephant and envelope.* Grand Haven, MI: School Zone Publishing.

Grover, M. (1993). *The accidental zucchini: The unexpected alphabet.* San Diego: Harcourt Brace Jovanovich.

Hague, K. (1986a). *Alphabears.* New York: H. Holt.

Hague, K. (1986b). *Numbears.* New York: H. Holt.

Lunn, C. (1989). *Bobby's zoo.* Chicago: Children's Press.

McPhail, D. (1989). *Animals A to Z.* New York: Scholastic.

Merriam, E. (1989). *Where is everybody?* New York: Simon & Schuster.

Nightingale, S. (1992). *Pink pigs a plenty.* San Diego: Harcourt Brace Jovanovich.

Shelby, A. (1994). *Potluck.* New York: Orchard Books.

Sloat, T. (1989). *From letter to letter.* New York: Puffin Unicorn.

OTHER FAVORITES

Brett, J. (1990). *Goldilocks and the three bears.* New York: G.P. Putnam's Sons.

Brown, M. (1957). *The three billy goats gruff.* San Diego: Harcourt Brace Jovanovich.

Carle, E. (1987). *The very hungry caterpillar* (Rev. ed.). New York: Philomel Books.

Carlstrom, N.W. (1992). *Baby-o.* Boston: Little, Brown.

De Paola, T. (1975). *Strega nona.* Englewoods Cliffs, NJ: Prentice Hall.

Galdone, P. (1970). *The three little pigs.* New York: Houghton Mifflin.

Galdone, P. (1975). *The little red hen.* New York: Scholastic.

Kalmain, M. (1988). *Hey Willy, see the pyramids.* New York: Penguin.

Keats, E.J. (1962). *A snowy day.* New York: Viking.

McCloskey, R. (1942). *Make way for ducklings.* New York: Viking.

McDermott, G. (1972). *Anansi the spider.* New York: Puffin Books.

McDermott, G. (1993). *Raven: A trickster tale from the Pacific Northwest.* San Diego: Harcourt Brace Jovanovich.

Perry, S. (1995). *If.* Venice, CA: Children's Library Press.

Piper, W. (1954). *The little engine that could.* New York: Platt & Munk.

Seeger, P. (1986). *Abiyoyo.* New York: Collier-Macmillian.

Sendak, M. (1973). *Where the wild things are.* New York: Harper & Row.

Shaw, C. (1947). *It looked like spilt milk.* New York: Harper & Row.

Slobodkina, E. (1987). *Caps for sale.* New York: Harper Trophy.

Steptoe, J. (1988). *Baby says.* New York: Lothrop.

Testa, F. (1993). *Time to get out.* New York: Tambourine Books.

Tharlet, E. (1993). *I wish I were a bird.* New York: North South Books.

WORDLESS PICTURE BOOKS

Hoban, T. (1983). *I read symbols.* New York: Greenwillow Books.
Mayer, M (1967). *A boy, a dog and a frog.* New York: Dial.
Mayer, M. (1971). *A boy, a dog, a frog and a friend.* New York: Dial.
Shories, P. (1991). *Mouse around.* New York: Farrar, Strauss & Giroux.
Turkle, B. (1976). *Deep in the forest.* New York: Dutton.

FOREIGN LANGUAGE

Delacre, L. (1989). *Arroz con leche: Popular songs and rhymes from Latin America.* New York: Scholastic.
Dunham, M. (1987). *Colors: How do you say it? English, French, Spanish, Italian.* New York: Lothrop, Lee, & Shepard Books.
McNaught, H. (1973). *500 palabras nuevas para ti (500 words to grow on).* New York: Random House.
Wyndham, R. (1968). *Chinese Mother Goose rhymes.* New York: Philomel Books.
Yolen J. (1992). *Street rhymes around the world.* Honesdale, PA: Wordsong.

TACTILE PICTURE BOOKS IN BRAILLE

Keller, H. (1993). *Geraldine's blanket.* Louisville, KY: American Printing House for the Blind.
Stratton, J., & Wright, S. (1991). *Bumpy rolls away.* Louisville, KY: American Printing House for the Blind.
Wright, S. (1991). *Silly squiggles.* Louisville, KY: American Printing House for the Blind.
Wright, S. (1993). *That's not my bear.* Louisville, KY: American Printing House for the Blind.
Wright, S., & Pester, E. (1991). *The longest noodle.* Louisville, KY: American Printing House for the Blind.

OTHER MATERIALS

Althouse, R. (1981). *The young child: Learning with understanding.* New York: Teachers College Press.
Borgia, E. (1996). Learning through projects. *Scholastic Early Childhood Today, 10,* 22–29.
Bricker, D., & Cripe, J.J. (1992). *An activity-based approach to early intervention.* Baltimore: Paul H. Brookes Publishing Co.
Clark, K. (1994). How do caterpillars make cocoons? *Dimensions of Early Childhood, 22,* 5–9.
Edwards C., Gandini, L., & Forman, G. (1993). *The hundred languages of children: The Reggio Emilia approach to early childhood education.* Norwood, NJ: Ablex.
Geller, L.G. (1985). *Wordplay and language learning for children.* Urbana, IL: National Council of Teachers of English.
Hartman, J., & Eckerty, C. (1995). Projects in the early years. *Childhood Education, 71,* 141–147.

Katzen, M., & Henderson, A. (1994). *Pretend soup and other real recipes: A cookbook for preschoolers and up.* Berkeley, CA: Tricycle Press.

Linder, T.W. (1993). *Transdisciplinary play-based assessment: A functional approach to working with young children* (Rev. ed.). Baltimore: Paul H. Brookes Publishing Co.

Maxim, G. (1997). Developmentally appropriate maps skills instruction. *Childhood Education, 73,* 206–211.

Morrow, L.M. (1989). *Literacy development: Helping children read and write.* Englewood Cliffs, NJ: Prentice Hall.

Neuman, S.G., & Roskos, S. (1993). *Language and literacy learning in the early years: An integrated approach.* San Diego: Harcourt Brace Jovanovich.

Seefeldt, C. (1992). *The early childhood curriculum: A review of current research* (2nd ed.). New York: Teachers College Press.

Strickland, D.S., & Morrow, L.M. (Eds.). (1989). *Emerging literacy: Young children learn to read and write.* Newark, DE: International Reading Association.

Yopp, H. (1992). Developing phonemic awareness in young children. *The Reading Teacher, 45*(9), 696–703.

Index

Page references followed by *t, f,* or *n,* indicate tables, figures, or footnotes, respectively.

Acknowledgments, 31
Activities
    components of, 39–41
    curriculum features, 5*t*, 6–7
    description of, 39
    implementing, 39–44
        suggested sequence for,
        44
    metalinguistic awareness,
        133–199
    oral language, 201–282
    parent's guide to, 327–360
    print/book awareness,
        45–132
    starting, 43–44
    see also specific activities
Activity planning forms, 41,
    42*f*
Adaptations, 41
Administration
    helpful scenarios, 293–295
    procedures and protocol,
        292–295
    suggested protocol for,
        292–295
Adult–child interaction, 6
    behaviors, 39–41
Alliteration, 16, 135
    activities, 137
    assessment procedures, 308
    definition of, 361
    goals and objectives, 137
    see also Alphabet/allitera-
        tion, additional
        resources
Alphabet/alliteration, addi-
    tional resources, 366
Alternatives, reducing, 32
Analytic discourse, *see* Inter-
    pretive/analytic dis-
    course
Anecdotal notes, 21
    forms for recording, 21,
        22*f*
Animals, Going Places—The
    Zoo activity, 337

Art
    area for, 38
    Museum Exhibit activity,
        126–128
Art Portfolios activities, 330
Assessment, 6, 19–25
    portfolio, 20
    procedures for, 8
Awareness
    of graphic symbols
        activities, 49
        assessment procedures,
            298–299
        goals and objectives, 49
    metalinguistic, 3–4, 15–17
        activities, 133–199
        assessment procedures,
            303–312
        behaviors and concepts, 14*t*
        definition of, 362
        goals and objectives,
            136–137
        Metalinguistic Awareness
            Checklist, 197*f*–198*f*,
            323*f*–324*f*
    print/book, 2–3, 14–15
        activities, 45–132
        assessment procedures,
            296–302
        behaviors and concepts,
            14*t*
        goals and objectives,
            48–50
        Print/Book Awareness
            Checklist, 130*f*–131*f*,
            321*f*–322*f*
    word, 16, 134
        assessment procedures,
            306
        behaviors and concepts,
            14*t*
        goals and objectives, 137

Bedtime activities, 328
Behaviors, adult–child inter-
    active, 39–41

Blending, 16–17, 135
    activities, 137
    assessment procedures,
        309–310
    definition of, 361
    examples, 293
    goals and objectives, 137
    Guess the Word (Blending)
        activity, 179–180
    I'm Thinking of a . . .
        (Blending by Cate-
        gory) activity, 181–183
Blocks
    Blocks activity, 98–100
    playing with, 293–294
    Recording Constructions
        activity, 101–103
Book awareness, *see*
    Print/book awareness
Book Buddy activity,
    222–224
Book conventions
    activities, 49
    assessment procedures,
        297–298
    definition of, 361
    goals and objectives, 49
Book narrative skills
    activities, 204
    assessment procedures,
        314–315
    goals and objectives, 204
Book review forms, 216, 217*f*
Books
    Enacting Storybooks activ-
        ity, 218–221
    favorite, 366
    Getting to Know Books
        activity, 334
    Making Books activity,
        87–90
    My Very Own Book activ-
        ity, 347
    playing with, 294
    The Rhyming Book activ-
        ity, 159–161

Books—*continued*
Shared Storybook Reading
activity, 51–55
tactile picture books in
braille, 366
Talking About Books activity, 213–216
wordless picture books,
367
Braille picture books, 366
Brainstorming activity,
263–266

Categorical organization, 18
activities, 204
assessment procedures, 317
definition of, 361
I'm Thinking of a . . .
(Blending by Cate-
gory) activity, 181–183
Sorting Objects activity,
94–97
Checklist
Ladders to Literacy Preschool,
291–326, 321*f*–326*f*
Metalinguistic Awareness,
197*f*–198*f*, 323*f*–324*f*
Oral Language, 280*f*–281*f*,
325*f*–326*f*
Print/Book Awareness,
130*f*–131*f*, 321*f*–322*f*
Scaffolding Strategies, 132*f*,
199*f*, 282*f*
Child-responsive teaching
strategies, 8
Child's experience, relating
to, 31
Children's books, *see* Books
Clap the Syllables activity,
150–152
Clarification requests, 31
Classroom Post Office activity,
81–83
Classrooms
example floor plan, 37*f*
guidelines for arranging,
36–38
literacy-rich environment
in, 6, 35–39
Cognition, 362
Cognitive structuring, 31–32
description of, 29
examples, 33, 34
Collecting data, 20–24
for individualized educa-
tion program (IEP)/
individualized family
service plan (IFSP),
24–25
Comments, 295
anecdotal notes, 21
forms for recording, 21, 22*f*

Communication materials, 24
Compound words, 361
Concrete, making more, 32
examples, 34
Construction
Let's Draw the Building You
Made! activity, 339
Recording Constructions
activity, 101–103
Context
decontextualization, 19,
203
assessment procedures,
317–319
decontextualized language,
361
Continuous sounds, 361
Contradictions, 32
examples, 34
Conventions
book, 49
assessment procedures,
297–298
definition of, 361
goals and objectives, 49
of representing in print, 15,
48
Conversation skills, 18
Conversations
activities, 204
assessment procedures,
316–317
goals and objectives, 204
Cooking
Following Recipes activity,
60–63
Recipes activity, 351
Snack/Lunch Menu activ-
ity, 56–59
Co-participation, 33
Cultural sensitivity, 7

Dance activity, 338
Data collection, 20–24
individualized education
program (IEP)/individ-
ualized family service
plan (IFSP), 24–25
Decentration, 361
Decontextualization, 19,
203
activities, 204–205
assessment procedures,
317–319
goals and objectives,
204–205
Decontextualized language,
361
Demands, levels of, 40
Descriptions, 29
Development
of early literacy, 13–25

zone of proximal develop-
ment (ZPD), 27
Developmental appropriateness, 6, 8
Diaries activity, 331
Dictations, 21–24
Direct questioning, 33
examples, 34
Discourse
interpretive/analytic, 19
activities, 205
assessment procedures,
319–320
definition of, 361
goals and objectives, 205
literate, 18–19, 203
assessment procedures,
316–320
behaviors and concepts,
14*t*
definition of, 362
goals and objectives,
204–205
Dramatic play, 38
Enacting Storybooks activity, 218–221
Pretend Play—Magic Pass-
word activity, 193–195
helpful scenario, 293–294
parent version, 341
Pretend Play—The Store
activity, 190–192
Showtime activity, 276–278
Drawing, 21
Art Portfolios activity, 330
Draw a Picture activity, 332
Let's Draw the Building You
Made! activity, 339
Recording Constructions
activity, 101–103

Early literacy
assessment of, 6
behaviors and concepts, 14,
14*t*
collecting data, 20–24
development of, 13–25
goals and objectives, 48–50,
136–137, 203–205
Early literacy observation
forms, 21, 22*f*
for metalinguistic aware-
ness, 196*f*
for oral language, 279*f*
for print/book awareness,
129*f*
Ecological sensitivity, 6
Elicitations, 33
Emergent literacy, 1–2
definition of, 361
Enacting Storybooks activity,
218–221

Encouragements, 31
  examples, 33, 34
Environment, literacy-rich, 6,
    35–39
  example floor plan, 37f
  guidelines for creating,
    36–38
Environmental print, 361
Environmental sounds
  activities, 136
  assessment procedures, 303
  goals and objectives, 136
Evaluation
  assessment, 6, 19–25
    procedures for, 8
  portfolio assessment, 20
  of yearly progress, 25
Evaluations (strategy), 31
Experience, matching inter-
    ests and, 32
  examples, 33
Explanations, 29–31

Families
  parent activities, 41
  parent's guide to activities,
    327–360
  suggestions for including,
    8
Feedback, providing, 31
  description of, 28–29
  examples, 33, 34
Feeling Objects activity,
    231–233
Fictional stories, narrations of
  activities, 204
  assessment procedures,
    315–316
  goals and objectives, 204
Figures and blocks, play with,
    293–294
Fill in the Blanks activity,
    84–86
First Sound activity, 333
First Sound Song activity,
    175–178
Following Recipes activity,
    60–63
Food
  Following Recipes activity,
    60–63
  Food Talk activity, 210–212
  Recipes activity, 351
  Snack/Lunch Menu activ-
    ity, 56–59
Foreign language resources,
    366
Formal assessment proce-
    dures, 8
Forms
  activity planning, 41, 42f
  book review, 216, 217f

Ladders to Literacy Preschool
    Checklist, 291–326,
    321f–326f
  Metalinguistic Awareness
    Checklist, 197f–198f,
    323f–324f
  observation, 21, 22f
    for metalinguistic aware-
      ness, 196f
    for oral language, 279f
    for print/book aware-
      ness, 129f
  Oral Language Checklist,
    280f–281f, 325f–326f
  Print/Book Awareness
    Checklist, 130f–131f,
    321f–322f
  for recording anecdotal
    notes, 21, 22f
  Scaffolding Strategies
    Checklist, 132f, 199f,
    282f
From This to That activity,
    267–270

Games
  Rhyming Games activity,
    162–164
  Word to Word Matching
    Game: First Sound
    activity, 184–186
Getting to Know Books activ-
    ity, 334
Goals and objectives
  metalinguistic awareness,
    136–137
  oral language, 203–205
  print/book awareness,
    48–50
  restating, 32
Going Places—The Library
    activity, 335
Going Places—The Museum
    activity, 336
Going Places—The Zoo activ-
    ity, 337
Grandparents, activities with,
    328
Graphic symbols, awareness
    of
  activities, 49
  assessment procedures,
    298–299
  goals and objectives, 49
Graphics
  activities, 49
  assessment procedures,
    296–297
  goals and objectives, 49
Group instruction, 7–8
Guess the Word (Blending)
    activity, 179–180

Guidelines for child-respon-
    sive teaching strate-
    gies, 8
Heterogeneous groups, 7–8
Home activities
  home links, 41
  Print in the Home activity,
    349

I Found . . . activity, 76–78
I See, You See activity,
    234–236
IEPs, see Individualized edu-
    cation programs
IFSPs, see Individualized fam-
    ily service plans
I'm Thinking of a . . . (Blend-
    ing by Category) activ-
    ity, 181–183
Implementation, 35–44
Individual differences,
    responsiveness to, 6–7
Individualized education pro-
    grams (IEPs), goals and
    objectives
  data collection for, 24–25
  documenting and monitor-
    ing progress on, 24–25
  identification of, 24
  recommendations for, 8
Individualized family service
    plans (IFSPs), goals
    and objectives
  data collection for, 24–25
  documenting and monitor-
    ing progress on, 24–25
  identification of, 24
  recommendations for, 8
Informal assessment proce-
    dures, 8
Information talk, 31
Instructing (strategy), 32–33
  description of, 29
  examples, 33, 34
Instruction
  curriculum features, 5t, 7–8
  group, 7–8
Instructional program deci-
    sion making, 25
  suggestions for, 25
Integration with other curric-
    ula, 8
Intentions, semantic, 362
Interaction
  adult–child behaviors,
    39–41
  Book Buddy activity,
    222–224
Interests and experience,
    matching, 32
  examples, 33

Interpretation of meaning, 31
    examples, 34
Interpretive/analytic dis-
    course, 19
    activities, 205
    assessment procedures,
        319–320
    definition of, 361
    goals and objectives, 205
Interviews, 24
Interviews activity, 256–258
Invented spelling, 361

Journals
    Diaries activity, 331
    My First Journal activity,
        118–121

Knowledge
    general, curriculum fea-
        tures, 5t, 5–6
    Let's Find Out! activity,
        271–275
    What Does This Mean?
        activity, 250–252

Labels
    Name Cups activity, 79–80
    superordinate level,
        362–363
    That's My Name activity,
        357
Ladders to Literacy Preschool
    Checklist, 130f–131f,
        197f–198f, 280f–281f,
        291–326, 321f–326f
    administration procedures
        and protocol, 292–295
    characteristics of, 291–292
Ladders to Literacy preschool
    curriculum
    activity features, 5t, 6–7
    description of, 5–8
    development research, 8–9
    general knowledge fea-
        tures, 5t, 5–6
    implementing, 35–44
    instructional features, 5t,
        7–8
    integration with other cur-
        ricula, 8
    major features, 5, 5t
    theoretical and research
        bases, 2–4
Landscapes and Maps activ-
    ity, 122–125
Language
    conventions of represent-
        ing in print, 15, 48
    decontextualized, 361
    foreign, resources for, 366
    oral, 4, 17–19

activities, 201–282
    area for, 38
    assessment procedures,
        313–320
    behaviors and concepts,
        14t
    Early Literacy Observa-
        tion Form, 279f
    goals and objectives,
        203–205
    Oral Language Checklist,
        280f–281f, 325f–326f
    Say it Fast activity, 352
Language documentary data,
    20–24
Let's Dance! activity, 338
Let's Draw the Building You
    Made! activity, 339
Let's Find Out! activity,
    271–275
Let's Say it Another Way!
    activity, 253–255
Let's Use Words to Describe
    . . . ! activity, 340
Letter identification
    activities, 49
    assessment procedures,
        299–300
    goals and objectives, 49
Letter Sound of the Week
    activity, 171–174
Letters
    Magnetic Letters activity,
        342
    single
        activities, 50
        assessment procedures,
            302
        goals and objectives, 50
Letter–sound correspon-
    dence, 15
    assessment procedures, 302
    behaviors and concepts, 14t
    goals and objectives, 50
Listening
    Listening to Songs activity,
        147–149
    What Did You Hear? activ-
        ity, 228–230, 358
Literacy
    centers, 39
    definition of, 362
    development
        early, 13–25
            knowledge about, 6
            supporting, 5–8
        early
            assessment of, 6
            behaviors and concepts,
                14, 14t
            collecting data, 20–24
            development of, 13–25

goals and objectives,
    48–50, 136–137,
    203–205
observation forms, 21,
    22f, 129f, 196f, 279f
emergent, 1–2
    definition of, 361
Ladders to Literacy Preschool
    Checklist, 291–326,
    321f–326f
Ladders to Literacy preschool
    curriculum
    description of, 5–8
    development research,
        8–9
    implementing, 35–44
    theoretical and research
        bases, 2–4
    materials for, 24
    new perspective on, 1–2
Literacy-rich environment, 6,
    35–39
    example floor plan, 37f
    guidelines for creating,
        36–38
Literate discourse, 18–19,
    203
    assessment procedures,
        316–320
    behaviors and concepts, 14t
    definition of, 362
    goals and objectives,
        204–205
Logical relationships, 31
    examples, 34
Long Jump activity, 114–117
Snack/Lunch Menu activity,
    56–59

Magic Password activity,
    193–195
    helpful scenario, 293–294
    parent version, 341
Magnetic Letters activity, 342
Making Books activity, 87–90
Making Signs activity, 64–67
    parent version, 343
Many Ways to Write activity,
    68–71
Maps and mapping
    Landscapes and Maps
        activity, 122–125
    Mapping the Territory
        activity, 344
Matching Game: First Sound
    activity, 184–186
Matching interests and expe-
    rience, 32
    examples, 33
Materials, 39
    additional resources,
        366–367

literacy and communication, 24
Meaning, interpretation of, 31
examples, 34
What Does This Mean? activity, 250–252
Measuring activity, 345
Memory, holding in, 32
description of, 29
Memory for sounds, 16, 134
assessment procedures, 303–305
behaviors and concepts, 14t
goals and objectives, 136
Messages
I Found . . . activity, 76–78
Morning/Afternoon Message and News activity, 72–75
Writing Messages activity, 360
Metacognition, 362
Metalinguistic awareness, 3–4, 15–17
activities, 133–199
assessment procedures, 303–312
behaviors and concepts, 14t
definition of, 362
Early Literacy Observation Form, 196f
goals and objectives, 136–137
Metalinguistic Awareness Checklist, 197f–198f, 323f–324f
Miniature toys, playing with, 187–189
Modeling, 32–33
examples, 33, 34
peer, 34
Morning/Afternoon Message and News activity, 72–75
Movie Reviews activity, 259–262
parent version, 346
Multicultural sensitivity, 7
Museums
Going Places—The Museum activity, 336
Museum Exhibit activity, 126–128
Music and songs
Clap the Syllables activity, 150–152
First Sound Song activity, 175–178
Let's Dance! activity, 338
Listening to Songs activity, 147–149

Musical Instruments activity, 141–143
Rhythmic Activities activity, 144–146
Sing a Song activity, 354
My Dream activity, 243–245
My First Journal activity, 118–121
My Very Own Book activity, 347

Names
Name Cups activity, 79–80
That's My Name activity, 357
Narrations of fictional stories
activities, 204
assessment procedures, 315–316
goals and objectives, 204
Narrations of real events
activities, 204
assessment procedures, 314
goals and objectives, 204
Narrative skills, 17–18, 202–203
assessment procedures, 314–316
behaviors and concepts, 14t
book
activities, 204
assessment procedures, 314–315
goals and objectives, 204
goals and objectives, 204
News activity, 72–75
Notes
anecdotal, 21
forms for recording, 21, 22f
for scoring, 295
Nursery Rhymes activity, 156–158, 348

Observation forms, 21, 22f
for metalinguistic awareness, 196f
for oral language, 279f
for print/book awareness, 129f
Obstacle Course activity, 111–113
Open-ended questioning, 29–31
description of, 28
examples, 33
Oral language, 4, 17–19
activities, 201–282
areas for, 38
assessment procedures, 313–320
behaviors and concepts, 14t

Early Literacy Observation Form, 279f
goals and objectives, 203–205
Say it Fast activity, 352
Oral Language Checklist, 280f–281f, 325f–326f
Organization
categorical, 18
activities, 204
assessment procedures, 317
definition of, 361
I'm Thinking of a . . . (Blending by Category) activity, 181–183
Sorting Objects activity, 94–97
Orienting, 33
examples, 34
Outside activities, 329

Parent activities, 41
Parent's guide, 327–360
Participation, 33
Peer modeling, 34
Perception and memory for sounds, 16, 134
assessment procedures, 303–305
behaviors and concepts, 14t
goals and objectives, 136
Phonemes, 15n
activities, 136
assessment procedures, 304–305
definition of, 362
goals and objectives, 136
Phonological skills, 16–17
assessment procedures, 306–312
behaviors and concepts, 14t
goals and objectives, 137
Phonology, 362
Photography activity, 91–93
Phrases
activities, 136
goals and objectives, 136
metalinguistic awareness of, 304
Physical education
Long Jump activity, 114–117
Obstacle Course activity, 111–113
Physical environment
classrooms, 36–38, 37f
literacy-rich, 6, 35–39
Picture books
in braille, 366
wordless, 367
see also Books

Pictures
  activities, 49
  assessment procedures, 296
  goals and objectives, 48
Planning, 29
Planning forms, 41, 42*f*
Play
  activities, 48
  assessment procedures, 296
  with books, 294
  dramatic, 38
    Enacting Storybooks activity, 218–221
    Pretend Play—Magic Password activity, 193–195, 293–294, 341
    Pretend Play—The Store activity, 190–192
    Showtime activity, 276–278
    with figures and blocks, 293–294
    goals and objectives, 48
    with paper and crayons, 294–295
    Play with Miniature Toys activity, 187–189
    Playing with the Sounds of Words activity, 165–167
    Water Play: Floating Objects activity, 240–242
Points, 295
Portfolio assessment, 20
Portraits activity, 225–227
Post Office activity, 81–83
Pragmatic skills, 362
Predictions, 29
  examples, 33
Preschool Checklist, *see Ladders to Literacy* Preschool Checklist
Pretend Play—Magic Password activity, 193–195
  helpful scenario, 293–294
  parent version, 341
Pretend Play—The Store activity, 190–192
Print, 15, 48
  assessment procedures, 297–301
  behaviors and concepts, 14*t*
  environmental, 361
  goals and objectives, 49–50
  Print in the Home activity, 349
  Print in the World activity, 350
Print/book awareness, 2–3, 14–15
  activities, 45–132

  assessment procedures, 296–302
  behaviors and concepts, 14*t*
  development of, 46
  Early Literacy Observation Form, 129*f*
  goals and objectives, 48–50
Print/Book Awareness Checklist, 130*f*–131*f*, 321*f*–322*f*
Purpose statements, 39
Puzzles activity, 153–155

Questioning
  direct, 33
    examples, 34
  open-ended, 29–31
    description of, 28
    examples, 33

Rainy day activities, 328
Reading activity, 51–55
Rearranging elements, 32
Recipes
  Following Recipes activity, 60–63
  Recipes activity, 351
Recording Constructions activity, 101–103
Reducing alternatives, 32
Referent, 362
Relating to child's experience, 31
Relationships, logical, 31
  examples, 34
Relatives, activities with, 328
Reminders, 32
Representations
  conventions of representing in print, 15, 48
  Sound Representations activity, 138–140
  symbolic, 14–15, 47–48
    assessment procedures, 296–297
    behaviors and concepts, 14*t*
    definition of, 363
    goals and objectives, 48–49
Research, 8–9
  bases, 2–4
  theory, 7
Resources, 365–368
Responsiveness
  guidelines for teaching strategies, 8
  to individual differences, 6–7
Restating goals, 32

Reviews
  book review forms, 216, 217*f*
  Movie Reviews activity, 259–262
  parent version, 346
Rhyming, 16, 134–135
  activities, 137
  additional resources, 365
  assessment procedures, 306–308
  examples, 293
  goals and objectives, 137
  Nursery Rhymes activity, 156–158, 348
  The Rhyming Book activity, 159–161
  Rhyming Games activity, 162–164
  Tell Me a Word that Rhymes with . . . ! activity, 356
Rhythm
  Let's Dance! activity, 338
  Rhythmic Activities activity, 144–146
Rules (strategy), 31
  examples, 34

Say it Fast activity, 352
Scaffolding
  categories, 28–33
  continuum of strategies, 29, 30*f*
  definition of, 362
  example interactions, 33–35
  role of, 27–34
Scaffolding Strategies Checklist, 132*f*, 199*f*, 282*f*
Science Projects activity, 107–110
Scoring
  notes for, 295
  points, 295
Scribbling activity, 353
Segmentation, 17, 135–136, 310–312
  activities, 137
  additional resources, 366
  definition of, 362
  examples, 294
  goals and objectives, 137
  syllable, 366
Semantic intentions, 362
Semantics, 362
Sensitivity, multicultural, 7
Sentences, oral
  activities, 203–204
  assessment procedures, 313
  goals and objectives, 203
Sequencing, 32
  examples, 33

Shared Storybook Reading
     activity, 51–55
Show and Tell activity,
     206–209
Showtime activity, 276–278
Signs activity, 64–67
     parent version, 343
Sing a Song activity, 354
Skills
     conversation, 18
     narrative, 17–18, 202–203
          assessment procedures,
               314–316
          behaviors and concepts,
               14t
          goals and objectives, 204
     phonological, 16–17
          assessment procedures,
               306–312
          behaviors and concepts,
               14t
          goals and objectives, 137
     pragmatic, 362
     tactile
          Feeling Objects activity,
               231–233
          picture books in braille,
               366
Snack/Lunch Menu activity,
     56–59
Song
     First Sound Song activity,
          175–178
     Listening to Songs activity,
          147–149
     Sing a Song activity, 354
Sorting Objects activity, 94–97
Sound-based nature of writ-
     ing, 48
Sound Isolation activity,
     168–170
Sound Representations activ-
     ity, 138–140
Sounds
     continuous, 361
     environmental
          activities, 136
          assessment procedures,
               303
          goals and objectives, 136
     First Sound activity, 333
     Letter Sound of the Week
          activity, 171–174
     letter–sound correspon-
          dence, 15
          assessment procedures,
               302
          behaviors and concepts,
               14t
          goals and objectives, 50
     perception and memory
          for, 16, 134

assessment procedures,
     303–305
behaviors and concepts,
     14t
goals and objectives, 136
Playing with the Sounds of
     Words activity, 165–167
single
     activities, 50
     assessment procedures,
          302
     goals and objectives, 50
Sound Isolation activity,
     168–170
stop, 362
Special Words activity,
     246–249
Spelling, invented, 361
Stop sounds, 362
Stories, narrations of
     activities, 204
     assessment procedures,
          314, 315–316
     goals and objectives, 204
Story structure and genre,
     202–203
     definition of, 362
Storybooks
     Enacting Storybooks activ-
          ity, 218–221
     Shared Storybook Reading
          activity, 51–55
     Storybook Reading Rou-
          tines activity, 355
Structure, story, 202–203
     definition of, 362
Structuring, cognitive, 31–32
     description of, 29
     examples, 33
Summaries, 32
Superordinate level labels,
     362–363
Support(s)
     for literacy development,
          5–8
     most helpful, 295
Syllables
     Clap the Syllables activity,
          150–152
     segmentation of, 366
     Syllable Puzzles activity,
          153–155
Symbolic representation,
     14–15, 47–48
     assessment procedures,
          296–297
     behaviors and concepts, 14t
     definition of, 363
     goals and objectives, 48–49
Symbols
     definition of, 363
     graphic, awareness of

activities, 49
assessment procedures,
     298–299
goals and objectives, 49
Syntax, 363

Tactile skills
     Feeling Objects activity,
          231–233
     picture books in braille,
          366
Talk
     Food Talk activity, 210–212
     information, 31
     Talking about Books activ-
          ity, 213–216
     see also Oral language
Task demands, levels of, 40
Task regulation, 32
     description of, 29
     examples, 33, 34
Teaching
     child-responsive strategies,
          8
     see also Instruction
Tell Me a Word that Rhymes
     with . . . ! activity, 356
That's My Name activity, 357
Theoretical bases, 2–4
Theoretical framework, 11–44
Thinking aloud, 31
Toys, miniature, 187–189
Travel activities, 329
     Going Places—The Library
          activity, 335
     Going Places—The Museum
          activity, 336
     Going Places—The Zoo
          activity, 337
Treasure Boxes activity,
     237–239
Treasure Hunt activity,
     104–106

Vocabulary, 17, 202
     assessment procedures, 313
     behaviors and concepts, 14t
     goals and objectives,
          203–204

Water Play: Floating Objects
     activity, 240–242
What Did You Hear? activity,
     228–230, 358
What Does This Mean? activ-
     ity, 250–252
What Will Happen Next?
     activity, 359
Word awareness, 16, 134
     assessment procedures, 306
     behaviors and concepts, 14t
     goals and objectives, 137

Word to Word Matching
    Game: First Sound
    activity, 184–186
Wordless picture books, 367
Words
  assessment procedures,
      302, 306
  compound, 361
  metalinguistic awareness of
    activities, 136, 137
    assessment procedures,
      303–304
    goals and objectives, 136,
      137
  oral
    activities, 203–204

assessment procedures,
    313
  goals and objectives, 203
perception and memory
    for, 134, 136
print/book awareness of
  activities, 50
  goals and objectives, 50
Special Words activity,
    246–249
see also Vocabulary
Writing, 21
  activities, 49–50
  assessment procedures,
      300–301
  goals and objectives, 49

Scribbling activity, 353
  sound-based nature of, 48
Writing centers, 38
Writing Messages activity,
    360

Yearly progress evaluation,
    25
Young children, supporting
    literacy development
    in, 5–8

Zone of proximal develop-
    ment (ZPD), 27
ZPD, see Zone of proximal
    development